TITANIC
SHIP of LOST ILLUSIONS

To all those friends who have offered support and
encouragement over the years.

And on the deck of the drumming liner
Watching the furrow that widens behind you,
You shall not think 'the past is finished'
Or 'the future is before us'.
                    T.S. Eliot, *Four Quartets*

TITANIC
SHIP of LOST ILLUSIONS
A FLOATING MICROCOSM OF EDWARDIAN SOCIETY

KEVIN BROWN

PEN & SWORD
HISTORY
AN IMPRINT OF PEN & SWORD BOOKS LTD.
YORKSHIRE - PHILADELPHIA

First published in Great Britain in 2025 by
Pen & Sword History
An imprint of Pen & Sword Books Limited
Yorkshire – Philadelphia

Copyright © Kevin Brown 2025

ISBN 978 1 03611 972 0

The right of Kevin Brown to be identified as Author of this work has been asserted by him in accordance with the Copyright, Designs and Patents Act 1988.

A CIP catalogue record for this book is available from the British Library.

All rights reserved. No part of this book may be reproduced, transmitted, downloaded, decompiled or reverse engineered in any form or by any means, electronic or mechanical including photocopying, recording or by any information storage and retrieval system, without permission from the Publisher in writing. No part of this book may be used or reproduced in any manner for the purpose of training artificial intelligence technologies or systems.

Typeset in INDIA by IMPEC eSolutions
Printed and bound in England by CPI (UK) Ltd.

The Publisher's authorised representative in the EU for product safety is Authorised Rep Compliance Ltd., Ground Floor, 71 Lower Baggot Street, Dublin D02 P593, Ireland.
www.arccompliance.com

For a complete list of Pen & Sword titles please contact:

PEN & SWORD BOOKS LIMITED
47 Church Street, Barnsley, South Yorkshire, S70 2AS, England
Email: enquiries@pen-and-sword.co.uk
Website: www.pen-and-sword.co.uk

or

PEN AND SWORD BOOKS
1950 Lawrence Road, Havertown, PA 19083, USA
Email: uspen-and-sword@casematepublishers.com
Website: www.penandswordbooks.com

Contents

List of Illustrations		vi
Preface		ix
Chapter One	Sunken Palace of the Sea	1
Chapter Two	Manly Heroes in Evening Suits	27
Chapter Three	The Shame of Survival	59
Chapter Four	Dutiful and Undaunted en Deshabille	93
Chapter Five	Class, Prejudice and Conflict	122
Chapter Six	Heroes or Incompetents	152
Chapter Seven	Deathly Distinction and Discrimination	180
Notes		206
Bibliography		231
Index		235

List of Illustrations

1. *Women and Children First* by Fortunino Matania, a representation of true manliness. (*Wikicommons, public domain*)
2. 'The Great *Titanic* Disaster', a photo montage centred on Captain Smith, the wireless operator and the lifeboats, images of negligence or duty? (*Library of Congress, LC-USZ62-61940*)
3. The airy drawing office of Harland & Wolff, where the sleek *Titanic* was designed under the supervision of Thomas Andrews and Roderick Chisholm, both lost with the Guarantee Group. (*Wikicommons, public domain*)
4. A marvel of modernism under construction. (*LC-USZ62-26743*)
5. A giant of modern technology whose propellers dwarfed the Harland & Wolff workers who built her. (*LC-USZ62-34781*)
6. The *Titanic* after her launch. (*LC-USZ62-56585*)
7. The Grand Staircase, the most recognisable emblem of the opulence of *Titanic* and a fitting backcloth for social display, although photographs of it come from *Olympic*. (*LC-USZ62-26812*)
8. The feminine and refined atmosphere of the Veranda Café and Palm Court. (*LC-USZ62-116095*)
9. An athletic man following the cult of keep fit was accommodated in the gymnasium, similar to the one on *Olympic*. (*LC-USZ62-26823*)
10. The Smoking Room, a bastion of masculinity, both its virtue and vices, identical to the room on *Olympic*. (*LC-USZ62-26825*)
11. The Great Promenade Deck, usually a scene of calm but one of confusion during the sinking. (*LC-USZ62-116096*)
12. Naval architect Thomas Andrews, the abstemious, clean-cut practical man of action. (*Wikicommons, public domain*)
13. Archie Butt, military aide to Presidents Roosevelt and Taft, the epitome of swaggering martial masculinity. (*LC-USZ62-116070*)

14. John Jacob Astor, 'the world's greatest monument to unearned income', tainted by the scandal of his divorce and marriage to the much younger Madeline, and in need of redemption. (*LC-USZ62-91221*)
15. Charles M. Hays, eulogised as a great entrepreneur though his railway empire was unstable. (*McCord Stewart Museum II-199189.0*)
16. The successful businessman, athlete and clubman as the embodiment of Anglo-Saxon manliness, Thornton Davidson. (*McCord Stewart Museum II-186045*)
17. The self-effacing scion of robber barons, Harry Widener was reincarnated as a new type of sensitive cultural hero. (*Wikicommons, public domain*)
18. Exquisitely tailored Victor Peñasco could pose as the gallant romantic lead, only for someone else's corpse to be purchased as proof of his death. (*Wikicommons, public domain*)
19. The *Denver Post* hired actors to reconstruct the alleged shootings of Italian passengers on *Titanic*, 19 April 1912. (*Library of Congress newspaper collection, public domain*)
20. Class and gender conflict was rife in the lifeboats. (*LC-USZ62-93570*)
21. The unsinkable Margaret Brown and Captain Rostron of *Carpathia*, both of whom saved lives and helped the survivors by their decisive leadership. (*LC-USZ62-47788*)
22. The plucky Countess of Rothes, a lady bountiful and the equal of any man. (*Wikicommons, public domain*)
23. Lucy Duff-Gordon, the fashion designer and dutiful wife determined to survive alongside her husband and contemptuous of women who left their husbands to die. (*LC-USZ62-135822*)
24. Charlotte Collyer and her daughter, clutching a White Star blanket from the wreck, survived but her husband perished. (*LC-DIG-ggbain-19397*)
25. The Navratil orphans of the *Titanic*, abducted by their father and at first feared unidentifiable. (*LC-USZ62-56585*)
26. *Titanic* survivors who came through their ordeal respectably dressed and without a scratch, George and Dorothy Harder with Sallie Beckwith on *Carpathia*. (*LC-USZ62-56452*)
27. Survivors on the deck of *Carpathia* were still distinguished by their social status whether wearing evening dress or dressing gown. (*LC-USZ62-56453*)

28. Stuart Collett, saved by his chivalry as an escort. (*LC-USZ62-85391*)
29. The heroic casualty Harold Bride, Marconi operator, whose feet were so badly frostbitten he had to be carried up a ramp. (*LC-USZ62-85392*)
30. Stewards Frederick Dent Ray, Andrew Cunningham and William Burke ready to justify their own survival at the American Inquiry in Washington, DC, 27 April 1912. (*LC-DIG-hec-00940*)
31. Men and women of all classes waiting for news at White Star Offices. (*LC-DIG-ggbain-10349*)
32. Journalists dominated the crowds waiting to greet survivors in New York. (*LC-USZ62-26635*)
33. Harold Cottam, Marconi operator on *Carpathia*, was overawed when questioned by the Senate Inquiry. (*LC-USZ62-68080*)
34. The guilty men? Bruce Ismay (far right) and White Star Line officials. (*LC-DIG-hec-00933*)
35. No mercy for Bruce Ismay under grilling during the Senate Inquiry at the Waldorf Astoria. (*LC-DIG-ds-13444*)
36. 'Which? Fate or Economy in Lifeboats', a cartoon criticising the cause of the loss of life on such a large scale. (*LC-USZ62-121019*)
37. The corpses of the recovered victims were embalmed on *Minia* and the other rescue ships, but only first-class passengers enjoyed the luxury of a coffin. (*Wikicommons, public domain*)
38. The Women's Monument to the *Titanic* heroes in Washington, DC, an accolade to the ideal of the manly man. (*LC-DIG-ggbain-21094*)
39. The Congressional Medal presented to Captain Rostron by President Taft featured heroic images of the male victims. (*LC-DIG-hec-01690*)

Preface

Another book on *Titanic* almost seems superfluous. The ship could have sunk many times over with the combined weight of them. The *Titanic* industry began immediately after the wreck. There were instant best-sellers, pop-up books of sometimes dubious merit and veracity, much like the newspaper reporting of the day, though illustrating the attitudes and social assumptions of the time, which is my focus here and which should give a different slant to the many depictions of gallantry, high society and steerage courage or cowardice that have dominated many of the books on the subject. Popular ideas about the *Titanic* have also been heavily conditioned by sensational cinema treatments of the sinking, where there is a real danger of reducing the tragedy to a soap opera. The first exploitative film on the subject, *Saved from the Titanic*, now lost, appeared within a month of the disaster and starred the actress Dorothy Gibson wearing the white silk evening dress, cardigan and polo coat in which she had been rescued. French and German films soon followed in 1912. The opportunity to depict the sinking as the result of British upper-class greed and stupidity prompted the Nazi propaganda film *Titanic* in 1943. A personal drama centred on a fictitious estranged married couple played by Clifton Webb and Barbara Stanwyck took centre stage in *Titanic* in 1953, though some real crew and passengers were depicted in bit parts. Perhaps the most accurate and one of the most affectionately remembered of the films was *A Night to Remember*, based on Walter Lord's eponymous book in 1958, with Kenneth More as the heroic Second Officer Lightoller. However, the popularity of this drama-documentary was to be eclipsed by James Cameron's 1997 blockbuster featuring a fictional and doomed inter-class affair between invented characters played by Leonardo DiCaprio and Kate Winslet in lavish settings. It all keeps the liner alive in the popular memory. A fresh look at the subject and new appraisal is always welcome, even if for some avid readers of anything *Titanic*-related there may be a sinking feeling at yet another tome.

In examining the world and social relationships and attitudes brought into focus by the *Titanic* disaster, the almost overwhelming volume of contemporary newspaper reports and survivor testimonies offers invaluable clues. It is very much biased towards stories of the actions of first-class passengers, the celebrities of the day, and to the experiences of the more articulate survivors. With so many contradictory and conflicting perceptions by different individuals, it is hard to reconstruct a coherent and definitive narrative of what actually happened as objective truth. However, it is the assumptions behind those differing and sometimes opposing viewpoints that can be most revealing about not just the individual witnesses but also the society of the time. Even where the press, in the absence of hard facts, made up or embellished witness stories, these untrustworthy fables reflect underlying realities of social expectations. Narratives are built around contemporary expectations of manliness and *noblesse oblige*. Whether or not the manufactured heroes and villains of that fateful night acted according to their presumed roles is another matter. Contemporary critics of that narrative, including suffragists, social reformers, socialists, trade unionists and cynics, are equally revealing with their alternative interpretations.

I have enjoyed the opportunity to discuss some of my ideas on class and gender distinction on *Titanic* through talks I have given for Camden Local Studies and Archives Centre, Camden History Society and the Belfast Titanic Society. Not only does talking on the subject and, even more so, responding to searching questions help to clarify and illuminate ideas, but the audiences for such lectures can raise interesting new areas to be researched or offer different ways of looking at the material. Considering the number of enthusiasts there are with encyclopaedic knowledge of such arcane subjects as who was in which cabin or the quality of steel used for the rivets, it is not surprising that my talks on *Titanic* attracted good turnouts, whether in person or online, and happily, they were well received and led to other bookings to speak. My own interest is in the overall picture of a society that the sinking offers rather than the minutiae, but that all adds to the understanding of what was going on. I wish to thank the people who organised these talks, specifically Tudor Allen (who also read the early draft of this book), Aidan McMichael, Malcolm Holmes, Lindsay Douglas, and David and Ruth Hayes, as well as the people who came to them and shared their breadth of knowledge and enthusiasm.

It takes some enthusiasm if not dedication, supposing it can be called that, to get up early in the morning while suffering from Covid-19 to be interviewed on *Times Radio* on the 110th anniversary of the sinking about why the *Titanic* disaster still attracts so much interest today and how notions of chivalry and cowardice were played out. Only after the interview was over and I had gratefully retreated back to bed did it occur to me that I had broadcast at exactly the same time as the ship went down 110 years earlier. Maybe I am a *Titanic* aficionado after all. I won't admit to nerd!

Certainly, I have been to a number of touring *Titanic* exhibitions over the years, though many of them seem to cover the same familiar territory in all too similar ways. The 1994 'Wreck of the Titanic' exhibition at the National Maritime Museum in Greenwich was perhaps the first major showing of artifacts, including passengers' suitcases, clothes and documents, recovered from the ocean bed. Over the ensuing decades, I have been to comparable exhibitions, from 'Titanic: The Artifact Exhibition' at the 02 Arena (formerly the Millennium Dome) in 2010 to 'Titanic: The Exhibition' at Surrey Quays in 2022, with the by now almost obligatory mock-ups of first-class and steerage cabins, White Star china, the iconic deckchairs waiting to be rearranged, a wall of ice, and yet another selection of the personal belongings of the victims and survivors. Such exhibitions, more than anything else, do tend to forge an imaginative personal link between the visitor and the passengers and crew of the doomed ship, though it is only the link with the shipwreck that raises many of these commonplace items above the mundane.

Questions quite rightly have been raised about the ethics of displaying for what amounts to the entertainment of the paying public the personal effects of victims of the *Titanic* salvaged from the debris field. The travelling bags, jewellery, wallets, suits, shirts, ties, blouses, dresses, nightclothes, hats, coats and stockings brought up from the wreck may tell us a lot about the characters of the people to whom they belonged, but they are only of interest because of the sensational scale of the disaster, and the original owners of this luggage would have been appalled at the invasion of their privacy. Would the victims of a more recent air crash wish their clothes and personal belongings to be put on public display after recovery from the crash site? There is something voyeuristic about it. There is a strong feeling among many, including Dr Robert Ballard, who rediscovered the wreck site in 1985, that *Titanic* is a gravesite to be respected. However, in 1994, salvage rights were granted to RMS Titanic Inc., which recovered and conserved thousands of items ostensibly to preserve their educational and cultural value, though they were put on public display for profit. The question remains one of whether or not the recovered effects tell us anything about the ship and the people it carried that would not be available elsewhere and thus have a unique educational and historical value. The answer is that, whilst they may give an eerie connection with their original owners, there is little emblematic of the society that produced them that could not be found elsewhere.

Museums devoted to *Titanic* exist all over the world, especially in the United States, a number of them in places where there is no real link with the ship itself except the enthusiasts who established and patronise them. However, there are some museums that do have a very real association. Foremost among these is Titanic Belfast, close to the slipways where *Titanic* and her sister ships *Olympic* and *Britannic* were built and to the impressively huge Hamilton Graving Dock. The emphasis in this iconic piece of modern architecture, reflecting not only the size and form of the liner but also its modernism, is rightly on the construction and design of the ship set in its Belfast context. Nearby it is possible to explore the Harland & Wolff headquarters building, adapted as the stylish Titanic Hotel with the magnificent, light-filled drawing offices now housing a bar and reception rooms whilst the restored board room, presentation room and the offices of Lord Pirrie and Thomas Andrews give a feeling of the building in its heyday. Thomas Andrews, teetotaller, naval architect and the head of the drawing office who went down with his creation, might not have approved of guests drinking at the bar now occupying his former workplace; he would certainly have approved of the restoration and return to Belfast of the tender *Nomadic*, even if it did have a bar for first-class passengers waiting to board *Titanic* at Cherbourg. In many ways, Titanic Belfast makes the complementary displays at the Northern Ireland Transport Museum redundant and suggests that the collections be brought together. Similarly, the Sea City Museum in

Southampton concentrates on the local connections of crew and suppliers, and the Merseyside Maritime Museum stresses the strong Liverpool links. Add in the *Titanic* collections at the National Maritime Museum and the material culture of *Titanic* is easily and enjoyably explored. The memory of those who lost their lives on the liner and the fervent desire to memorialise them can also be explored all over the world, especially in Southampton, London, New York and Washington, DC, together with the graves and cenotaphs of these men and women. A particular favourite of mine is the Phillips Memorial Cloister, an Arts and Crafts structure and Gertrude Jekyll-designed garden at Godalming, Surrey, in memory of radio operator Jack Phillips.

As always, I wish to thank the staff of libraries consulted, particularly the British Library, National Maritime Museum and the National Archives. Thank you is also due to Robert Gardiner and Julian Manning of Seaforth Publishing, with whom I have worked on a number of books with a saltwater theme over the past fifteen years, and who recommended this book to Pen and Sword, introducing me to Heather Williams as editor, whom I also wish to thank for her help. I would like to thank Linne Matthews for copyediting and Jon Wilkinson for a striking book jacket design.

With this book, I have enjoyed the luxury of being able to consult virtually documents digitised by the Library of Congress, the Public Archives of Nova Scotia and the National Archives of the United States of America in Washington, DC and New York. It may make life much more convenient and will ease the lives and wallets of many historians able to conduct that research from home in the future, but it is not the same as actually physically handling the building blocks of history, just as perusing an electronic book cannot match the pleasure of reading a printed one. Researching and writing a work of history involves travel over time and space, and physical connection with the evidence of the past. That is not something I would wish to lose for myself nor see others deprived of.

There is always an excitement to sharing a love of history with others, whether in person, online or in print. None of these activities is solitary as they all involve human interaction of one kind or another. They can also lead to the unexpected. When ending an online talk on *Titanic*, just as I delivered my final remarks, my screen went dead, and I lost internet connectivity. It was an appropriately dramatic end to the presentation, effectively my going down with the ship. Luckily, it was recorded and, after re-joining for questions, I later discovered that I had spoken my final words before I vanished spectacularly from the screen. Such theatrical incidents can also enliven a talk given before a live audience. In 2015, I delivered a special memorial lecture on the seventy-fifth anniversary of the sinking of the *Arandora Star* – a difficult task as the audience included relatives of the interned Italian men who lost their lives, and I wanted to be sensitive to their feelings whilst still trying to tell the truth about what actually happened in the context of 1940. Just as I was describing what it must have been like for the drowning victims as the torpedo struck, a light fitting at the back of the hall crashed down from the ceiling – unintended special effects. Perhaps I should avoid sinkings and shipwrecks in future!

Kevin Brown
2 January 2024, London

Chapter One

Sunken Palace of the Sea

On the crowded deck of the doomed *Titanic*, soon to sink on a starry night, a debonair young man in a fashionable dinner jacket blows a farewell kiss to a well-dressed, attractive young woman boarding a lifeboat. Almost forgotten in his other hand is his life jacket trailing on the deck. Further along the deck, a man wearing a chef's hat and carrying a coil of rope, in a disciplined line of crew members, turns to look at the glamorous couple with an expression of disbelief at such a romantic and affected gesture from his social betters in the middle of such a crisis. Behind the gallant stands a man covering his face with his hands, recognising his own plight and likely fate. A man in a cap and heavy overcoat, with his life jacket on, clutches a small case and stares at a woman's abandoned shoe on the deck. Meanwhile, a man in his pyjamas urges his reluctant wife to board a lifeboat. His overcoat lies on the rail. An older couple hug each other. All the while, officers load the lifeboats with women and children as passengers of all classes look on with serious expressions on their faces as if realising that death was imminent for most of them. Stoicism is the order of the day. The man in the dinner jacket stands as the representative of an ill-fated class, impeccably turned out and maintaining a stiff upper lip and chivalrous attitude to the end.[1]

It would be all too easy to dismiss this romantic tableau by the artist Fortunino Matania, first published in *The Sphere* in May 1912, as nothing more than a sentimental, somewhat mawkish imagining of an idealised scene of the last hours of *Titanic* far removed from reality. Yet the artist had based the scene on his own cross-examination of a witness, a bedroom steward who had survived the sinking:

> The scene was vividly impressed on the steward's mind and he was able to correct costume and grouping as the reconstruction proceeded,

down to the smallest detail ... The shoe lying on the deck is no artist's invention. The passenger in his dinner jacket stood here as shown, not wearing his lifebelt, but holding it as he kissed what was to be a last farewell to his wife.

As the artist worked on his reconstruction of the tragic events, 'every point, from the positions and attitude of the people to the angle of the davits and position of the boats, was fought out' between the eyewitness and artist, with the unnamed steward correcting details as they proceeded with such comments as, 'No, the man stood here – a foot more to the right.'[2] The people shown were real passengers and crew, dressed and acting as they were as they faced death. Yet the entire picture is still an artistic composition – the exquisitely dressed and stoical couple in evening dress are a contrast with the man in pyjamas pleading with his companion to enter a lifeboat and the more despairing passengers of lower social standing. It represents a truth but an artistic version of that truth. As such, it epitomises a panoramic vision of contemporary society at a moment of crisis reduced to the confined world of *Titanic* in which myth and reality co-exist.

The magnificent ship was a floating microcosm of pre-Great War society, from the very rich to the poor. Its fate was one of hubris for the wealthy, and the death of so many ambitions and dreams among passengers and crew. There were people of all social classes among the passengers and crew, representing a cross-section of society, whose experiences of the voyage differed greatly according to their place in a very stratified community. Although he never saw the ship itself, Matania represents its appearance with a degree of accuracy, the atmosphere of its sinking and the diversity of those aboard. The scene may be dominated by the attractive, young first-class couple, as indeed, the wealthy and glamorous have tended to monopolise the contemporary reporting of the disaster and modern images of the ship, but behind them is a wide range of people, less conspicuous but very much brought to life as individuals by the details that emerge from deeper scrutiny of the picture.

In many ways, *Titanic* reflected the hierarchies and social order of the world its passengers came from:

> Veritably, on a small scale the *Titanic* was a nation. She had her government and social classes and every man to his duty. She was sailed by an aristocracy, the trained and tried captain and his officers ... the chances of destruction are, of course, minimised when sailed by a nautical aristocracy. And, conversely, they would be illimitably increased if a vessel were sailed by the contradictory and clamorous counsels of her democracy, the passengers and crew.[3]

It was a world in which everyone was assumed to know their place, though they might have an inflated idea of where they stood in the order of things or might aspire to something better. They had their dreams and their own self-images. Yet, this tightly ordered world of a ship was illusory, just as the world it reflected was much messier than shipboard society. Essentially, it should be seen as a theatrical set that reflected a particular image but where reality intruded as the stagecraft collapsed. The events of 15 April 1912 revealed the realities behind that imagined world as individuals tried to live up to the values they believed had characterised their lives and as they faced up to the realities of their situation. We get a snapshot of that society under pressure, revealing not only how people wished to be seen but also the reality beneath the façade.

Luxury and comfort characterised *Titanic* at all levels, though tempered by what was deemed appropriate to each class. Class distinction indeed pervaded the whole ship. For the wealthiest passengers, it was a familiar if idealised world but one without the inconveniences of everyday life. First-class passengers, accommodated in luxurious suites, staterooms and cabins on the upper decks, were pampered as soon as they stepped aboard so that they 'may skate, dance, smoke, swim, dive, and practise the arts of physical culture at their will'.[4] There were even kennels for their pet dogs, though some passengers preferred to keep their pets with them in their cabins. The American artist Frank Millet was irritated by 'a number of obnoxious, ostentatious American women, the scourge of any place they infest and worse on shipboard than anywhere', many of whom 'carry tiny dogs, and lead husbands around like pet lambs'.[5] Governess Elizabeth Shutes was more elegiacal as she recalled 'happy, laughing men and women constantly passing up and down those broad, strong staircases, and the music went on and the ship went on'.[6] It was said of these passengers by a contemporary that:

> They had heard the ship described as a floating hotel; but as they began to explore her they must have found that she contained resources of a perfection unattained by any hotel, and luxuries of a kind unknown in palaces. The beauties of French chateaux and of English country-houses of the great period had been dexterously combined with that supreme form of comfort which the modern English and Americans have raised to the dignity of a fine art. Such a palace as a great artist, a great epicure, a great poet and the most spoilt and pampered woman in the world might have conjured up from their imagination in an idle hour was here materialized and set, not in a fixed landscape of park and woodland, but on the dustless road of the sea, with the sunshine of an English April pouring in on every side, and the fresh salt airs of the Channel filling every corner with tonic oxygen.[7]

The cabins for these wealthy travellers were sumptuously decorated and furnished, and 'everywhere comfortable oaken bedsteads gave place to furniture in the famous suites beloved by millionaires'.[8] Ida Straus was impressed by a ship 'so huge and so magnificently appointed' and was pleased that 'our rooms are furnished in the best of taste and most luxuriously and they are really rooms not cabins'.[9] Lucy Duff-Gordon, a fashion designer, 'entranced with the beauty of the liner' and the novelty of having strawberries for breakfast in April, was especially delighted with her 'pretty little cabin with its electric heater and pink curtains' in which it was a pleasure to go to bed.[10] She felt that 'it all looked so homely and pretty, just like a bedroom on land, that it did not seem possible there could be any danger'.[11] For the wealthiest passengers, 'a suite of rooms magnificently furnished, consisting of two bedrooms, sitting-room, private bath, and valet's room, communicating with a private promenade and thus securing absolute privacy throughout the voyage, can be obtained at a cost of £870.'[12] The staterooms were decorated in an eclectic variety of styles, most of them imposing and regal rather than homely, including Italian Renaissance, Tudor, Jacobean, Queen Anne, Georgian, Regency, Adams, Hepplewhite,

Colonial, Old Dutch, Early Dutch, Louis XIV, eighteenth-century French and Second Empire pastiches. Frank Millet was reminded of English country houses he had visited as a guest and was very impressed by his own stateroom:

> As for the rooms they are larger than the ordinary hotel room and much more luxurious with wooden bedsteads, dressing tables, hot and cold water, electric fans, electric heater and all. The suites with their damask hangings and mahogany oak furniture are really very sumptuous and tasteful. I have the best room I have ever had in a ship and it isn't one of the best either, a great long corridor in which to hang my clothes and a square window as big as the one in the studio alongside the large light. No end of furniture, cupboards, wardrobe, dressing table, couch. Not a bit like going to sea.[13]

The first-class passengers enjoyed lavish meals in the formal Jacobean-style dining room, where dressing for dinner was as strictly observed as on land, before the gentlemen retired to the mahogany-panelled Smoking Room with its open fire, and the ladies to one of the public reception lounges or the quieter reading and writing room. An orchestra played in the public areas and both men and women would congregate in the reception room outside the restaurant for concerts after dinner as well as to socialise in a setting that for once was not segregated by sex. In all the regal public spaces, 'the soft sweet odours of rare flowers pervaded the atmosphere.'[14] In that lounge or crush room they could listen to *The Tales of Hoffman* and *Cavalleria rusticana*.[15] Archibald Gracie recalled, 'On these occasions, full dress was always *en règle*; and it was a subject both of observation and admiration, that there were so many beautiful women – then especially in evidence – aboard the ship.'[16] May Futrelle recalled the Sunday evening dinner as 'a rare gathering of beautiful women and splendid men' and that it would be 'hard to find in one place a crowd which would better typify the highest type of American manhood and womanhood'. It was a setting where the women 'fondly wore their latest Parisian gowns. It was the first time that most of them had the opportunity to display their newly acquired finery.'[17]

Even more luxurious was the à la carte restaurant, decorated in Louis XVI style, where passengers could dine even more extravagantly for an extra cost, though at the end of the voyage they could reclaim the price of the meals they had missed in the dining room. The Café Parisien and the Veranda Café also offered refreshment in a more informal setting. Decorated with ivy creepers on a French-style trellis, the Café Parisien was considered an 'extremely attractive' place in which to meet.[18] Sir Cosmo and Lady Duff-Gordon dined in the restaurant on the last night and 'everybody was very gay and at neighbouring tables people were making bets on the probable time of this record-breaking run.'[19] Mahala Douglas remembered:

> The tables were gay with pink roses and white daisies, the women in their beautiful shimmering gowns of satin and silk, the men immaculate and well-groomed, the stringed orchestra playing music from Puccini and Tchaikovsky. The food was superb: caviar, lobster, quail from Egypt, plovers' eggs, and hothouse grapes and fresh peaches.

Yet the memory for her was bittersweet, since:

> As far as I have been able to learn, not a man in that room, all those who served, from the head steward down, including Mr. Gatti, in charge, the musicians who played in the corridor outside, and all the guests were lost – except Sir Cosmo Duff-Gordon, Mr. Carter, and Mr. Ismay.[20]

The Smoking Room evoked the atmosphere of a Pall Mall gentleman's club and:

> The apartment was a lounge where a couple of hundred guests might rest in cosy chairs. Its walls were panelled with rich, dark wood, exquisitely inlaid with mother-of-pearl. It spoke of wealth, refinement, luxury. It was a place for millionaires of taste and millionaires of beauty.[21]

Such a setting was very familiar to passengers like Tyrell Cavendish, a member of the Carlton and Windham clubs in London. Where it differed from a London club was that it was not exclusive like Windham's, where membership was limited to 600 and which offered 'a convenient and agreeable place of meeting for a society of gentlemen, all connected with each other by a common bond of literary or personal acquaintance'.[22] Denizens of Montreal clubland, like ambitious stockbroker Thornton Davidson, or of similar societies in New York and Washington popular with Anglophiles like Clarence Moore, would have felt at ease in such a congenial setting, though they risked meeting with men who might have been blackballed by the clubs to which they belonged at home. It may have emanated the illusion of being a private club but it still offered an aggressively masculine sanctum and the opportunity for congenial companionship. Archibald Gracie:

> invariably circulated around during these delightful evenings, chatting with those I knew, and with those whose acquaintance I had made during the voyage. The recollections of those with whom I was thus closely associated in this disaster, including those who suffered the death from which I escaped and those who survived with me, will be a treasured memory and bond of union until my dying day. From the palm room, the men of my coterie would always go to the smoking room, and almost every evening join in conversation with some of the well-known men whom we met there.[23]

First-class passengers could also keep themselves fit in a well-equipped gymnasium, invariably casually dressed in suit, collar and tie, or in skirt, coat and bonnet that now seems the height of discomfort and formality. Thomas McCawley, the 36-year-old:

> instructor ran here and there, looking the very picture of robust rosy-cheeked health and fitness in his white flannels, placing one passenger on the electric horse, another on the camel, while the laughing group of onlookers watched the inexperienced riders vigorously shaken up and down as he controlled the little motor which made the machines imitate so realistically horse and camel exercise.[24]

As the ship was about to go down, the physical training instructor manfully remained at his post and gave guidance on the use of the mechanical horses and parallel bars to those who sought distraction from their fate. In addition to the gymnasium, the more energetic passengers could play squash in the racquets court or enjoy the swimming pool and Turkish bath. Archibald Gracie, a devotee of the cult of physical efficiency, was determined to make full use of all these facilities:

> When Sunday morning came, I considered it high time to begin my customary exercises, and determined for the rest of the voyage to patronize the squash racquet court, the gymnasium, the swimming pool, etc. I was up early before breakfast and met the professional racquet player in a half hour's warming up, preparatory for a swim in the six-foot deep tank of salt water, heated to a refreshing temperature. In no swimming bath had I ever enjoyed such pleasure before. How curtailed that enjoyment would have been had the presentiment come to me telling how near it was to being my last plunge, and that before dawn of another day I would be swimming for my life in mid-ocean, under water and on the surface, in a temperature of 28 degrees Fahrenheit![25]

Just as impressive as the public rooms were the up-to-date medical facilities, which not only complied with Board of Trade regulations and the scale of medicines, medical instruments and medical comforts to be carried on passenger ships, but even exceeded them. The medical team on board *Titanic* was led by the 62-year-old senior surgeon William Francis Norman O'Loughlin, who had practised medicine at sea for over forty years. He was ably assisted by 37-year-old John Edward Simpson, a territorial captain in the Royal Army Medical Corps who had originally gone to sea on account of his own ill health, and who had responsibility for the health of the second- and third-class passengers and of the crew. Both of these doctors had previously served together on *Olympic* and both were to go down with *Titanic*. They were aided by a hospital steward, William Durnford, and two stewardesses, one acting as nurse-stewardess for the first-class passengers and the other, Catherine Wallis, as matron for the immigrant passengers in third class, many of whom she had to teach how to use a flush lavatory.[26]

Hospital facilities, like everything else on board ship, were strictly segregated. The second- and third-class passengers had their hospital wards on D Deck near the galley, where there were also two isolation rooms for infectious cases, whilst the crew had their own small sick bay close to their quarters, and the third-class passengers had their own hospital wards. The surgeons worked from a dispensary and surgery near to their cabin berths, though first-class ticketholders expected to receive treatment in their own cabins. These medical facilities were little used on the ill-fated maiden voyage. The only recorded casualty during the voyage was when a first-class passenger, Irene Harris, fell on the grand staircase and broke her arm, but accounts differ as to whether the assistant surgeon Simpson set her arm in plaster, or whether she insisted on being treated by a fellow passenger, a New York orthopaedic surgeon, Henry William Frauenthal. Ironically, Dr Frauenthal himself was to break the ribs of a fellow passenger and knock her unconscious, when he leapt aboard a two-thirds-full lifeboat as the ship went down, in a successful attempt to save himself. Another first-class passenger, Charlotte Drake Cardeza, preferred to rely on her own medical chest, which she took on board with her luggage of fourteen trunks, four suitcases and three crates.[27]

The wealthiest passengers were travelling with their personal valets and maids, who, needing to be close to their masters and mistresses to attend them, were accommodated in first-class cabins and had their own dining room. Chauffeurs were often booked in as second-class passengers, their services being redundant at sea. When not required by their employers, the maids could enjoy the voyage, though not without some work. Nellie Barber was allowed time to herself by her mistress Julia Cavendish on the Sunday of the voyage:

> it was a nice day, and after breakfast I went up on board to sit in a deckchair and get on with some needlework. Next to me sat the millionaire, Mr Jacob Astor. All that afternoon was spent in reading and sitting in a deckchair in the warm Atlantic breeze.

Mrs Cavendish told her that 'there was a service in the lounge if I wanted to go to it. I did not go.'[28] George and Edith Vanderbilt's footman, Edwin Wheeler, travelled in second class without any real duties other than to escort the Vanderbilts' luggage during the voyage as his employers were travelling on *Olympic*; he was lost with the Vanderbilt baggage after what had amounted to a holiday for him.[29] Similarly, Frank Stanley, chauffeur to Washington Roebling, had sailed on an earlier ship to New York from Rotterdam with his employer's Fiat car.[30] Wheeler was able to socialise with fellow second-class passengers. Benjamin Guggenheim's French chauffeur, René Pernot, shared a table in the dining saloon with the Harts from Ilford.[31]

Second-class passengers had their own dining saloon, lounges, library and smoking room, all comfortably appointed but less lavishly than those in first class. Journalists commented that 'lifts and lounges and libraries are not generally associated in the public mind with second class yet in the *Titanic* all are found' and 'it needed the assurance of our guide that we had left the saloon and were really in second class'.[32] Grocer Harvey Collyer felt that the magnificence of the ship would spoil him for any future travel: 'I can tell you we do swank, we shall miss it on the trains as we go third on them.'[33] His wife Charlotte found the food 'too heavy and rich', but admitted that 'no effort was spared to serve even to the second-class passengers on the Sunday the best dinner that money could buy'.[34] The library was a:

> beautifully furnished room, with lounges, armchairs, and small writing- or card-tables scattered about, writing-bureaus round the walls of the room, and the library in glass-cased shelves flanking one side, – the whole finished in mahogany relieved with white fluted wooden columns that supported the deck above.[35]

The cabins for second-class passengers were plainer and smaller but were considered to be the equivalent of first-class accommodation on other ships. Lawrence Beesley, a widowed science teacher, wrote to his son that 'my cabin is ripping, hot and cold water and a very comfy looking bed and plenty of room'.[36]

Steerage passengers, dignified with the status of third class, were on the lower decks in cramped cabins for two, four or six passengers, and in small dormitories reserved for single men. These cabins had little space for more than bunk beds, albeit ones with red-and-white coverlets, unlike the comfortable rooms of their social superiors. Third-class facilities were altogether basic with a general public room, two dining saloons, offering two sittings for meals and in which single men were strictly segregated from unmarried women and married couples, a promenade, and a smoking room. Each class of passenger was strictly segregated from the others, separated by locked gates in compliance with American immigration regulations, which later made evacuation from the sinking ship more difficult than it ought to have been. The accommodation was generally considered 'comfortable' and for the 'hundreds of English, Dutch, Italian and French mingling in happy fellowship', in the opinion of observers, 'the *Titanic* was a wonder'.[37] What was on offer to them was superior to what was found on other liners. Laura Mae Cribb immediately 'became aware that there was a difference between the accommodations of the two ships for the same class of passengers' when she was taken aboard *Carpathia* and found 'such things as table linens and other homelike features were missing in our new habitations'.[38]

As well as carrying emigrants, *Titanic* was also transporting cargo in its hold in addition to the luggage of passengers that was not required during the voyage. As a Royal Mail ship, she carried 3,435 bags of mail, sorted by British and American post office staff. Some passengers were also shipping larger items as freight. William Carter was taking his prized Renault car back to Philadelphia with him. Margaret Brown had three crates of architectural models of ancient buildings intended as a donation to Denver Museum. Mauritz Håkan Björnström-Steffansson was to put in an insurance claim for $100,000 in compensation for the loss of the massive neoclassical oil painting *La Circassienne au Bain*, by Merry-Joseph Blondel.[39] More mundane cargo included fabrics, stocks of velvet, goat skins, jute bagging, cognac and other alcoholic drinks, shelled walnuts, olive oil, anchovies, cheese, vinegar, jam, mushrooms, ostrich plumes and consignments of books. One diamond merchant lost stock insured for £18,000 on a ship, which, 'freighted with millionaires and their wives, is a little diamond mine in itself'.[40]

An expensive and intricately bound copy of *The Rubáiyát of Omar Khayyám*, known as The Great Omar, was one of the more unusual victims of the *Titanic*. Embellished with over 1,000 jewels, 5,000 leather inlays and 100 square feet of gold leaf, it took the Holborn-based bookbinding firm of Sangorski & Sutcliffe two years to make. Its covers were decorated with three golden peacocks, associated with bad omens and portents. John Stonehouse, manager of Sotheran's bookshop, who commissioned The Great Omar, considered it to be 'the finest and most remarkable specimen of binding ever designed, or produced, at any period, or in any country'. It was offered to the Royal Library at Windsor but Sir John Fortescue, the King's Librarian, rejected it as 'the most eminent failure, perhaps, that I ever saw ... absolutely inappropriate, ineffective and insignificant, and to me personally a positive distress'. Its asking price of £1,000 was too high for the British book market. It was sent to New York to be auctioned but returned when the duty on it was considered too high for Sotheran's to pay, and it was finally sold at Sotheby's for £450, a fraction of its cost, to Gabriel Weis, an American book dealer and acquaintance of Harry Widener, a wealthy bibliophile travelling on the *Titanic*. The book sank with the ship. Ten weeks later, the bookbinder Francis Sangorski was drowned in the sea at Selsey Bill while on holiday. A second version of the binding was burned in the Blitz. It all made for the legend that The Great Omar was cursed. Perhaps rather than being cursed, the book could be said to represent the hubris of the wealthy first-class passengers, their extravagance and inherent vulgarity of their flamboyant lifestyles unlimited by cost.[41] The fate of the book was shared by a number of wealthy and prominent bibliophiles and book collectors on board, among them the quietly studious Harry Widener, his fellow Philadelphian William Crothers Dulles, who collected equine-related books and prints, the British business and civic leader Christopher Head, a collector of books, prints and modern art, and William Augustus Spencer, a connoisseur of fine bindings.

Luxury indeed pervaded the entire ship just as surely as the scent of flowers disguised the smell of new paint everywhere. After the sinking of this ship with its wealthy patrons there was a suggestion that 'the provision of Turkish baths, gymnasiums and other so-called luxuries involved a sacrifice of some more essential things, the absence of which was responsible for the loss of so many lives', but there was actually enough space for lifeboats amidst the overwhelming opulence. These luxuries were extras for the comfort and convenience of passengers. They did not take up space that could have been occupied by lifeboats. The failure of the White Star Line was in not providing enough lifeboats, not in lacking the space for them.[42]

It was a marvellous illusion of 'the luxurious hotel transferred to the ocean, the glittering lobster palace afloat'.[43] This façade gave a false sense of security to passengers, as Joseph Conrad recognised:

It is in more ways than one a very ugly business, and a mere scrape along the ship's side, so slight that, if reports are to be believed, it did not interrupt a card party in the gorgeously fitted (but in chaste style) smoking-room – or was it in the delightful French café? – is enough to bring on the exposure. All the people on board existed under a sense of false security. How false, it has been sufficiently demonstrated.[44]

Edward Talbot, Bishop of Winchester, denouncing the 'hyper-luxuries' enjoyed by the wealthy, preached that 'the *Titanic* in name will stand for a monument of warning to human presumption' and was 'a mighty lesson against our confidence and trust in the strength of machinery and money'.[45]

G.K. Chesterton indeed believed that the luxury made passengers and crew alike ignore the risks of sea travel:

The very lines of the boat have the swift poetry of peril; the very carriage and gestures of the boat are those of a thing assailed. But if you make your boat so large that it does not even look like a boat, but like a sort of watering-place, it must, by the deepest habit of human nature, induce a less vigilant attitude of the mind. An aristocrat on board ship who travels with a garage for his motor almost feels as if he were travelling with the trees of his park. People living in open-air cafes sprinkled with liqueurs and ices get as far from the thought of any revolt of the elements as they are from that of an earthquake under the Hotel Cecil. The mental process is quite illogical, but it is quite inevitable. Of course, both sailors and passengers are intellectually aware that motors at sea are often less useful than life-boats, and that ices are no antidote to icebergs.[46]

Behind the opulent façade lay what was considered a technological marvel of its day. Innovation was essential to maintaining White Star's position as a major shipping line and to Harland & Wolff's reputation as a shipbuilder.[47] *Titanic* was powered by two reciprocating four-cylinder, triple-expansion steam engines and one centrally placed low-pressure Parsons turbine, each of which drove a propeller. Reciprocating engines by themselves were not powerful enough to propel an *Olympic*-class liner and a similar combination of engines on *Laurentic* in 1909 had shown the possibilities for greater efficiency.[48] The furnaces powering the engines and electric generating plant required over 600 tons of coal a day to be shovelled into them by hand by 176 firemen.[49] Combustion gases were vented from the boilers through three of *Titanic*'s four distinctive 81 feet 6 inches high funnels. The fourth funnel was a dummy used for ventilation and contained a staircase for crew, though it primarily served an aesthetic function in making the ship look more powerful and distinguished. It was observed that if the funnels were placed horizontally, each could hold a dinner party for fifty people and that they were wide enough to easily allow two tube trains to pass through.[50]

An electrical control panel worked all the fans, generators and lighting on the ship, as well as regulating the condensers that turned steam back into water. The ship had a system of heating and pumping water to all parts of the vessel through a complex network of pipes and valves. The main water supply was taken aboard while *Titanic* was in port, but for emergencies the ship had a distillation plant to desalinate seawater. A network of insulated ducts conveyed warm air, driven by electric fans, around the ship. There was a central clock on the bridge that allowed the captain to adjust all the clocks on the ship to a new time zone. The most up-to-date navigational equipment was supplied, allowing the officers to calculate the position of the ship, the distance travelled, speed and depth of water.[51]

The latest in wireless telecommunications was installed, capable of transmitting messages for 500 miles during the day and 2,000 miles at night with the transmitter's antenna strung between the ship's masts. The transmitter was one of the first Marconi installations to use a rotary spark gap, which gave *Titanic* a distinctive musical tone that could be distinguished readily from other signals. Manned by two young and highly trained Marconi operators, this was a communications marvel that encouraged passengers to send not only business messages but also frivolous Marconigrams as the latest novelty for their friends. As there was not yet an established practice of keeping a clear channel for emergency communications, this meant that urgent warnings could get lost easily amidst the congestion of Morse code traffic.[52] Only with the 1912 Radio Act, signed by President Taft in August 1912 and informed by the deficiencies of shipboard wireless communications revealed by the experience on *Titanic*, was there a restriction on the wavelengths that could be used by amateur radio hams. Other provisions of the Radio Act required all radio operators to be licensed, passenger ships to carry at least two operators who could maintain a continuous watch and be alert for distress signals, and to have auxiliary electrical power supplies to enable the radio apparatus to be operated continuously for at least four hours in an emergency.[53] For passengers on *Titanic*, the latest in radio technology allowed them to stay connected with the rest of the world, though it was deemed a luxury rather than an essential. Soap manufacturer Thomas Pears sent a message on 13 April that was not received by his company until 15 April. His rather inconsequential message intended for his family that all was well only took on a significance later.[54] Department store owner Isidor Straus and his wife Ida enjoyed communicating by wireless telegraphy with their son and daughter-in-law travelling to Europe on *Amerika*.[55] Harold Bride, the junior of the two operators, remembered:

> We had been sending out scores of private messages and messages from the captain to his chiefs in New York and Liverpool – the next moment we send out an urgent distress call. The ships in the vicinity could not believe it. I think that is the reason why there was such a silence after our first call.[56]

As a precaution against damage from running aground, *Titanic* was provided with a double bottom but not with a double hull, which had been specified by Cunard for *Lusitania* and *Mauretania*. Divided into watertight compartments by fifteen steel bulkheads, *Olympic* and *Titanic* were designed so that any two compartments could be flooded without compromising the safety of the ship. Each watertight bulkhead door, which could be controlled from the bridge, would automatically close if any compartment became flooded by more than 6 inches of water. If the bow was damaged by a collision, the ship could stay afloat even with the first four compartments flooded, and if the side of the ship was gashed, with any two of its central compartments flooded. However, to save costs, these bulkheads did not extend to the full height of the hull and if more than two compartments were flooded, the water would flow over the top of a bulkhead and flood the next compartment. This proved a design flaw when *Titanic* struck an iceberg and six of the watertight compartments were damaged. As the weight of the water drew the ship down at the bow, each compartment was successively flooded. In such a situation, the pumps were ineffective.[57]

Watertight compartments might have delayed the sinking but could not prevent it, and 'in this lamentable case these bulkheads served only to prolong the agony of the passengers who could not be saved', in the opinion of Joseph Conrad. He was equally dismissive of the claims of experts that it was impossible to remedy the design defects where water from one flooded compartment overflowed to another with:

> continuous bulkheads – a clear way of escape to the deck out of each water-tight compartment. Nothing less. And if specialists, the precious specialists of the sort that builds 'unsinkable ships', tell you that it cannot be done, don't you believe them. It can be done, and they are quite clever enough to do it too. The objections they will raise, however disguised in the solemn mystery of technical phrases, will not be technical, but commercial.[58]

It had seemed unthinkable that *Titanic*, with its watertight compartments, should sink, but it was still necessary to comply with Board of Trade regulations on the provision of lifeboats. Alexander Carlisle, general manager at Harland & Wolff until 1910, as well as Lord Pirrie, chairman of the shipbuilding company, aware that new regulations for the greater provision of lifeboats on the larger liners were being considered by the Board of Trade, proposed that *Titanic* be supplied with forty-eight or even a generous sixty-four lifeboats. He got the designers 'to design me davits which would allow me to place, if necessary, four lifeboats on each pair of davits, which would have meant a total of over 40 boats'.[59] Carlisle's proposals were rejected by Pirrie and Bruce Ismay as soon as it became obvious that the regulations would not be changed, and the provision of lifeboats was cut from forty-eight to twenty, which was still more than the sixteen mandated by the Board of Trade for a ship of this size. Whilst the pairs of davits for raising and lowering four lifeboats could be supplied at no additional cost and ensured that if in future the Board of Trade did increase its requirements, *Titanic* would be ready for compliance, the immediate additional cost of greater lifeboat provision was considered needless expense. The davits for them were there but not the extra lifeboats that had the capacity that could have saved most of the passengers and crew. Carlisle was only too aware that:

> The White Star and other friends give us a great deal of liberty, but at the same time we cannot build a ship any bigger than they order, or put anything in her more than they are prepared to pay for. We have a very free hand, and always have had; but I do not think that we could possibly have supplied any more boats to the ship without getting the sanction and the order of the White Star Line.[60]

Titanic and her sister ships *Olympic* and *Britannic*, the *Olympic*-class ships built by Harland & Wolff, were the White Star Line's answer to competition in the lucrative transatlantic emigration market. Although promotionally the emphasis was placed on *Titanic* as a luxury means of transport for the wealthy, it was actually as an emigrant ship that it was expected to make money. Profit depended on the high-volume sales of steerage tickets, not on the high ticket costs of first class, which demanded more expensive facilities than those expected by third-class passengers. Although conditions were an improvement over what they had been in steerage over the previous century and White Star was taking them further in terms of comfort, they were still economical to provide.[61] The splendour of elite travel was a gilding meant for prestige rather than great profit. Competition was fierce. In 1907, the launch of the Cunard liners *Lusitania* and *Mauretania* posed a challenge to the White Star Line's drive to dominance of the market.

Cunard enjoyed the privilege of subsidies from the British government for the building of new ocean liners in an attempt to maintain British primacy in Atlantic traffic. In 1902, Cunard was provided with an annual subsidy of £150,000 and a low-interest loan of £2.5 million for the construction of the two superliners, the Blue Riband winners *Lusitania* and *Mauretania*, each capable of reaching a speed of 26 knots. In time of war, these ships could be requisitioned by the Royal Navy and adapted for battle. Their design had to meet with Admiralty approval. At the same time as guaranteeing extra support in war, the subsidies supported national prestige in shipping and ensured that Cunard remained a British company rather than fall into the hands of American big business.[62]

In many ways, the British government subsidies for Cunard were a response to the formation in 1902 of the International Mercantile Marine Company, an attempt by American financier and banker John Pierrepoint Morgan to establish a trust that would monopolise North Atlantic shipping. It was formed of the International Navigation Company, comprising the Red Star and American lines, the Atlantic Transport Line, the Leyland Line and the White Star Line, and acted as a holding company. Each company retained its own identity and sailed under its own country's flag but was owned by a single trust. Morgan hoped to dominate transatlantic shipping through interlocking directorates and contractual arrangements with the railroads.[63] Nevertheless, there was concern that:

> It is nothing but a mere pretence to say that through the technical wording of the Company's Act they are in any sense British, though through this technicality they are allowed to fly the British flag, a fact which most people regard as nothing less than a public scandal.[64]

Profit-sharing arrangements were made with the German Hamburg-Amerika and the North German Lloyd lines.[65] This relationship with these other companies was close enough for Johan George Reuchlin, managing director of Holland America Line, to travel on *Titanic* to investigate the possibility of his company running a steamer service from Antwerp and Rotterdam through the Panama Canal, as well as checking out the *Olympic*-class liners built by Harland & Wolff.[66] Philadelphia traction magnate Peter Widener was a major shareholder and director of the International Mercantile Marine Company and an associate with Morgan in the United States Steel Corporation; his son George, himself a member of the board of the Fidelity Trust Company of Philadelphia, which had provided finance for the company, was a passenger on the maiden voyage with his wife and son. J.P. Morgan had also been expected to sail but had cancelled his passage shortly before embarkation.[67]

Although initially opposed to joining the International Mercantile Marine Company, Joseph Bruce Ismay, president of White Star, served as its president from 1904 until 1913. The White Star Line was very much the creation of Ismay's father, Thomas Ismay, who in 1867 had bought the name, flag and goodwill of a bankrupt packet company. Under him, White Star gained its reputation for stable and comfortable ships, and it was claimed that 'Mr Ismay was, in truth, the inventor of luxurious ocean travel'.[68] Bruce Ismay, 'a cultured cosmopolitan, if you like, but not a strong ruler of strong men', succeeded his father in 1899 and continued the emphasis on comfort over speed.[69] In 1907, the main operational base of the line was moved from Liverpool to Southampton. A weekly service would sail from Southampton every Wednesday and head across the English Channel to the French port of Cherbourg that evening, before calling at Queenstown (since renamed Cobh) the following morning. On return eastbound crossings, ships did not call at Queenstown and instead landed at Plymouth, before proceeding to Cherbourg and Southampton. Southampton was closer to London than Liverpool, which reduced the travelling time for wealthier passengers. The terminal at Cherbourg would be convenient for passengers travelling in Europe, both emigrants and the wealthy travelling by train from Paris. This was the route to be taken by *Titanic* on her maiden voyage.[70]

Since the time of Thomas Ismay, White Star had enjoyed a close relationship with the Belfast shipbuilding firm of Harland & Wolff, founded in 1861 and headed since 1895 by James William Pirrie as chairman. Pirrie built up the firm into a leading shipbuilding company and placed an emphasis on the construction of large and technologically advanced vessels. He played a leading role in the design of the *Olympic*-class ships along with Alexander Carlisle but kept firm control of all financial matters in his own hands. The newspaper editor and journalist W.T. Stead described Lord Pirrie as:

> the greatest shipbuilder the world has ever seen. He has built more ships and bigger ships than any man since the days of Noah. Not only does he build them, but he owns them, directs them, controls them on all the seas of the world.[71]

He was also one of the leading figures in the International Mercantile Marine Company alongside Ismay, Widener and Morgan. It was only the need to rest in order to recover from a prostate operation that prevented him from sailing on *Titanic*, which he and Ismay had conceived as a means of consolidating the business future of White Star and mounting an effective challenge to Cunard.[72]

The new ships were to be on a hitherto unparalleled grand and lavish scale, at 840 feet long and of 52,000 gross tonnage, outdoing the Cunarders.[73] When launched in 1911, *Titanic* was to be even larger than when first planned: 882 feet 9 inches long, 92 feet broad, 175 feet high, with a gross tonnage of 46,328. The emphasis was on size and luxury since the new White Star ships could not match the speed of their rivals. Instead, *Titanic* was promoted as a monument to modernity, shown in publicity brochures and postcards vertically between a group of four New York skyscrapers and a number of historical monuments including the pyramids that themselves were the height of innovation and technological progress, as well as great size, in their own time. It represented a continuity of technological advance from Ancient Egypt to the latest developments.[74] Lord Pirrie believed that with the building of these mammoth ocean liners there was 'no limit to the size of ship except that imposed by accommodation in shipbuilding yards and docks'.[75] However, not everyone agreed that the potential to build ever bigger and more extravagantly was unbounded. Charles Hays, the railroad magnate, himself a builder on a large scale, warned only hours before the sinking of:

> the White Star, the Cunard and the Hamburg-American lines now devoting their attention to a struggle for supremacy in obtaining the most luxurious appointments for their ships, but the time will soon come when the greatest and most appalling of all disasters at sea will be the result.[76]

However, Pirrie's confidence in progress remained boundless and was to be unchallenged until disaster struck. Yet despite her size, *Titanic* was expected to 'reign supreme as the largest vessel in the world' for only a year until the completion of the Hamburg American liner *Imperator*.[77] Just as there was an arms race between Britain and Germany to build bigger and better naval vessels, there was also a race to launch prestige ships between the rival shipping companies of the two nations.

The Harland & Wolff shipbuilding facilities on Queen's Island, Belfast, needed to be upgraded before work could begin on the new and massive

Olympic-class ships. Four of the existing slipways were replaced by two larger slips, over which was erected a gigantic steel gantry carrying a system of cranes and travelling frames and accessed by electric elevators and walkways. This Arrol Gantry, named after the Glaswegian engineering firm of Sir William Arrol and Company that had designed it, was so huge it could be seen from most parts of Belfast. The Thompson Graving Dock, built by the Belfast Harbour Commissioners as the largest dry dock in the world for ship repairs, was extended in size to accommodate the *Olympic*-class ships; opened in 1911, it was to be where *Titanic* was to have her propellers fitted and a final coat of paint applied in February 1912, following her launch on 31 May 1911 and subsequent fitting out.[78] Already ports were preparing for the advent of this new generation of super ships. The Belfast Harbour Commission had deepened the Victoria Channel by dredging it to a depth of 32 feet below high-water levels 'in anticipation of the demand for greater water draught that will be made by the new mammoth White Star liners *Olympic* and *Titanic*, and the even greater vessels that are expected to follow them'.[79] At Southampton, a new deep-water dock was built, the Trafalgar Dock was reconstructed to accommodate the ships, and it was proposed that the channel in Southampton Water be deepened and that 'all the work that has to be done will be completed before the *Titanic* and *Olympic* come round from Belfast'.[80] The dock facilities in New York would also need to be extended in order to handle these 'ocean-going leviathans of much greater dimensions than any yet attempted'.[81]

Titanic and *Olympic* were planned and constructed at the same time. The design of the two ships was the responsibility of the naval architects, marine engineers and draftsmen working in the two spacious, lofty and well-lit drawing offices in the Harland & Wolff headquarters building at the shipyard. *Olympic* was started first and any change of design for *Titanic* was noted on the *Olympic* plans. Only if the differences were considerable would a separate plan be made for *Titanic*. Such alterations included extra cabins replacing unused deck space, two first-class suites and the installation of sliding glass windows, known as Ismay screens, on the promenade on A Deck. In the Mould Loft, the lines of the cross-section of the ship would be chalked at full size and the length at quarter scale in order to fix any mistakes made by the draftsmen from working on a small scale. Models of the ship were also made. Precision was the order of the day under the supervision of Thomas Andrews, Pirrie's nephew:

> big and strong, a paint-smeared bowler hat on his crown, grease on his boots and the pockets of his blue jacket stuffed with plans, now making his daily rounds of the yards, now consulting his chief, now conferring with a foreman, now interviewing an owner, now poring over intricate calculations in the drawing office, now superintending the hoisting of a boiler by the 200-foot crane into some newly launched ship by a wharf.[82]

As much attention was given to the design and construction of two tenders, *Nomadic* and *Traffic*, as to the simultaneous building of *Olympic* and *Titanic*, all under the supervision of Thomas Andrews and to the same exacting standards as the ships they were to serve. Unlike Southampton and Queenstown, the port at Cherbourg was too shallow to allow the great transatlantic liners to berth, so tenders were built to carry passengers from the quay to the outer harbour where they could board their ship. *Nomadic* was used for first- and second-class passengers, segregated from each other by the engine room and sliding grilles on the upper deck. *Traffic* carried the third-class passengers separately from their social superiors. It was intended that, unlike previous tenders, *Nomadic* should reflect the grandeur of the ocean liners to give a taste of what was to come with ornate plasterwork and carved oak and mahogany corbels. Like the liners it served, it too represented progress and the power of modern technology. Thomas Andrews was pleased to see in Cherbourg that 'the two little tenders looked well'. He also believed that 'the weather is fine and everything is shaping for a good voyage'.[83]

Not everyone shared his confidence in progress and technical excellence. Joseph Conrad deplored the materialism implicit in the faith most people had in the power of technology just as much as he condemned the materialism of the opulent trappings that disguised the mechanics of a modern ship:

> You build a 45,000 tons hotel of thin steel plates to secure the patronage of, say, a couple of thousand rich people (for if it had been for the emigrant trade alone, there would have been no such exaggeration of

mere size), you decorate it in the style of the Pharaohs or in the Louis Quinze style – I don't know which – and to please the aforesaid fatuous handful of individuals, who have more money than they know what to do with, and to the applause of two continents, you launch that mass with two thousand people on board at twenty-one knots across the sea – a perfect exhibition of the modern blind trust in mere material and appliances. And then this happens. General uproar. The blind trust in material and appliances has received a terrible shock.[84]

Thomas Hardy also decried in 'The Convergence of the Twain' the arrogance that resulted in *Titanic* coming to rest 'in a solitude of the sea deep from human vanity, and the Pride of Life that planned her' where 'over the mirrors meant to glass the opulent the sea-worm crawls' and 'jewels in joy designed to ravish the sensuous mind lie lightless'. In his poem, the manmade beauty and materialism of the *Titanic* is destined to meet its match in the elemental forces of nature, 'and as the smart ship grew in stature, grace, and hue, in shadowy silent distance grew the Iceberg too'. Technological achievement and flawless luxury are ultimately insignificant. Yet the fish in the ocean ask the question 'what does this vain-gloriousness down here?'[85]

The apparent perfection that underlay a belief in the indestructability of the ship was illusory. Not everything on *Titanic* was finished to the expected standards, not surprisingly in the rush to be ready for the maiden voyage. Eleanor Cassebeer complained that 'while the ship was fitted up most sumptuously one could not help but notice that she was not prepared to sail'. Thomas Andrews, with whom she shared a table at dinner, was said to have told her that 'the only reason they allowed her to go when they did was that the sailing date had already been fixed and they just simply had to start'. The frames for printed notices were on the cabin walls but there were no instructions in them. She could not easily find her life jacket.[86] She was not the only one to notice signs that work on preparing the ship was incomplete or hastily done. Imanita Shelley was moved to a second-class cabin that 'looked in a half-finished condition' after complaining that she and her mother, Lutie Parrish, had originally been placed in a cabin too small for two women. An inveterate complainer, Mrs Shelley had then been transferred with her mother to a cabin that 'though large and roomy, was not furnished in the comfortable manner as the same accommodation procured on the Cunard and other lines' as well as not being 'finished' to a satisfactory standard. Suffering from tonsillitis, she was ordered to stay in her cabin but found the room service inadequate because the stewardess was unable to find a tray for her meals so had to take each plate or dish to her one by one. Bedroom steward George Beedem was also unhappy with his working equipment and told his family that 'what with no dusters or anything to work with I wish the bally ship at the bottom of the sea'.[87] Even the second-class ladies' toilet was incomplete with some of the fixtures in crates waiting to be installed.[88] The ornate carved wooden panel showing 'Honour and Glory Crowning Time', which was prominent on the first-class staircase, was incomplete because there had not been time to set a clock into the panel and a mirror had been substituted until the clock could be installed.[89] Nellie Barber, maid to Julia Cavendish, indeed remembered that some of the first-class areas seemed to be in an unfinished state.[90] Stewardess Violet Jessop saw these criticisms as an insult to Thomas Andrews and the shipbuilders and refuted Nellie Barber's memories, but finding the faults was why Andrews and his Guarantee Group of workers from shipbuilders Harland & Wolff were on board.[91]

There were problems with the heating throughout the ship. Mrs Shelley had asked the steward to have the heat turned on because her cabin was too cold, only to be told that the heating system for the second-class cabins was not working. Only three second-class cabins had any heat at all but were so hot that the purser had ordered that all the heating should be turned off with the result that 'the rooms were like ice houses all of the voyage'. Conditions in steerage were no better.[92] The first-class staterooms had electric heaters so could be kept warm, although some passengers felt the need to ask the stewards if they were safe to use.[93]

Crew members were also not altogether satisfied with their accommodation on a new ship. Captain Smith's personal steward or 'Tiger', James Paintin, who previously had served Smith on both *Adriatic* and *Olympic*, complained, 'What a fine ship this is, much better than the *Olympic* as far as passengers are concerned, but my room is nothing near so nice, no daylight, electric light on all day, but I suppose it's no use grumbling.'[94] Although 'the accommodation is far in excess both as regards size and fittings of any other British packet carrying a sea post office on the Atlantic', the postal clerks were unhappy with their mess room, which was used as a thoroughfare to the valets' and ladies' maids' dining room, and complained that the noise from third-class passengers prevented them from enjoying a decent night's sleep.[95] Sixth Officer James Moody considered that 'my room is no bigger than a broom cupboard' and found it difficult to find his way around such a 'big omnibus' which needs '85 clocks and 16 pianos to furnish it'.[96] He was luckier than most of the crew who were accommodated in dormitories. Thomas Andrews was keen to improve crew accommodation but it remained the case that 'no place can be so utterly devoid of glory, of comfort and privacy and so wretched a human habitation as the usual ship's glory hole', as stewards' quarters were known, and in such areas 'all that was low in men seemed to gain the upper hand'.[97]

Contemporary observers, however, were impressed by the facilities on board *Titanic* and considered that 'it is scarcely a compliment to the *Titanic* to say that she is like a sumptuous hotel afloat', comments frequently made about the ship, since 'most of the London hotels are far less sumptuous'. It was generally agreed that:

> the millionaire who pays his £850 for a private suite with a promenade deck of his own, or the third-class passenger who takes his ease in the spacious smoke room which is part of his lot, could scarce expect to find afloat better value for money.[98]

There was no thought that such value for money and luxury appropriate to class might also involve risk of shipwreck. When asked at the British inquiry into the sinking whether it was the view of the White Star Line 'that the *Titanic* was unsinkable', Bruce Ismay's reply was that 'we thought she was' – a false sense of confidence successfully sold to trusting passengers.[99]

The grandeur of *Titanic* provided a stage set against which those on board could act out for a time an idealised version of their lives in the self-contained environment of the ship until disaster revealed what lay behind their own façades. The grand staircase allowed wealthy women to display their finest dresses and for high society to flaunt its wealth. Honeymoon couples such as

Victor and Pepita Peñasco, Lucian and Eloise Smith, and Daniel and Mary Marvin could start out their all-too-short married lives, and tennis player Karl Behr was able to woo his future wife Helen Newsom, in a suitably romantic and glamorous setting. Clubbable businessman Thornton Davidson was able to press palms in the discrete and dignified Smoking Room, where industrial and business magnates such as George Widener, John Thayer and Charles M. Hays held court. Social climbers like Alfred Nourney, masquerading in a fancy wardrobe as a German baron, could act out their fantasies and professional gamblers could select their prey. Philanderers Benjamin Guggenheim and Quigg Baxter could indulge their mistresses. In second class, passengers could enjoy a genteel, more leisurely life than at home. Even the more austere setting of steerage offered a tableau of lower-class gaiety, as observed by Lawrence Beesley looking down from second class to the lower deck, in which:

> the third-class passengers were enjoying every minute of the time: a most uproarious skipping game of the mixed-double type was the great favourite, while 'in and out and roundabout' went a Scotchman with his bagpipes playing something that Gilbert says 'faintly resembled an air'.[100]

The bagpipe player, Eugene Daly, was actually an Irish wool heaver and mechanic who had played a lament on his traditional Irish uilleann pipes as the ship left Queenstown. Behind the scenes, personal dramas involving child abduction, mistresses, business dealings and social scandal took place. Soon, the magnificence of *Titanic* became the backcloth to scenes of tragedy and life-or-death drama. Matania's depiction of one moment on deck evokes the society aboard *Titanic* and the theatricality of its end, which came when, at about twenty minutes before midnight on 14 April, RMS *Titanic*, on its maiden voyage from Southampton to New York, struck an iceberg on its starboard side and sank at about twenty past two on the morning of 15 April 1912.

Chapter Two

Manly Heroes in Evening Suits

Visions of elegant gentlemen, formally dressed in conservative white tie evening dress or the newly fashionable tuxedos favoured by more stylish and sartorially daring younger men like Matania's young gallant in his illustration of *Women and Children First*, bravely and insouciantly sacrificing themselves to certain death while waving off their loved ones, have become an enduring if somewhat clichéd image of the last hours of the supposedly unsinkable *Titanic*. The heroism of these first-class passengers was lauded in the popular press even before the journalists had the opportunity to interview any survivors or learn any detail of what had actually happened, starting an almost mythical narrative continued by the accounts of survivors and the embellishments of reporters. Second Officer Charles Lightoller reinforced this picture of stoicism:

> There had been no lamentations, no demonstrations either from the men passengers as they saw the last life-boat go, and there was no wailing or crying, no outburst from the men who lined the ship's rail as the *Titanic* disappeared from sight. The men stood quietly as if they were in church.[1]

Charles Weikman, the ship's chief barber, particularly remembered:

> Mr. Widener and his son Harry at the rail. They were all aiding and giving words of cheer to the heart-broken women, whose sobs and pleadings rose above the noise of the screeching davits as the boats were being lowered. During all this time the vessel had been settling slowly and now it was noticed that it had commenced to sink faster. Those of us who remained on board must die.[2]

The journalist Marshall Everett fulsomely considered that 'the Wideners of Philadelphia are a hearty race. Their money has not sapped their manhood.'[3] There was comfort that 'in the midst of harrowing recitals shines the heroism of American manhood, which protected the weak and helpless'.[4] Léontine Pauline Aubart, mistress of financier Benjamin Guggenheim, especially remembered the demeanour of British gentlemen, happily stating in a newspaper interview that:

> I, who am a patriotic French woman say that never can I forget that group of Englishmen – every one of them a perfect gentleman – calmly puffing cigarettes and cigars and watching the women and children being placed in the boats.[5]

Inevitably, all attention was on the most illustrious and prominent of the passengers in first class, men whose names were well known and whose activities were often reported in newspapers. It was these men who were noticed by their fellow passengers and whose heroic deaths could sell newspapers. British newspapers noted that 'the majority of the well-known people on board belonged to New York rather than to London', yet still churned out stories about the wealthy and glamorous victims of both nations.[6] The *Washington Post* described how:

> Americans and Englishmen of fame and wealth – Archibald Butt, William T. Stead, Clarence Moore, John Jacob Astor, F.D. Millet, George D. and Harry Widener among them – from the deck of the *Titanic* watched the last lifeboat disappear and went to heroes' graves marked by the depthless sea.[7]

The same names of wealthy men dying heroically were repeated incessantly in different accounts of the sinking with the effect that chivalric self-sacrifice came to be equated with wealth and social position. The columnist Elbert Hubbard lamented that:

> The Strauses, Stead, Astor, Butt, Harris, Thayer, Widener, Guggenheim, Hays, I thought I knew you because I had seen you, realized somewhat

of your able qualities, looked into your eyes and pressed your hands, but I did not guess your greatness.⁸

The *Philadelphia North American*, a newspaper that was usually critical of big business and supported organised labour against the industrial magnates, did not stint in its praise of the conduct of men whose conduct as employers it rarely defended:

> John Jacob Astor, true to his record of patriotism and gallantry in 1898, smiling and waving farewell to the young wife soon to be a mother; Archie Butt, that loveable, debonair gentleman of the South, well called by Admiral Dewy 'nature's nobleman', calmly controlling with perfect courtesy the well-nigh frenzied women, and placing them in safety; George Widener, kissing his wife goodbye and with reassuring word falling back into the line, busied with the work of rescue, and beside him his son, as true a man as his brave father; John B. Thayer, surrendering a place of safety in favour of Mrs Thayer's serving-maid; Ryerson, Dulles, Williams, Sutton, and Brewe – all these, with hundreds of others, are on a roll of nobility that history will preserve.⁹

Their ruthlessness and sharp business practices in life, along with any moral or social failings, were atoned for by the noble and exemplary manner of their deaths. One of the early, near contemporary books on the sinking by Logan Marshall stressed that they were powerful business and industrial leaders but showed the best side of such capitalists at a time when there was criticism of their harsh treatment of their workers:

> There were men whose word of command swayed boards of directors, governed institutions, disposed of millions. They were accustomed merely to pronounce a wish to have it gratified. Thousands 'posted at their bidding'; the complexion of the market altered hue when they nodded; they bought what they wanted, and for one of the humblest fishing smacks or a dory they could have given the price that was paid to build and launch the ship that has become the most imposing

mausoleum that ever housed the bones of men since the Pyramids rose from the desert sands. But these men stood aside – one can see them! – and gave place not merely to the delicate and the refined, but to the scared Czech woman from the steerage, with her baby at her breast; the Croatian with a toddler by her side, coming through the very gate of Death and out of the mouth of Hell to the imagined Eden of America.[10]

A less heroic, less idealistic image of these same rich and powerful men as they faced death was offered by the journalist and proponent of spiritualism W.T. Stead's daughter Estelle, who in 1922 published what she claimed was her father's account of the afterlife communicated through a series of seances:

Here were hundreds of bodies floating in the water – dead – hundreds of souls carried through the air, alive; very much alive, some were. Many, realising their death had come, were enraged at their own powerlessness to save their valuables. They fought to save what they had on earth prized so much. The scene on the boat at the time of striking was not pleasant, but it was as nothing to the scene among the poor souls newly thrust out of their bodies, all unwillingly.[11]

Among them were men and women who 'were in agony of doubt as to their people left behind and as to their own future state', many of them 'almost mental wrecks. They knew nothing, they seemed to be uninterested in everything, their minds were paralysed.' Once these 'living dead' had all been collected, they were transported together through the air on a gigantic platform to another world where they parted company and individually could be purified as free agents. Dressed as they had been in life with their own clothing transported with them, they gradually lost their corporeal desires and habits such as smoking, alcohol and overeating while they were offered the opportunity to refine their worldly interests in a more ethical manner, be they in the academic or business worlds. In this fantastical view of the world, it was only after death that the wealthy, avaricious, grasping and ruthless were purged of their sins rather than through their self-sacrifice of dying chivalrously as the popular press had suggested in

1912. Nevertheless, redemption of more than reputation was on offer in the spiritualist world. In the real world, it was reputation that mattered.

The wealthiest man on the *Titanic* was in desperate need of the redemption and rehabilitation offered by a conspicuous act of gallantry and a virtuous death. Business magnate, real estate developer, investor, writer, lieutenant colonel in the Spanish American war, John Jacob Astor has been dismissed as an aimless dilettante and 'the world's greatest monument to unearned income', earning him the uncomplimentary nickname of 'Jack Ass-tor'. He was the author of a science-fiction novel about life on Saturn and Jupiter in the year 2000. He also patented several inventions, including a bicycle brake, a 'vibratory disintegrator' used to produce gas from peat moss, and a pneumatic road-improver. He was the builder of two luxurious New York hotels, the Astoria and the St Regis, patronised by the fashionable and wealthy including some of his fellow travellers on *Titanic*. Despite such prominence, he remained difficult to know. To journalist Filson Young he was 'like a polite skeleton in his own gay house; an able but superficially unprepossessing man, so rich that it was almost impossible to know accurately anything about him – a man, I should say, to whom money had been nothing but a handicap from his earliest days'.[12] Despite money having seemingly brought him little pleasure, he was assiduous in increasing his wealth. A slum landlord who ignored calls to improve the living conditions of his tenants, he opposed the redevelopment of North Manhattan for fear that his rental income would fall if the tenements he owned were less overcrowded.

It was not his lack of social conscience that had brought him social ostracism but his personal life. In 1909, he had divorced his first wife after eighteen years of marriage and within two years had scandalised New York society by marrying Madeleine Forge, a woman twenty-nine years younger than him and at 18, a year younger than his son Vincent, the reluctant best man at the wedding. Keenly aware of public criticism, he had announced defiantly that:

> Now that we are happily married, I don't care how difficult divorce and remarriage laws are made. I sympathize heartily with the most straitlaced people in most of their ideas, but believe that remarriage should

be possible once, as marriage is the happiest condition for the individual and the community.[13]

It was not how his marriage was generally viewed and to escape the ignominy the Astors had wintered in Europe and Egypt before returning to the United States for the birth of their first child and in the hope that the scandal of their marriage might have been forgotten. They were accompanied by Astor's valet, Victor Robbins, Mrs Astor's maid, Rosalie Bidois, her nurse, Caroline Louise Endres, and their pet Airedale terrier, Kitty. Only Madeleine, her nurse and her maid survived.

Captain Smith was said to have warned Astor individually about the collision with the iceberg. The Astors waited in the gymnasium for the loading of the lifeboats and sat on the mechanical horses. Astor, ever the man of practical science, even demonstrated to his wife the structure of the lifebelts by slicing through the lining of one with his penknife. Archibald Gracie later claimed to have helped Astor to place his wife into one of the lifeboats. Astor had then asked if he could join her as she was pregnant, but was told that 'no man is allowed on this boat or any of the boats until the ladies are off'. He accepted this instruction but, fully expecting that he was in no personal danger, asked for the number of the lifeboat to help him find his wife once the emergency was over. He was last seen smoking and talking with the writer Jacques Futrelle on the starboard bridge wing.[14]

Many survivors spoke of how Colonel Astor had personally helped them into lifeboats, including making sure that Ida Hippach and her 17-year-old daughter Jean took the last two places in the final lifeboat despite their reluctance to do so and ordered the crew to wait until the two women had joined the lifeboat.[15] It was alleged that he had willingly surrendered his place in a lifeboat so that women and children might be saved.[16] Astor was said to have given a military salute to his wife before bidding her a last farewell.[17] George Harder remembered him putting a woman's hat on a small boy so that the child would be allowed to enter another boat disguised as a girl.[18] Philip Mock claimed to have seen him 'in the water clinging to a raft with William Thomas Stead, though their feet became frozen and they were forced to release their hold'.[19] As well as heroically saving other passengers, he was also said to have attempted to save the dogs aboard *Titanic*, including his own terrier Kitty, by opening the kennels to give the animals a chance of survival. Once the social pariah, he was now eulogised. The Twaalfskill Golf Club of Kingston, New York, declared that his last hours had been characterised by 'that self-sacrifice, heroism, and chivalry which are the distinguishing characteristics of American manhood'.[20] Flags were at half-mast for his funeral. Only through a seemingly heroic death was he once more accepted by society.

The mining and smelting tycoon Benjamin Guggenheim was another wealthy passenger whose private peccadillos were atoned by his death. The Hebrew Technical Institute in New York was to lament that 'we cannot but feel that a career full of possibilities of larger achievement and rich in promise of even broader service to his fellow-men has been cut short by a ruthless and needless catastrophe', though he was hitherto remembered for his genial personality and generous impulses rather than for any prior solid achievement.[21] He had boarded *Titanic* with his latest mistress, French singer Léontine Aubart. His bedroom steward, Henry Etches, testified that Guggenheim and his valet and secretary, Victor Giglio, had assisted the officers in ensuring that women and children were safely aboard the lifeboats. He had reassured his mistress and her maid that they would all soon be reunited safely, before retiring to his stateroom with Giglio so that master and servant could change into full evening dress, declaring that 'we've dressed up in our best and are prepared to go down like gentlemen'. He also asked Etches to tell his much-neglected wife back in New York that his last thoughts were of her and their daughters. It was also important that she and the world should know that 'I've done my best in doing my duty'[22] and 'that I played the game straight to the end and that no woman was left on board this ship because Ben Guggenheim was a coward'.[23] In apparently acting in this way he gave the defining image of the death of a gentleman, albeit one reflected in his choice of fine clothing and the importance of looking good rather than in action, and ensured that his own reputation would be more than that of a serial philanderer.

Charles Hays, a railroad magnate, seems to have had an exemplary family life and did not board *Titanic* with any imputations of personal moral failings, but he was beset by business worries, which potentially could have ruined him, but were forgotten for a time when he lost his life saving weaker women and children. Hays was president of the Grand Trunk Railway of Canada, with a brief to introduce modern and more aggressive, less scrupulous business practices that were at the time standard in the United States but not so familiar in Canada, where more gentlemanly British ways of operating were more widespread. He had grandiose ambitions for a transcontinental railway that would open up the prairies, for which he enjoyed federal government support from Prime Minister Sir Wilfrid Laurier, though the constant demands of Hays for government subsidies for his railway expansion were to split Laurier's cabinet.[24] Hays, who brooked no interference with the way in which he ran his railway, also ran roughshod over organised labour, resulting in a localised strike in Ontario in 1905 and a bitter national dispute in 1910. His disdain for organised labour was such that he was described as 'heartless, cruel and tyrannical'.[25]

By 1912, the Grand Trunk Railway was facing insolvency in the face of increasing costs stoked by rising wages, higher prices for materials and the insistence of Hays on 'building to the highest standards'. In 1912, Hays travelled to London for a directors' meeting at which he insisted that only by upgrading rolling stock, double tracking and by building a chain of luxury hotels across Canada could bankruptcy be averted. He was keen to return to Canada for the opening of his flagship hotel, the Château Laurier in Ottawa, at the end of April and also to see one of his daughters, who was having a difficult pregnancy. He happily accepted an invitation to return on *Titanic* as the guest of Bruce Ismay, only paying incidental expenses for his retinue and himself, including his wife, daughter and son-in-law, his wife's maid and his private secretary, Vivian Payne, who was regarded as almost a surrogate son to Hays and 'had the knack of making friends without any effort on his part, and attracted to himself everyone with whom he came into contact'.[26]

In the immediate aftermath of his death, Hays was eulogised as one of Canada's greatest railway magnates. On the day of his funeral:

> from Montreal to Chicago, from New Brunswick to the Pacific coast, in all the thousands of miles of sidings and branch lines owned and operated by the Grand Trunk Railway, in every Grand Trunk Depot, at every Grand Trunk crossing, action ceased for the space of five full

minutes as the Grand Trunk Railway system paid its respects to the memory of its great departed chief.[27]

However, his policies resulted in the collapse of the company in 1919, partly because he had committed the board to expensive undertakings and guarantees without fully informing his fellow directors of the consequences.[28]

James Clinch Smith's reputation had been besmirched by association with a scandal rather than direct involvement in it, but all was now wiped clean and forgotten in the circumstances of his death. His brother-in-law, the architect Stanford White, had been murdered at the opening of a new musical comedy at Madison Square Garden in 1906. Not only was Smith a witness but he had been deep in conversation with the murderer, Harry K. Thaw, before the deed and was called on to testify at the trial, which brought this quietly conservative man into the limelight. Although 'there are no stories of heroics concerning his conduct during those awful final hours', the *New York Times* still surmised that 'he must have fulfilled the law of "women and children first", going silently into eternity'.[29]

Dying as a gentleman was integral to contemporary codes of manliness. A young doctor travelling in second class, Alfred Pain, although Canadian by birth and upbringing was described by St George's Benevolent Society as having:

> acted the part of a true born Englishman. He played the man among that noble band of heroes who have thrilled the whole world by their glorious death. He has upheld the most splendid tradition of our race, and the joy of it can never die. The heart of every member of our society throbs in sympathy.[30]

It was important to his friends and family that Pain should have lived up to the gentlemanly code even in his death.

The contemporary cult of manliness and ideas of selfless masculinity defined the narrative into which the heroism of the men who died in the sinking of *Titanic* were slotted.[31] Elites were glorified with their notions of duty, fair play, generosity, restraint and self-sacrifice suggesting how a true gentleman should behave. In adversity, he was stoical and displayed an Anglo-Saxon stiff upper lip to the world.[32] He was chivalrous to women, though this may have marginalised the role of what patronisingly was seen as the weaker sex. He was active and cut a dashing and fine figure in action. The character of the manly man was formed through education and an emphasis on sporting activity and athleticism. The British public schools had fostered these traits in such men as Tyrell Cavendish, educated at Harrow, Christopher Head at Lancing, and Thomas Pears at Clifton College, as did American elite private schools such as the Hill School in Pottstown, Pennsylvania, where both Washington Roebling and Harry Widener had been educated. Widener, noted for his retentive memory of baseball averages, the stage roles of his favourite actors and complex bibliographical detail, had gone on to study at Harvard, where the majority of his courses were in History with others taken in English, Fine Arts and Greek, reflecting his personal interests, but he also took an active part in student life, athletics and drama, developing the persona of manliness in himself expected in a student of the time. He played hockey as a freshman. He was a member of the Hasty Pudding Theatricals, the debating society of The Institute of 1770, the Fencing Club and the final club, Phi Delta Psi, known as the Owl Club.[33] At Berkeley, Walter Clark was heavily involved in the social life of student fraternities, with their arcane rituals, heavy drinking and exclusivity, as was Richard Frazar White at Bowdoin. White's trip to Europe with his father and return home on *Titanic* was to celebrate his graduation. His *alma mater* mourned 'the early death of a brilliant student, a popular and loyal undergraduate, and a true son of Bowdoin'.[34]

Membership of the right clubs was essential for most gentlemen, both to confer social status but also for the conduct of business. Thornton Davidson, the stockbroker son-in-law of railroad mogul Charles Hays, was 'a valued member of the club life' of Montreal whose membership of the St James, Racquet, Montreal Hunt, Montreal Jockey, Montreal Polo, Royal St Lawrence Yacht, Manitou and Canada clubs, and the Montreal Amateur Athletic Association, meant that by the age of 31 he was 'regarded as one of the shrewdest and most progressive of the younger members of the Stock Exchange'. The thrusting and energetic ambition of the successful businessman was seen as an essential attribute of a gentleman in the elite Anglo-Protestant society of Montreal, though business failure was seen as a sign of weakness if not effeminacy. Davidson was ever on the lookout for opportunities and ways of ensuring his personal success. The social contacts he made as a sporty and convivial clubman were useful for him in 'promoting various financial undertakings' and clinching hardheaded deals.[35] In this, he was representative of the spectacularly successful but unscrupulous and self-assured stockbrokers of the gilded age, though in his case greatly aided by the political connections of his father, Chief Justice Davidson, and father-in-law Charles Hays. Boldly and brashly, he had announced his arrival in London on the *Lusitania* on 4 March 1912 'for the purpose of establishing a financial connection in London and Paris' by placing an advertisement in *The Times*.[36] It was inevitable that after his death he should be lauded by his peers as having been 'foremost among the younger generation of business men in Montreal' and as a young man with a 'strength of character which manifests itself in the highest type of manhood when a crisis arises' and who had 'attained a high standing in the financial circles of the city, but whose untimely death in the sinking of the steamship *Titanic*, April 15, 1912, ended a career that had not only been successful, but gave great promise for the future'.[37]

Most of the men who perished on *Titanic* were said to have shown equally great promise for the future, though in many cases with less evidence to show for it than Thornton Davidson. Quigg Baxter, a fellow Canadian and also from Montreal, had squandered his opportunities, having dropped out of his studies in Applied Science at McGill University and dabbled as a hockey coach before applying his energies to alcohol and hedonism. His father, 'Diamond Jim' Baxter, a diamond broker and banker, had brought shame on the family in 1900 after being convicted and imprisoned for five years for embezzling $40,000 from his bank. Now aged 24, Quigg was travelling home from Europe with his mother and sister, but unbeknown to them he had also booked a cabin for his Brussels cabaret singer mistress Berthe Mayné, whom he planned to marry in Montreal. The three women met for the first time when he escorted them all to the same lifeboat. He retained his insouciance to the end, his sister remarking that 'while he didn't relish being parted from us, he bade me farewell bravely'. He also handed his mother his hip flask filled with brandy only to be thanked with reprimands for his heavy drinking, which he cut short with his farewell:

'Êtes vous bien maman? Au revoir, bon espoir vous-autres.' It was his parting shot at his overly critical mother as he was never to be seen again.[38]

Sporting prowess was considered important in the character building of a gentleman. Alfred Pain, a 24-year-old doctor returning as a second-class passenger to Hamilton, Ontario, after working at King's College Hospital in London, was extolled as:

> a model of Canadian manhood – 6 foot tall, broad and straight, pure in thought and keen in life, loving and gentle; ever thinking of the happiness of others, planning for the pleasure of friends and of the parents and brother for whom he lived; kind to those around him, especially if afflicted or needy – a gentleman in every true sense of the word.

Although his main interest outside medicine was music, he was also 'an ardent lover of clean sports', such as cricket, football, rifle shooting, yachting and all water sports. During his voyage home, he organised games on deck to keep his fellow passengers amused.[39]

Whilst for a canny businessman like Thornton Davidson participation in such sports as riding, hunting, polo, racquets, tennis, hockey and yachting gave him opportunities to forge business contacts, for others it offered an activity to break up the idleness of a leisured life. Clarence Moore was returning from a trip to buy foxhounds in England for the Loudon Hunt in Virginia, of which he was hunt master. He was described as 'the most daring horseman I have ever seen, and yet one could not call him reckless. He knew every phase of fox hunting, which was his greatest hobby.'[40] A member of the New York Yacht Club, the Travellers' Club of Paris, and the Metropolitan, the Chevy Chase and the Alibi clubs of Washington, he was said to be 'one of the best-known men in Washington' and 'one of the best-known sportsmen in America'.[41] Billy Carter actually aped the manners of the English aristocracy. He had dropped out of the University of Pennsylvania so that he could devote the majority of his time to hunting and polo. He was returning home to Pennsylvania after a year in England, where he had rented Rotherby Manor in Leicestershire for the hunting season.[42]

Many of the real English gentlemen their American counterparts tried to equal believed that they had a duty to contribute to local or national politics.

Tyrell Cavendish, a country gentleman devoted to the sport of hunting and fishing so beloved by his peers, was also keenly interested in politics and was actively seeking nomination for a safe Tory parliamentary seat. His friend Norman Carlyle Craig, Unionist MP for the Isle of Thanet, booked a passage on *Titanic* at the same time as Cavendish and his American wife Julia, but did not travel 'in view of the present political situation' regarding Irish Home Rule.[43] Cavendish, who 'had a keen sense of humour and was very amusing and a good speaker', according to his wife, was robbed of realising his political ambitions by his early death at sea.[44]

Christopher Head, a London barrister, insurance broker and an underwriter for Lloyds of London, travelling on maritime insurance business to New York and on to the West Indies, by contrast, had already made his mark in local government as Mayor of Chelsea and a Municipal Reform Party councillor allied to the Conservatives. Critics alleged that 'he would gladly have governed all Chelsea in the spirit of the benevolent despot' with his 'impractical or even quixotic' views and that he hoped to 'awaken public spirit on behalf of the country's defensive forces'. He was especially interested in town planning, the preservation of open spaces for the public benefit, libraries, education and civic art. A member of the Burlington Fine Arts Club, Head was a connoisseur and collector of art, particularly modern art, and closely involved in artistic circles in Chelsea, which gave him an advantage in taking a leading role in Mansion House plans for a national monument to the late king, Edward VII. He himself was the subject of a bronze statue showing him as an unpretentious, almost louche young man in a lounge suit, exhibited in 1909 by Kathleen Scott, who later sculpted a more heroic monumental representation of Captain Edward Smith equal in power to her public memorials to her explorer husband Robert Falcon Scott and his Polar colleague Edward Wilson, who also lost their lives in 1912. Head, who with his close friend Cuthbert Heath pioneered the use of statistics to assess the probability of risks in catastrophe insurance against hurricanes and earthquakes, was cautious enough to insure his own life 'against ocean accidents' for £25,000 before his trip on *Titanic*. The main beneficiary was his wife Ethel, whom he had married in 1910 very soon after her divorce on the grounds of her adultery was finalised.[45] His journalist friend Filson Young described him as:

typical of that almost anonymous world that keeps the name of England liked and respected everywhere. ... Christopher Head was mild and unassuming, and one of the most attractive of men, for wherever he went he left a sense of serenity and security; and he walked through life with a keen, observant intelligence.[46]

For wealthy younger men, motor sports and speed offered a new excitement that was modern and in keeping with the optimism of the age. Crated up among the cargo was Billy Carter's 25 horsepower Renault car, which he was taking home with him from Europe. Washington Roebling II, 'a daring driver' and athlete, and his widowed friend Stephen Blackwell were themselves returning from a motoring trip around Europe, but Roebling's Fiat car and chauffeur were on a different ship. 'Washy' Roebling, nephew of a Civil War hero and builder of the Brooklyn Bridge, was a young engineer who, in collaboration with the French automobile designer Etienne Planche, designed and built his own Roebling-Planche racing car, which he drove to take second place in the Vanderbilt Cup Race in Savannah in 1911 only for it to fail to start when entered for the American Grand Prix. As the dashing general manager of the Trenton-based Mercer Automobile Company, which manufactured high-end racing cars, he test-drove every car himself. After the sinking, his family believed that their 'only hope lay in the fact that Mr Roebling was a true sportsman and his training as an auto driver would stand him in good stead at the time of trouble enabling him to keep cool'.[47]

Thomas Pears's faith in the efficiency and infallibility of new technology was to be sadly misplaced. A clean-cut young soap manufacturer who preferred fast vehicles to slow ocean liners, Pears revelled in fast racing cars and motorcycles. He had the medals he was awarded for taking part in two twenty-four-hour car runs from London to Edinburgh in 1908 mounted as napkin rings. Despite not having shown any interest in sport as a boy at Clifton College before going briefly to Cambridge on a science scholarship, he was a keen sportsman and active supporter of the Pears' Athletics Club at the soap works he managed at Isleworth as a progressive employer interested in the welfare of his employees as befitted an active Anglican and the son of Andrew Pears, who had a reputation as a 'stalwart radical' as chairman of the Brentford

Liberal Association and an alderman on Middlesex County Council. With his wife Edith, he was on a business trip and, ever the consummate businessman, despite having failed to be elected to his father's seat on the board of his family firm, he was unhappy to find bars of 'Vinolia Otto Toilet Soap – perfect for sensitive skins and delicate complexions' in his stateroom rather than Pears soap, which his own company manufactured. At first, it was believed that Pears, whom his former headmaster believed had 'no doubt, like others, helped those who were weaker in their hour of danger, and borne himself as all would wish to do in the face of a great danger', had survived the sinking.[48] On 13 April he had sent a Marconigram to his colleagues and family with the message 'All well' but it was not received until after his death and raised false hopes of his survival. Subsequent Marconigrams informed their families that 'Edith safe, all hope for Tom', followed by a report that both were missing and finally, that Edith was now with friends in New York but that there was no news of the fate of her husband.[49] The latest technology had merely sown confusion and false intelligence. It was also to propagate fake news about the survival of the ship and all its passengers in the immediate aftermath of the sinking to such an extent that the British consul-general in New York complained that 'a great deal of pain was caused to the public by the improper use of wireless' and that 'amateurs with imperfect instruments picked up parts of messages and piecing them together sent messages that were far from true'.[50]

Budding cinematographer Daniel Marvin, like Tom Pears, was also an enthusiast for motorcycling and was an active member of the New York Motorcycle Touring Club. However, his main passion was for cinematography and movie cameras. The son of the founder of the early motion picture production houses American Mutoscope and the Biograph Company, Marvin also had ambitions to be a filmmaker. He was a friend of Thomas Edison. His wedding was restaged for the camera and could be claimed to be the first to be 'cinematographed'. With him on his honeymoon was a movie camera, which he was seen using on the voyage home. He was said to have entrusted the reel of film to his wife Mary as he saw her off in a lifeboat, but its subsequent fate remains unknown. Had it survived, it would have been a remarkable record of the fatal voyage and might have suggested the actual talent of a man who came to be seen as a lost film director or movie studio mogul.[51]

Although speed and the latest in technological advances were important to many younger passengers, there is no evidence that *Titanic* was building up speed in an attempt to break records for the Atlantic crossing. Railway tycoon Charles Hays feared that 'the White Star, the Cunard, and Hamburg-American Lines are devoting their attention and ingenuity in vying with one another to attain the supremacy in luxurious ships and in making speed records. The time will come soon when this will be checked by some appalling disaster,' though he was also convinced that *Titanic* would stay afloat for ten hours, which should have been long enough for the rescue of all the passengers.[52] The White Star Line stressed comfort and reliability above the record-breaking crossings publicised by rivals Cunard. That didn't stop passengers from making bets on how quickly the ship would reach New York. It was noted by passenger Archibald Gracie that the captain had each day improved upon the previous day's speed, and prophesied that 'with continued fair weather, we should make an early arrival record for this maiden trip'.[53] Bruce Ismay, chairman and managing director of White Star, seems to have been keen to beat the crossing time of his own ship *Olympic*, and on Saturday, 13 April was overheard by Elizabeth Lines discussing with Captain Smith the possibility of getting to New York before the scheduled time: 'Well, we did better to-day than we did yesterday, we made a better run to-day than we did yesterday, we will make a better run to-morrow. Things are working smoothly, the machinery is bearing the test, the boilers are working well' and that 'We will beat the *Olympic* and get in to New York on Tuesday'.[54] Ismay admitted that 'it was our intention, if we had fine weather on Monday afternoon or Tuesday, to drive the ship at full speed. That, owing to the unfortunate catastrophe, never eventuated.'[55] Nevertheless, it was believed that *Titanic* was going too fast through the ice field.

Risk-taking and gambling were characteristic of many of the first-class passengers. Aboard ship their favourite resort was the Smoking Room, decorated to resemble one of the gentlemen's clubs of Mayfair, where they could be all boys together, enjoying cigars, strong spirits and cards, free of the presence of women. When the iceberg struck, there were at least seven games of cards in progress. Playing seven-card stud were Manhattan lawyer and Yale tennis champion Karl Behr, financier Richard Beckwith, Edwin N. Kimball, president of the Hallet, Davis Piano Company in Boston, and hotel owner

Alexander T. Compton. Nearby, a game of bridge was being played by Hugh Woolner, Mauritz Björnström-Steffansson, Jim Smith and Edward Kent. After attending a dinner hosted by Eleanor Widener in the à la carte restaurant in honour of Captain Smith, her son Harry was ending the evening with a game of bridge whist with Archie Butt and Billy Carter, who had also been guests at the Widener dinner party, a group joined by Clarence Moore. Butt's friend, the artist Frank Millet, was playing cards with New York broker Frederick Hoyt. Colonel Alfons Simonius-Blumer, president of the Swiss Bankverein, Dr Max Staehelin-Maeglin, director of the Swiss Trust Company, and Maximilian Frölicher-Stehli, a manufacturer and importer for the R. Stehli-Hausheer & Sohn silk mill in Zurich, were quietly playing a more discrete game of bridge as befitted Swiss businessmen. Alfred Nourney, posing as a German aristocrat, Baron von Drachstedt, was trying to win money from two businessmen, jeweller Henry Blank and fur importer William Greenfield. Nourney may have been a conman, but he was a novice compared to three professional gamblers, George Brereton, Charles H. Romaine and Harry Homer, who had snared two unwary passengers, Howard Case and Walter Clark, as their prey in a game of auction bridge. It was a typical night for hardened bridge players.

Walter Miller Clark was a young chancer, 'extremely popular in the social and business life of Los Angeles', whose run of luck only went so far. He survived the 1906 San Francisco earthquake when a student at Berkeley, only to go down with the *Titanic*, the sinking of which interrupted his game of auction bridge with cardsharps.[56] Manager of the Los Alamitos Sugar Company in Los Angeles, son of railroad developer James Ross Clark and nephew of Montana copper magnate William Andrews Clark, a Democratic senator found guilty of bribery, whose son Charles, a fellow hard drinker and gambler, was his closest friend, Walter Clark enjoyed the high life his wealth afforded him. He was alleged to have been drunk when he entered the Smoking Room in search of a game of cards after dinner as his wife Virginia had told him to 'go to the smoking-room and play bridge, but, above all things, cautioned him under no circumstances to wake her up when he came down for the night'.[57] An inveterate gambler, Clark's poker chips together with a pair of his gold cufflinks made from Turkish coins, his gold lapel pins, a brass shaving stick canister still containing the shaving soap he used and Virginia's locket and powder compact were later found in his wife's bag in the wreckage close to where their cabin would have been.[58] The professional gamblers had already lured Howard Brown Case, London manager of the Vacuum Oil Company, into playing with him and young Clark was soon identified as an easy target to be fleeced in their 'stiff game'.[59]

Even collision with an iceberg was not enough to rouse seasoned card players from their game. Virginia Clark had to go twice to the Smoking Room door to attract the attention of her husband when she became alarmed about what was happening and had been told by a fellow passenger that everyone should put on their life jackets. Only at her second attempt did he react and heed her warnings.[60] Spencer Silverthorne was watching the game and 'when the crash came I said: "We've hit something," and went out on the starboard side to look. None of us was alarmed. It occurred to me that we might have bumped some small craft.' The players returned to the Smoking Room and resumed their game to the impatience of one of them who had stayed at the table the whole time totally uninterested in anything beyond winning.[61]

A similar attitude of indifference to anything beyond the cards in hand prevailed among the poker players in the second-class Smoking Room. Most of them were young men 'full of hope for their prospects in a new world, mostly unmarried, keen, alert, with the makings of good citizens'. Unlike their counterparts in first class, no one had remembered or recorded their names and very few, if any, of them survived. They had not interrupted their games even 'when one of them had seen through the windows an iceberg go by towering above the decks'. One man joked that the iceberg had probably scratched some of the new paint on the ship and that the captain would wait until it had been touched up before going any further. Another asked one of his friends to run along the deck and pick up some ice for his glass of whisky.[62] It was a story also told of John Jacob Astor and other passengers in first class known to be fond of ice in their Scotch. It reflected a belief that all was well and would make for a good anecdote to be retold in clubrooms in the future.

Harry Widener, dedicated bibliophile and occasional dilettante businessman, cavalierly dismissed the dangers of sinking as 'ridiculous' to fellow passenger Dr Henry Frauenthal, an attitude that Frauenthal believed 'probably describes the mental state of nearly everyone on the boat, thinking that it was impossible for anything serious to happen to this paragon of modern ship architecture'.[63] It was not the first time Widener had been involved in a collision at sea. In September 1911, he was sailing to New York on board *Olympic* when it collided with HMS *Hawke* in the Solent and had to return to Southampton. Then it was nothing more than an inconvenience and, taking advantage of family influence and connections, he was able to return by tug ahead of his fellow passengers to Southampton and take the next sailing on *Mauretania* with his uncle Joseph.[64] Surviving one accident at sea gave him a false sense of security. Now his luck was running out.

Milton Long, considered to be 'a young man of delicate refinement and with the strength lent by increasing robustness … handsome to an unusual degree', was another survivor of a previous accident at sea. He had been aboard the steamer *Spokane* when she ran aground and was wrecked in Seymour Narrows, British Columbia, in 1911. Ever the accomplished raconteur, it was said that:

> His account of the wreck of the *Spokane* was graphic, but, more by the manner of his telling than by what he said, it was apparent that he had gone through the nerve-trying episode with a calmness which must have stood him in good stead in the last ordeal of the *Titanic*.[65]

Harry Molson, Canadian banker and bon vivant, was a veteran survivor of accidents at sea until he went down with *Titanic*. In 1899, he swam away from the sinking of the *Scotsman* in the Gulf of St Lawrence, and in 1904 swam to shore after jumping through his stateroom window dressed only in his shirt and trousers when the *Canada* collided with a collier in the St Lawrence River. He was last seen on *Titanic* taking off his shoes but this time there was no safety within swimming distance.[66]

Titanic had narrowly avoided a collision with the liner *New York* on leaving Southampton, which may have made many passengers feel complacent about the latest collision. Stockbroker Austin Partner had written to his wife telling her that:

> We nearly collided with a liner coming out of Southampton, the *New York*. She was moored so close to where we passed and broke away from

her mooring. She was only about three feet off us, such a shave, I was afraid we should have to go back, which would have been maddening.

Despite having 'a most comfortable room and the ship is quite the most luxurious I have ever been on', Partner was keen to complete his business in Canada and then return home to his wife, so 'I hope she will get there quickly'.[67] Lawrence Beesley, a school teacher travelling in second class, observed that:

> Unpleasant as this incident was, it was interesting to all the passengers leaning over the rails to see the means adopted by the officers and crew of the various vessels to avoid collision, to see on the *Titanic*'s docking-bridge (at the stern) an officer and seamen telephoning and ringing bells, hauling up and down little red and white flags, as danger of collision alternately threatened and diminished.[68]

It was noticeable that of all the passengers crowding the desk to observe the near collision with *New York* on leaving Southampton:

> no one was more interested than a young American kinematograph photographer, who, with his wife, followed the whole scene with eager eyes, turning the handle of his camera with the most evident pleasure as he recorded the unexpected incident on his films. It was obviously quite a windfall for him to have been on board at such a time. But neither the film nor those who exposed it reached the other side, and the record of the accident from the *Titanic*'s deck has never been thrown on the screen.[69]

The young cinematographer was most likely William Harbeck, a 45-year-old pioneer of motion pictures, including feature films, promotional shorts and travelogues, who was lost together with his two cameras, a number of completed movies and a younger woman, Henriette Yvois, travelling with him and presumed by Beesley to be his wife.[70]

Many of the passengers on *Titanic* were seasoned transatlantic travellers and as such did not expect any real threats on what might have been little more than a regular journey to them. Harry Widener and his parents had regularly travelled between North America and Europe. Maritime insurance broker Christopher Head, who 'spared himself neither time nor trouble in what he undertook whether in his public or private capacity', regularly travelled in trading vessels to extend his professional knowledge and 'he undoubtedly chose the *Titanic* as a means of gathering further experience'. Austin Partner of Tolworth, Surrey, himself was a globetrotting stockbroker with unrivalled knowledge of Canadian securities and investments, who had travelled on the *Mauritania* and *Lusitania*. His seventeenth Atlantic crossing, on *Titanic*, was destined to be his last. Ten days before boarding the ship he had started a new stockbroking job with brokerage firm Myer and Robertson and was travelling to Toronto and Winnipeg to familiarise himself with an affiliated firm, Robinson & Black. It was to be uncompleted business. He had recently joined the London Stock Exchange but his joining fee was reimbursed to his widow as his family was impoverished by his death.[71] Similarly, the last few months of his life was a round of transatlantic travel for millinery commercial traveller Ralph Giles. He went to New York on the *Olympic* on 14 February 1912, returning on the *Lusitania* in March. After another business trip to Paris, Giles purchased his second-class ticket, on the *Titanic*, to return to New York on her maiden voyage.[72]

It is little wonder that many seasoned travellers, rather than sacrificing themselves to save others, actually thought they would be safer on the ship than in a lifeboat. One second-class passenger refused to get out of bed and remarked to his friend, who was leisurely fastening his tie with a similar lack of urgency, 'You don't catch me leaving a warm bed to go up on that cold deck at midnight. I know better than that.'[73] Harry Widener and his father George had waited for an hour on the boat deck before they could escort his mother, Eleanor, and her maid to a lifeboat. Eleanor Widener's final view of her husband and son was of them leaning against the rail with their fellow Philadelphian John B. Thayer. It was a static picture that contrasted with the emphasis on frantic activity by the rich and famous to help women and children into the lifeboats, including some reports of the activities of the Wideners themselves. Later, Harry's acquaintance William Carter advised him to find a place on one of the lifeboats but he replied, 'I think I'll stick to the big ship, Billy, and take my chance.' He and his father were last observed by Second

Officer Charles Lightoller among those men who jumped from the ship at the very last moment as *Titanic* split in two and the funnel collapsed, crushing some of the passengers.[74]

Like Harry Widener, Walter Clark did not think himself in any danger by remaining on the ship. He had changed from his evening clothes into an ordinary woollen suit and his warmest, thickest underwear before going on deck on a cold night and he had made sure that his wife Virginia had enough money with her in case they were separated for any reason, but these were practical actions. The Clarks were travelling home in time for their son's second birthday after a trip to Europe and Egypt, the first holiday Walter had been able to take from work in over two years. His wife later recalled:

> Neither of us thought that there was any danger of our not meeting again. I know from the way he bid me good-bye that he felt no apprehension and fully expected to join me later. He did not kiss me good-bye, nor did he even say good-bye. I knew he had no more idea of the possibility of his being lost than had I.[75]

The belief that the ship could not sink was reflected in the first newspaper reports of the sinking. They could make for an interesting counterfactual, but had these reports been true, *Titanic* and the passengers on its maiden voyage would now be of little interest other than as illustrations of the long-lost splendours of the great ocean liners. Instead, they represent the lack of information immediately after the sinking and what now seems to be a pathetic optimism. No one believed that so many captains of industry and society figures could be wiped out simultaneously. It was widely reported that *Titanic* was still afloat despite the collision and was being towed into Halifax, that all passengers had been saved and that 'the women and children aboard are in the lifeboats, which are ready to be lowered at a moment's notice, but this will not be done until it is certain that the vessel is actually sinking'. Philip Franklin, the vice-president of International Mercantile Marine, even issued a statement that:

> We have nothing direct from the *Titanic*, but are perfectly satisfied that the vessel is unsinkable. The fact that the Marconi messages have ceased

means nothing; it may be due to atmospherical conditions, the coming up of the ships, or something of that sort. We are not worried over the possible loss of the ship, as she will not go down, but we are sorry for the inconvenience caused to the travelling public.[76]

This confidence in the invincibility of *Titanic* was very much the arrogance of the wealthy man who vainly thought himself untouchable and took for granted the luxuries of the gourmet meal, elegant evening clothes, fine cigars and liquors, and the games of cards in the all-male Smoking Room. His world was elitist and the brutality and hubris of his end would have seemed unthinkable to such a man imbued with a sense of *noblesse oblige* and oblivious to the possibility that wealth might count for nothing or that his perfect tailcoat or dinner jacket and unearned income could not save him from the same fate as lesser men. Yet reality quickly intruded and an attitude of stoicism replaced that of belief that all would be well and that there was nothing to worry about. As a well-bred English country gentleman, Tyrell Cavendish kissed his wife farewell with the words 'good-bye, dear I will be with you soon'. His wife remembered his assurances that:

> he would rather stay on the boat, thinking he would be safe. He told me to go and that he would stay on the ship with the other men. They were happy to see us lowered away in the boats and kept telling us they would be all right as the ship could not sink.

Cavendish's last known words to a fellow passenger before jumping ship were more realistic though still optimistic: 'Well, there are no more boats to fill, we will shake hands and hope that we will meet again soon.' Although one passenger helped into a lifeboat by Washington Roebling, Caroline Bonnell, believed that her protector 'little thought that the great boat would soon go down and that he would go with it', Edith Graham, another lady assisted by him and Howard Case, was struck by the men's cheerful acceptance of their plight:

> They shouted goodbye to us, and what do you think Mr. Case did then? He just calmly lighted a cigarette and waved us goodbye with his hand.

Mr. Roebling stood there, too — I can see him now. I am sure he knew that the ship would go to the bottom. But both just stood there.[77]

Patience and resignation were indeed the great manly virtues shown by many of the men who lost their lives, rather than frenzied activity or panic. It was a time when the heroes of the British Empire and in popular literature were seen as chivalrous medieval knights. Logan Marshall considered the gentlemen of *Titanic* to be greater than the heroes of the Middle Ages:

> Chivalry is a mild appellation for their conduct. Some of the knights of old were desperate cowards by comparison. A fight in an open field or jousting in the tournament did not call out the manhood in them as did the waiting till the great ship took the final plunge.[78]

Resignation to fate was a virtue not just limited to English and American passengers. It was also shown by a 24-year-old Spanish millionaire and man about town. Victor Peñasco was imbued with the code and values of a gentleman and of chivalry by upbringing. His father, Hilario Peñasco, a lawyer and conservative city councillor in Madrid, had built up a reputation as a historian of Madrid before his early death aged 34 when Victor was only 5, leaving his extensive collection of 2,658 books on the history of Madrid to the municipal library, including rare volumes from the sixteenth century. His stepfather, Julián Suárez Inclán, was a professional soldier, member of the Royal Academy of History and a military historian, whose brother-in-law was the liberal politician José Canalejas, who was prime minister from 1910 until his assassination in 1912. His reputation as a man of firm liberal principles and vast culture should have been an excellent example for his stepson, Víctor Peñasco, who would have been too young to remember his own distinguished father.[79]

However, Victor, a handsome, elegant and well-educated young man of 24, was a peacock more interested in buying jewellery for his wife, travelling around Europe on an extended honeymoon and cultivating his own elegant appearance by building an extensive wardrobe. Whereas his father Hilario Peñasco's memorial after his death at the age of 34 was the 2,658 books he left to the Madrid public library, the stylish son Victor was more appropriately for him celebrated by an exquisite silk *esmoquin* or smoking suit, made for him in Paris and kept by his family to remember him by after his loss at sea.[80] He was an athlete and sportsman, attributes of a gentleman, as well as an aesthete.[81] He had no need to work and his inherited wealth allowed him to indulge his love of travel and enjoy a life of leisure, which included appreciation of the finer things in life and a taste for fine tailoring. He was said to have polished his knowledge of English on his many visits to his London tailors in pursuit of perfection in his suits, shirts and ties. Appearance mattered to him. It was important that he should be depicted as a gentleman and a hero to the last, despite the flamboyance and the softness of his personal lifestyle. Peñasco came from a cultured background but his passion for fine clothing was indicative of a more effete, decadent Europe, yet he was reportedly last observed helping women and children passengers as a hero very much in the spirit of Benjamin Guggenheim and still the fastidious fashion plate in the fine tuxedo he had worn all evening. At one point, he was seen kneeling on the deck in an attitude of prayer while a Catholic priest, Thomas Byles, recited the Rosary and led prayers. A Spanish newspaper reported him as stoically saying that 'if he perished he would take his conscience calmly to eternity'.[82]

Inevitably, the Peñasco parting, with the young peacock seeing his wife into a lifeboat before stepping back in the knowledge that she would be saved though he would die, was depicted as a romantic tragedy with Victor as the dashing young knight errant, whose shining armour was his resplendent tuxedo. Both Victor and his wife Pepita looked younger than they were, their elegance exaggerating their youthfulness and innocence whilst masking their immaturity. In many accounts of the sinking, they are described as being only 18 and 17 rather than Victor's true age of 24 and Pepita's 22, and referred to as looking like children.[83] Their fate seemed even more tragic if they were even younger than they actually were with a happy life seemingly ahead of them. Victor Peñasco was also incorrectly described as the grandson of the Spanish prime minister, hinting at his lost potential of a prominent place in public life, though there was actually no sign of him yet showing any interest in following his real grandfather and father into politics or a business career, let alone historical writing.

Gentlemanly behaviour reinforced the heroic reputation of figures who were already admired for their dashing public images. Archie Butt, like Victor

Peñasco, was known for the splendour of his wardrobe and for the flamboyance of his lifestyle. Military aide-de-camp to Presidents Theodore Roosevelt and William Taft, he was a prominent figure in Washington society and made an impact on everyone who met him. He very much saw himself as the archetypical Southern gentleman, loyal still to the Confederacy that had surrendered shortly before his birth in Atlanta. After working as a journalist, he had come to the attention of Theodore Roosevelt during his military service in the Spanish–American War of 1898 and in the Philippines. Resplendent in 'raiment which puts out the eye of Rembrandt', whether in military uniform or in a flamboyant, brightly coloured civilian suit, Major Butt enjoyed being the centre of attention and hosted extravagant parties for politicians, judges, diplomats and 'the young fashionable crowd' at the Washington house he shared on occasion with the artist and ex-journalist Frank Millet, who was nineteen years older than him and married, attended by athletic Filipino youths. In need of a rest from his work for Taft, Butt had travelled with Millet to Rome and now was reluctantly returning to his White House duties.[84]

Butt's alleged actions during the sinking were the stuff of legend and based on expectations of how a military man should behave, especially one as dashing as Butt, who 'was here and there and everywhere, giving words of encouragement to weeping women and children, and uttering, when necessary, commands to keep weak-kneed men from giving in and rendering the awful situation even more terrible'.[85] He was said to have stood before the lifeboats with his gun or an iron bar in his hand as he 'defended the women and children from the maddened men in that part of the ship', ensuring that 'we will save their women and children as quickly as we will our own'.[86] President Taft eulogised him as having 'never lost under any conditions his sense of proper regard to what he considered the respect due to constituted authority'.[87] Tyrell Cavendish, as befitted his distant aristocratic connections and as an upright English gentleman, was also reported as having 'with revolver at hand, kept at bay men who were trying to pull women out of the lifeboats and take their places'.[88] Butt was even more the man of action, yet Archibald Gracie last saw him calmly sitting in the Smoking Room with Frank Millet, Clarence Moore and a fourth man whom Gracie did not recognise, and was not aware of any later reputable sightings of any of the men:

> All four seemed perfectly oblivious of what was going on the decks outside. It is impossible to suppose that they did not know of the collision with an iceberg and that the room they were in had been deserted by all others, who had hastened away. It occurred to me at the time that these men desired to show their entire indifference to the danger and that if I advised them as to how seriously I regarded it, they would laugh at me.[89]

It was perhaps a different reaction to danger than was expected of the dashing military man but it also reflected a type of discipline.

A good death could also exalt the memory and character of the aesthete and intellectual as much as it did that of the man of action, making him into a different kind of hero who could serve as a role model for a more cerebral and scholarly man. Young Harry Widener was a noted bibliophile already at the age of 27, yet it was only by his death that he would be remembered or known outside his small socially exclusive world. In death, he achieved a heroic status equal to that of Archie Butt, with whom he had spent his last evening. Amongst his latest acquisitions was a rare 1598 second edition of Francis Bacon's *Essaies* he had bought for £260 on his trip to London. When collecting his latest treasure, a very small pocket-sized book, he had told the bookseller Bernard Quaritch, 'I think I'll take that little Bacon with me in my pocket, and if I am shipwrecked it will go with me.'[90] He was said to have collected it from his cabin before the sinking so it may well have been in the pocket of his well-cut tuxedo as he died in the icy waters of the Atlantic. His body was not recovered. Edward Newton thought that it was appropriate that 'in poor Harry Widener's pocket there was a Bacon, and in this Bacon we might have read, "The same man that was envied while he lived shall be loved when he is gone."'[91] The bookseller A.S.W. Rosenbach mourned his client, saying 'young Lycidas had died utterly untowardedly', echoing the British press, which referred to him as an 'American Lycidas' thereby comparing him to the subject of Milton's poem who also drowned before his full promise could be realised. His most romantic gesture in life was to die with his copy of a valued book in his suit pocket, described by Rosenbach as 'the most touching, most pathetic, withal the most glorious incident in the romance of book collecting'.[92] As he was unknown in the wider world, his family and friends were able to build up a heroic posthumous image of him characterised by his love of books and gentlemanly ways.

Most of the books he had acquired on his trip to London were saved from the fate of Harry and his prized book. They were sent home in a tin-lined trunk on a different ship. However, there was another of his purchases that was to be lost with him. On board with him was a last-minute purchase, said to have been bought on impulse on the morning of his departure from London, a 1542 four-leaved octavo pamphlet, 'Heuy newes of an horryble erthquake in Scarbaria', sold as the only surviving copy. Happily, there were actually other copies in existence, one of which was later purchased by Harry's brother George and presented to the library at Harvard just as one of Harry's friends had obtained and presented a copy of the same edition of the Bacon essays to complete the collection as Harry would have wanted in recognition that his collection reflected the tastes, personality and ambitions of the young bibliophile.[93] However, in 1912, Harry Widener believed that his pamphlet was unique rather than merely rare, but there is no mention of him trying to save it, though, like the Bacon, it would have fitted easily into the pocket of his evening suit jacket. Instead, he is identified through association with Bacon's *Essaies* in the tributes paid to his memory just as it was hoped that his body might have been distinguished from the corpses of other elegantly dressed young men by the book in his pocket. A pamphlet on an obscure earthquake did not have the same literary or intellectual associations needed to eulogise a young collector.

The wealth accumulated by American robber barons and their offspring was used to build up vast collections of rare books. Like the emigrants travelling in third class, these books were being uprooted from an economically declining old world in Europe to the unfettered expansive United States. However, they were not intended for labour or reading. They did not form the working library of the scholar. Rather they were commodities for display to celebrate the taste and discernment of the collectors.[94] For Harry Widener, and his fellow collectors of the Gilded Age, his book collection was a form of conspicuous consumption, rarities to be admired more than to be read. The only writer he is known to have read himself was Robert Louis Stevenson, though he also enjoyed detective stories.[95] He claimed that he never travelled without a copy of *Treasure Island*, which he almost knew by heart, having read it at least seventy-one times.[96] In life and death, these books showed to the world the status and cultural pretensions of their owners as well as their wealth. In his acquisitiveness, Harry Widener, with his prized edition of Bacon 'tucked into a pocket of whatever finely-cut suit' he was wearing, has been charged that his 'accumulation of priceless antiquarian books kept him occupied and sailing the oceans in search of further acquisitions, and came a close second' to his fellow passenger John Jacob Astor as 'the world's greatest monument to unearned income'.[97] Even his hardheaded if indulgent grandfather was 'afraid that Harry will impoverish the entire family' with his passion for book buying.[98] Perhaps these books were regarded as objects of conspicuous consumption in the same way as Victor Peñasco's collection of suits and jewellery, against which the same charge of excess and privilege through inherited wealth could be made. After all, these collectors lived in an age of excess, but must be seen as atoning for their extravagance through a noble death.

Like his fellow Philadelphian Harry Widener, William Crothers Dulles was returning from a book-buying trip to England. A 39-year-old graduate supposedly of Yale and the University of Pennsylvania Law School who never practised as a lawyer, he collected equine-related books and art, which he stored in a specially built, fortified bunker at his country home at his horse-breeding establishment, Tophill Farm in Goshen, New York. He had the only key to the bunker that housed his collection but when his body was recovered and his clothing and effects itemised, the key to the vault, which he usually kept in his pocket, was missing, and locksmiths had to break in to recover his library of sporting books so that they could be auctioned off.[99] Another collector to lose his life, William Augustus Spencer, a collector of fine French bindings and a patron of some of the major bookbinders of his time, was more generous in wishing to share his passion for books after his death and bequeathed his collection in its entirety to the New York Public Library together with an endowment fund for the purchase of 'the finest illustrated books that can be procured' as his own chosen monument. This was less elitist than the beneficiary of Harry Widener's book-collecting activities, Harvard University.[100]

A private and reserved man in life, Harry Widener was to become 'immortal in his death'[101] as a public figure celebrated in a great library that perpetuated the philanthropy rather than the sharp, often unscrupulous business practices of both his paternal and maternal forebears, the Wideners and the Elkins, street car magnates from Philadelphia, with himself portrayed as the dedicated bibliographer and lover of Harvard. It was important to show his death in terms of a gentleman and scholar, an example that would be as much of a legacy as his collections. Not long before his death, Widener told one of his friends that:

> I do not wish to be remembered merely as a collector of a few books, however fine they may be. I want to be remembered in connection with a great library and I do not see how it is going to be brought about.[102]

He toyed with the idea of establishing a chair in bibliography, but it was his collections and a library that were to be his memorial. In his will of 1909 he gave instructions that his mother, to whom he had left all his property, an estate valued on probate at $150,000, when 'in her judgment Harvard University will make arrangements for properly caring for my collection of books she shall give them to said University to be known as the Harry Elkins Widener Collection'.[103] His life was a high price to pay for fame and the promise of immortality of reputation for a young man of whom it was said by a friend that 'a new acquaintance could spend half a day with him and never guess that Harry stood to inherit Philadelphia's largest fortune. He was totally unassuming, unpretentious, and never put on airs of any sort.'[104]

His grieving mother went further than even he had anticipated in recreating the shy, bookish young man as a new kind of hero and embodiment of noble sacrifice emerging from the wreckage of *Titanic*, a chivalrous cavalier of scholarship. At first, she had merely intended to build an extension to Harvard's existing Gore Hall but then resolved to erect a new library housing both her son's collection and the general library of Harvard. She chose the architect Horace Trumbauer, who had designed the sumptuous Lynnewood Hall and other houses for the Widener family, and personally made all decisions about the building, which she paid for directly.[105] At the heart of the building, dedicated in 1915, lay the English oak-panelled Widener Memorial Rooms housing Harry Widener's collection. His desk was sent up from Lynnewood and a 1913 portrait of a sensitive Harry by Gabriel Ferrier was placed in central position above the marble fireplace. Mrs Widener stipulated that fresh vases of cut flowers, originally roses and then carnations, should be kept on the tables. Harvard legend later claimed that this was because carnations were his favourite flower and 'Harry used to have carnations dyed crimson to remind him of Harvard', whose colour it was, and his mother kept up the tradition.[106] One visitor to the library commented that it was still as if Harry Widener lived among his books,[107] appropriately for a young man of whom it was said that 'his library was his bedroom, his study, his workshop'.[108] The completed library, however, was not as Harry Widener had left it, but was considerably augmented before its transfer to Harvard. Following the advice of her son's friend and mentor the bookseller A.S.W. Rosenbach, Eleanor Widener had obsessively purchased the rare books she believed her son would have wanted had he lived to create a library as idealised as the image of Harry as the scholarly hero and moral exemplar that she was intent on keeping alive. The poet and critic Edmund Gosse, who 'was drawn very tenderly out to him by his sweet exuberance of zeal', wrote of his friend as Marcellus, the lost nephew and heir to Augustus celebrated by Virgil and similarly commemorated by his mother building a library in his name.[109] Harry Widener's shrine was opened when Europe was at war, and once the United States had entered the war, the charming and unmartial young Widener was even to be seen as one of the first American war heroes who through his youthful idealism and collecting had helped to carry European civilisation from the old to the protection of the new world before offering an example of noble sacrifice.[110] The Harry Elkins Widener Library at Harvard put before students at the university Harry Widener had attended 'and loved a reminder of that noble company of men who from the decks of *Titanic* looked death in the face without flinching and without thought of themselves'.[111]

The rich may indeed be different in their view of life and conduct but they were just as fallible human beings as everyone else. However, these men who lost their lives on *Titanic* were to be immortalised as heroes by their contemporaries and by succeeding generations, as described in elegiac mood by survivor Elizabeth Dowdell:

It was pitiful watching the men who had to remain in absolute silence on deck, leaving their wives, sisters and children to face and battle with danger without their aid. ... Much should be said for the noble and heroic acts on the part of the men, and should ever remain in the reminiscences of the history of the world. Many a social leader or man of wealth grasped hold of the limbs of a labourer and sacrificed his life just to form a human ladder where women and children escaped from perishing.[112]

Whether in the traditional mould of the action man, courteous gentleman, romantic gallant or a new more cerebral role model, the men who lost their lives on *Titanic* were destined to be cast as heroes whatever the reality of their characters and behaviour may have been. Manliness mattered.

Chapter Three

The Shame of Survival

If the men who perished were lauded as heroes, universal opprobrium at worst and suspicion at best was heaped on those men who survived the sinking. The dead were all cast as heroes and the survivors seen as sinners and cowards. Filson Young, in one of the first instant accounts of the sinking to be published, recognised that:

> To say that all the men who died on the *Titanic* were heroes would be as absurd as to say that all who were saved were cowards. There were heroes among both groups and cowards among both groups, as there must be among any large number of men.

In contrast to the sensationalist newspaper accounts of countless acts of heroism ascribed to such eminent men as Jack Astor, Archie Butt and Tyrell Cavendish:

> There was no theatrical heroism, no striking of attitudes, or attempt to escape from the dread reality in any form of spiritual hypnosis; they simply stood about the decks, smoking cigarettes, talking to one another, and waiting for their hour to strike. There is nothing so hard, nothing so entirely dignified, as to be silent and quiet in the face of an approaching horror.[1]

As for the survivors, Young saw something pitiable in them:

> They were a poor remnant indeed of all that composite world of pride, and strength, and riches; for Death winnows with a strange fan, and although one would suit his purpose as well as another, he often chooses the best and the strongest. There were card-sharpers, and orphaned

infants, and destitute consumptives among the saved; and there were hundreds of heroes and strong men among the drowned. There were among the saved those to whom death would have been no great enemy, who had no love for life or ties to bind them to it; and there were those among the drowned for whom life was at its very best and dearest; lovers and workers in the very morning of life before whom the years had stretched forward rich with promise.[2]

For many of these men there was to be a lasting guilt for having survived as well as the ordeal of having to face the immediate shaming of the newspaper reporting that questioned why they had survived and better men than they had not. The writer May Futrelle bitterly asserted that 'the only men who were saved were those who sneaked into the lifeboats or were plucked up after the *Titanic* sunk'. Her husband having had no chance of being saved, she was especially indignant about the presence in her lifeboat of 'a first cabin passenger, who must have sneaked in, for there were no men allowed there'.[3]

Inevitably, the greatest attention was paid to the men in first class who were perceived to have not behaved in the manner expected of a gentleman. However, whereas the heroism of the better known and more prominent passengers in first class had drowned out the stories of lesser known people who went unnoticed or were of less interest to newspaper readers, the stories of second- and third-class survivors now received more attention as many of these men were called upon to explain why they had survived and were thus able to talk of their own experiences, though they were often vilified for living. Even then, first-class survivors were more vocal in defending their reputations and there were far fewer survivors in second and third class to tell their own stories had they been asked. One unidentified survivor was quick to defend his actions, both in terms of only entering a lifeboat when there were no women waiting for a place and of what his loss would have meant to his young family if they had been left fatherless:

'God knows I'm not proud to be here!' said a rich New York man. 'I got on a boat when they were about to lower it and when, from delays below, there was no woman to take the vacant place. I don't think any man who was saved is deserving of censure, but I realize that, in contrast with those who went down, we may be viewed unfavorably.' He showed a picture of his baby boy as he spoke.[4]

It was not a viewpoint that was to receive much public sympathy, certainly not in the popular press of the day.[5]

The high survival rate of first-class male passengers compared to men in the other classes suggests a different picture to that of the perception of the universal heroism of upper-class men in the conventional narrative constructed in the immediate aftermath of the disaster and perpetuated ever since. Despite the widespread reporting of the heroic deaths of the most prominent of the first-class passengers, 33 per cent of men in first class survived, representing 57 men out of 175 compared with only 46 per cent of women surviving in third class, 76 out of 165. By contrast, only 75, or 16 per cent, of the 462 men in third class survived. Second-class men had the least chance of survival, with only 14 men, or 8 per cent, of the 168 who boarded making it to New York. Only 4 women died in first class and 13 in second class, whilst only 1 child was lost in first class compared with 27 children, or 34 per cent, in third class. Overall, women and children survived at rates of about 75 per cent and 50 per cent respectively, whilst only 20 per cent of men survived.[6] Class and gender were important in determining who survived. Jacques Futrelle, a popular writer of detective stories, reassured his wife at the start of the voyage that 'they save the first-class passengers' when she asked him 'in case of trouble who do they save first?'[7]

It was noticed by the crew that 'the first few boats mostly contained "toffs"'.[8] Indeed, the first lifeboats to be launched, boats 1, 3, 5 and 7, were only filled with first-class passengers, but the fifth boat allowed in women from second class as well as some men. Lawrence Beesley thought that the procedure for loading the lifeboats was slanted against second-class passengers since:

If the second-class ladies were not expected to enter a boat from the first-class deck, while steerage passengers were allowed access to the second-class deck, it would seem to press rather hardly on the second-class men, and this is rather supported by, the low percentage saved.[9]

It is hardly surprising that in the aftermath of the sinking some people upgraded their bookings on other liners from second class to first, 'because if there is a wreck the first-class passengers will be taken off first'.[10]

Many of the second-class passengers waited for a lifeboat on the port side, where men were generally denied a place, so it is not surprising that only thirteen of the men in second class survived. They were there because 'a report went round among men on the top deck – the starboard side – that men were to be taken off on the port side' and it was 'assumed that women were being taken off on one side and men on the other'.[11] A second-class male passenger indeed had the lowest chance of survival of everyone on board the ship. Second-class passenger Lawrence Beesley described them as 'the average Teutonic crowd',[12] obedient to the orders they were given, whilst Lightoller said that 'the men all refrained from asserting their strength and from crowding back the women and children. They could not have stood quieter if they had been in church.'[13] Beesley also recalled that 'we stood there quietly looking on at the work of the crew as they manned the lifeboats, and no one ventured to interfere with them' and that 'the crowd of men and women stood quietly on the deck or paced slowly up and down waiting for orders from the officers'.[14]

It was later considered significant that many of the men travelling in second class were British and that British men had a greater likelihood of going down with the ship than other nationalities. Although the British made up 53 per cent of those on board, significantly fewer of them were among the 706 survivors, whereas about 25 per cent of passengers from the United States were saved, despite being a fifth of the total on board. The British survival rate has been estimated as 10 per cent lower than that of other men from other countries whereas male passengers from the United States had a 12 per cent higher probability of survival than the British. This has been linked with national characteristics and ideas of how a British gentleman should behave.[15] Bruno Frey of the University of Zurich, who analysed the comparative survival rates of different nationalities, surmised:

> The Americans at the time were not very cultured, while the English were still gentlemen. The British were much more aware of the social norms at the time. They would have been more likely to stand in a queue and wait their turn than Americans.[16]

However, this interpretation of the differing survival rates by nationality is built more on national stereotypes than on any hard evidence and to some extent perpetuates popular prejudice rather than reality.

Such notions of the superiority of the British gentleman had already been dismissed a month after the disaster by the playwright George Bernard Shaw:

> But is it necessary to assure the world that only Englishmen could have behaved so heroically, and to compare their conduct with the hypothetical dastardliness which lascars or Italians or foreigners generally – say Nansen or Amundsen or the Duke of Abruzzi – would have shown in the same circumstances?[17]

Arthur Conan Doyle challenged Shaw's interpretation of the xenophobia revealed by the sinking by reminding him 'that our sympathies extend beyond ourselves is shown by the fact that the conduct of the American male millionaires has been warmly eulogized as any single feature in the whole wonderful epic'.[18] For Conan Doyle, the men travelling in first class were all equally heroic.

The popular narrative of the heroism of men in first class was to be challenged momentarily in the early days after the sinking, though based on nothing but rumour in the absence of any firm information from eyewitnesses of what had happened. Lucy Duff-Gordon, with her own reputation to defend, argued that 'the wildest rumours as to "the scandalous conduct" of the "millionaires" … were sedulously fanned by the agitators' with wild rumours that 'a boatful of women had been turned out to make room for the pet dogs and luggage of Mrs. Astor'.[19] *The Irish Independent*, generally a supporter of business interests against organised labour, found satisfaction in reporting that:

> Strong men shed bitter tears as they realised that perhaps there was not so much to be proud of in the last hours of the *Titanic*'s male passengers for the reports stated that far from sacrificing their lives for the sake of the women folk many of the most prominent passengers fought like madmen and beat back the women in their efforts to obtain places in the lifeboats.

As a result of such ungentlemanly behaviour it was claimed that several of these eminent figures in society, including the otherwise much lauded John Jacob Astor and George Widener, had been shot by the ship's officers assisted by 'one or two heroes' including Archie Butt. The newspaper admitted that such stories were 'wild' but 'to the public mind they were quite believable'.[20]

Survivors were subsequently to suggest that at least one passenger in first class had been shot for trying to enter a lifeboat but without much supporting detail or corroboration from other eyewitnesses. Cecil Fitzpatrick, the engineers' mess steward, claimed that 'a saloon passenger tried to claim a seat in one of the boats. The officer told him to leave, and, as the man hesitated, the revolver rang out and his body fell in the sea.'[21] Tillie Taussig told reporters that there was still room for fourteen more on lifeboat 8 when it was lowered and that 'the men were pleading for permission to step in, and one came forward to take a place next to his wife. I heard a shot and I am sure it was he that went down.'[22]

Victor Peñasco has been identified circumstantially with that first-class passenger alleged to have been shot for trying to rush onto the lifeboat in order to be with his hysterical wife who was calling out his name frantically, but this is based on nothing other than a false assumption that a romantic, passionate Spaniard would be lacking in the fortitude of Anglo-Saxon men.[23] Although dressed as a gentleman, perhaps too fastidiously turned out, he was still seen as a foreigner who could never be accepted as quite the Anglo-American gentleman however well groomed and charming in manner he may have been. Considering that Mrs Taussig, who claimed to have seen a man shot, would have been aware that his wife Pepita, who was in the same boat, was hysterical at being parted from her husband and that Victor, something of a dandy, was so conspicuous for his good looks, glamour and stylish suits among the first-class passengers, had he rushed the boat and been shot she surely would have identified him. Other women in the lifeboat also would have been aware of his making a rash attempt to save himself only to be shot, and would have commented on it. If he indeed died in such a fashion, it would have amounted to murder. All Emma Bucknell noted was that he was 'held back by other men' when he tried to comfort his wife.[24] Rather everything else points to Victor Peñasco being an honourable gentleman in action as well as appearance, one considered more likely to surrender his place to a woman and child than show any sign of cowardice in a desperate attempt to maintain the all-important appearance of gallantry. In keeping with his personal chivalrous code of the hidalgo, this self-appointed hero in a tuxedo merged into the crowds on the deck so that his distraught wife could not follow him, determined that she survive even if he did not. His fortitude and stoicism contrasted with the tears and hysterics of his bride. He had seemed only too resigned to his fate in his last words to his wife: *'Pepita, que seas muy feliz.'* ('Be very happy, Pepita.')[25]

Whilst shots undoubtedly were fired as warnings by the officers, there is no firm evidence of any first-class passenger having been shot and most rather xenophobic tales of the shooting of men rushing the boats were centred on third-class passengers, especially foreigners. A *Daily Mail* editorial in April 1912 reflected the distrust of dashing non-Anglo-American passengers like Victor Peñasco travelling in first or second class when it wrote that:

> No other race of men at any rate excels our own in its respect for woman; the men of other races may have a more gallant bearing, but is there so much regard when it comes to the actual pinch? But always among our own race that disciplined cry goes up.[26]

Yet, however much suave foreign men might be distrusted, it was the lower-class passengers who were actually feared and discriminated against. Fifth Officer Harold Lowe admitted to having fired three shots when a crowd of 'Italians' on A Deck attempted to jump onto lifeboat 14 as it was being lowered for fear that the boat was overloaded and might buckle if anyone jumped down into it. However, he denied aiming the shots at any particular individuals and was adamant that he had not hit anyone. His account of his actions was corroborated by several crew members and passengers in the boat who confirmed that he had fired warning shots though he had threatened to shoot anyone who tried to get into the boat.[27] Charles Lightoller also had to brandish his unloaded revolver to prevent third-class passengers from rushing the last boat on the port side.[28] Jane Hoyt, a first-class passenger in Collapsible D, the last to leave from the port side, however, stated that it was Chief Officer Wilde who responded to attempts by 'steerage passengers' to get into the boat by pulling out his pistol and then he 'ordered every man in the boat to get out'.[29]

The official policy in determining who could have a place in a lifeboat was that women and children should board first, but the instruction was applied differently by the individual officers supervising the launch of the boats. To some extent, whether or not male first-class passengers were allowed into a lifeboat depended on whether they were on port or starboard. Captain Edward Smith issued orders to fill the lifeboats and 'put the women and children in and lower away'.[30] First Officer William Murdoch, in charge of loading starboard lifeboats, allowed men in once women and children were in the lifeboats, but Lightoller on the port side interpreted this as literally meaning 'women and children only', and resolutely excluded men, youths and even some boys, even when:

> I could have put more in that boat and could have put some men in, but I did not feel justified in giving an order for men to get into the boat, as it was the last boat as far as I knew leaving the ship, and I thought it better to get her into the water safely with the number she had in; or, in other words, I did not want the boat to be rushed.[31]

Despite fearing that the boats would be overwhelmed by a rush of men, Lightoller admitted that discipline was splendid, and that only had 'the men commenced to climb in when they heard there were no more women'.[32]

Many of the first-class male passengers accepted the decision that women and children should have priority in boarding the lifeboats with a certain insouciance and 'expressed their determination to take their chances with the steamer rather than embark in the lifeboats' in the belief, encouraged by the officers, that:

> Under the worst conditions possible the *Titanic* could not sink in less than eight or ten hours, and that a number of steamers had been communicated with by wireless and would be standing by to offer relief within an hour or two.[33]

Dr Dodge of San Francisco observed that 'men in evening clothes stood about chatting and laughing' throughout the proceedings of the night.[34]

Not all male passengers were happy about leaving their wives and initially attempted to accompany them into the lifeboats. Emma Bucknell remembered that:

Once a group of men shouted that they would not be separated from their wives if it became necessary to take to the boats and made a rush to find accommodations for themselves. The captain seemed to straighten out his shoulders and his face was set with determination. 'Get back there, you cowards,' he roared. 'Behave yourself like men. Look at these women. Can you not be as brave as they?' The men fell back, and from that moment there seemed to be a spirit of resignation all over the ship. Husbands and wives clasped each other and burst into tears.[35]

The number of young couples on honeymoon, mainly first-class passengers, who were allowed to escape together in lifeboats, is remarkable. In most cases, they had been allowed into the boats because there were no women to take up the places and it was hoped that allowing men to accompany their wives might encourage other women to follow their example. Dickinson and Helen Bishop were invited to enter lifeboat 7, one of the first boats to be launched after a call for brides and grooms. Mrs Bishop claimed that they joined three other couples and that the women on deck could not be persuaded to join them despite the available places. She remembered that 'someone said, "put in the brides and grooms first"',[36] though in giving evidence to the American Inquiry she was to change her story and claim that the couple were 'literally pushed to one of the first lifeboats launched. Nothing was said about "brides and grooms first".' The story that helped to exonerate her husband of any charges of cowardice was now that 'an officer took me by the arm and told me to get into the boat quietly, and my husband was pushed in with me'.[37] She was unhappy about leaving her dog Frou Frou behind but accepted that 'there would be little sympathy for a woman carrying a dog in her arms when there were lives of women and children to be saved'.[38]

The only other married couple actually on that lifeboat with them, John and Nelle Snyder, later claimed that John Snyder, a 24-year-old automobile dealer from Minneapolis, had been lifted into the boat by one of the officers despite his own reluctance to save himself:

I hesitated and probably would have waited as the others were doing, but someone, I think it was the petty officer, took my wife's arm and pulled her to the boat. I followed her and someone took my arm and pulled me so hard that I missed the edge of the boat with my foot and fell down into it.[39]

Despite this supposed manhandling and time in the lifeboat, the Snyders still managed to maintain a stylish appearance when photographed in the elegant clothes they were wearing when rescued on arrival at New York, with other survivors looking little the worse for their ordeal.

Indeed, many of the husbands saved alongside their wives were to claim that they had been unwillingly forced into the boats. Albert Dick was only saved because his wife Vera, 'while clinging to her husband in one last embrace was shoved into the boat by this officer. She dragged her husband in after her.' He was to excuse his presence in the lifeboat on the grounds of 'being the last man to enter the boat, and Mrs. Dick being the last woman on the deck, and as there were already four men in this boat besides sailors, I felt no compunction on being compelled to enter the boat'. He also claimed that he had wanted the boat to go back to pick up survivors from the water but, 'every other passenger with one voice descried this idea, and as I could not compel them to turn back we had to leave the struggling mass of humans to their fate.'[40]

George Achilles Harder was more honest in admitting that 'he owes his life, in all probability, to the fact that he was dressed at the time of the collision, took his wife to the deck and found practically an empty lifeboat and decided to get in with her'. He believed that they had survived because he was more aware of the dangers than many others who joked about having hit an iceberg and laughed at him for having put on his life jacket:

> It was not so heavy as to even wake up a great many passengers, and I might say right there that many of them never knew of the collision, and I believe sank while asleep. Some women have said that they were not even called by the stewards. Others, and these constitute the great majority, were told that there was no danger, not to hurry and not to be even the least bit perturbed. I went on deck, however, as I did not like the scraping sound that followed the thud, and when I reached there, they told me I had better get my life belt and I returned with my wife, both of us with belts on.

As a result of his caution and businesslike summing up of the situation, George and Dorothy Harder came through their ordeal 'without receiving as much as a scratch or a cold'.[41]

Henry Blank, a Newark jeweller, ascribed his survival to his curiosity in going on deck when trying to find out what had happened after he had been disturbed from his enjoyment of a cigar in the first-class Smoking Room by the collision and thereby being in exactly the right place to be given the chance to enter a lifeboat at a time when 'every woman and child in sight was ordered into the boats' and 'there were not enough there to fill the boats and in that way some of the men got a chance for their lives'. Freely admitting that 'I am not much of a sailor', although selected to help with the rowing, Blank went to pains to tell journalists later interviewing him, 'Now don't make me a hero.'[42]

Washington Dodge, a San Francisco doctor, claimed that he was pushed into a lifeboat full of panic-stricken, screaming women and children by a steward he knew from previous voyages on *Olympic* who exclaimed that 'he needed his help in caring for his helpless charges'.[43] Dodge was to insist that this was necessary because:

> the peculiar part of the whole rescue question was that the first boats had no more than thirty passengers, with four seamen to row, while the latter boats averaged from forty to fifty, with hardly one person aboard who knew how to move an oar.

In such a situation, he was obviously needed to save the women in that particular lifeboat and so when ordered by an officer 'some of you men tumble in', he had no qualms and 'I tumbled'.[44]

The Yale-educated lawyer and tennis player Karl Behr from New York was rescued in the same boat as the Harders together with the entire family and friends of Helen Newsom, the young woman he was courting. Having spent the evening in the Smoking Room with Helen's stepfather, realtor Richard Beckwith, who remained throughout his ordeal 'debonair and complaisant, his almost perpetual smile carving his cheeks into such a vision of happiness that it seemed almost impossible to consider him a survivor of such a shocking disaster',[45] Behr had been about to undress for bed when he felt the ship tremble and heard the engines stop. Replacing his collar, waistcoat and cutaway evening coat, he had gone to check on Helen and her family before going on deck to find out more about what had happened. Beckwith reported that he had seen water in the squash courts and Behr led the way to where he knew the lifeboats were located. Bruce Ismay, chairman of the White Star Line, told them to get into the lifeboats, but Behr and the Beckwiths were reluctant to follow his instructions because, 'the prospect of being lowered some eighty foot or more to the ocean in the dark was not alluring, and we all felt that nothing so far warranted such a risk; to our minds the idea of the *Titanic* sinking was preposterous.' Ismay repeated his instructions to board the lifeboat and Behr suggested to his companions that it might be the time to do what he said. Sallie Beckwith then asked him if all her party could get into the same boat together, including the men, to which he replied, 'Of course, Madam, every one of you.' The lifeboat then waited three minutes for anyone else to join them but Behr recalled that 'there was no one at all left around there'. Another man in the boat offered him his gun, with the comment that 'should the worst come to the worst, you can use this revolver for your wife, after my wife and I have finished with it.'[46]

Although not yet engaged, Karl Behr and Helen Newsom were to get married the following year. The popular press could not resist suggesting that they had realised that their future was with each other in the lifeboat. He was said to have proposed with words that now seem trite and tasteless: 'If we are saved Helen, as I am sure we shall be now, will you let me row by your side through life?' to which she sentimentally replied:

> I have known all along that you were big and strong and able, good and worthy, all that a girl could ask in a husband. I didn't know until this dreadful night that you were also a hero. I would sail by your side through eternity.[47]

Behr indeed may have cut a romantic and dashing figure in his elegant evening clothes holding his sweetheart's hand as they huddled, cold and wet, in the lifeboat that saved them, but it was not the time for a proposal, which was to come later. Karl Behr was conscious of not having played the hero and in his accounts of his experience was to make it clear that when he left the ship there were no women or children, nor indeed other men, waiting for a boat to safety. It is not surprising that he should have initially praised Bruce Ismay for having ordered him into a lifeboat, 'made sure that our crew was complete' and that 'everything was handled in the most perfect manner and discipline, thanks to Mr. Ismay', though he was later to be critical that Ismay had neglected to ensure that the lifeboats were full and insistent that Ismay had the overall responsibility for passenger safety. Despite a propensity to take a leading role in all his activities, whether guiding his friends to safety on *Titanic*, taking up the oars in the lifeboat or organising the survivors on *Carpathia*, Behr was to claim to have had no part in the decision not to go back for survivors: 'the officer in charge of our boat, seeing the men swimming in the water, refused to go back and I guess he was right, for he claimed we surely would have been swamped by the hundreds in the water.'[48]

It was important to survivors to stress that they were only obeying orders in boarding the lifeboats and that they had no idea that there was not enough capacity for everyone to be saved, but for others it was even more important to appear heroic by having jumped ship at the very last minute and struggled in the water until they could reach a raft. In this way they could see themselves and be seen by the world as heroes as great as the men who went down with the ship:

> Every man among the survivors acted as though it were first necessary to explain how he came to be in a lifeboat. Some of the stories smacked of Munchausen. Others were as plain and unvarnished as a pike staff. Those that were most sincere and trustworthy had to be fairly pulled from those who gave their sad testimony.[49]

Even men who had volunteered to man the boats because their rowing skills were superior to those of the crew were regarded with suspicion about their true motivation:

> When the first order was given for the men to stand back, there were a dozen or more who pushed forward and said that men would be needed to row the life-boats and that they would volunteer for the work. The

officers tried to pick out the ones that volunteered merely for service and to eliminate those who volunteered merely to save their own lives. This elimination process, however, was not wholly successful.[50]

The very act of volunteering was cause for suspicion about the courage of the men offering to help with the rowing. They were compared unfavourably with yachtsmen or rowers who stood back, such as Thornton Davidson, who was 'a sailor of intrepid daring and remarkable skill' prominent in the Royal St Lawrence Yacht Club, of which Harry Molson was commodore. Archie Butt urged his friend Clarence Moore, a member of the New York Yacht Club who 'could do most anything any true sportsman could', to man an oar in one of the last lifeboats to leave the ship, only to be told, 'No, major, I'll stay and take my chances with you; let the women go.'[51]

George Bernard Shaw, forthright as ever in his criticism of the popular attitudes to heroism and cowardice as reflected in press reports of the sinking, was perhaps more realistic in his attitude towards men who found themselves a place in a lifeboat:

> What is the first demand of romance in a shipwreck? It is the cry of Women and Children First. No male creature is to step into a boat as long as there is a woman or child on the doomed ship. How the boat is to be navigated and rowed by babies and women occupied in holding the babies is not mentioned. The likelihood that no sensible woman would trust either herself or her child in a boat unless there was a considerable percentage of men on board is not considered.[52]

His was a practical, unromantic view but it was counter to the unforgiving attitude of the day that made villains of most of the men who survived.

Arthur Peuchen, a Canadian businessman, had offered his services when Lightoller asked for sailors to man boat 6. As a former vice-commodore and rear commodore of the Royal Canadian Yacht Club, he considered himself a proficient yachtsman and was told by Lightoller that if he were a seaman enough to lower himself into the boat by a rope and help with the rowing he could take a place. However, once in the lifeboat, he was more reluctant to take an oar despite his later claims that his presence had been necessary to save the women passengers with him. He was accused of having 'said he was a yachtsman so he could get off the *Titanic*, and if there had been a fire, he would have said he was a fireman'. He even asked Lightoller to write him a note to say that he had only entered the boat under orders but even this was considered evidence that he should never have been in the lifeboat in the first place.[53] It is little wonder that Charles Eugene Williams, a physical education instructor at Harrow travelling in second class to defend his title as world champion racquets player, claimed to have survived by jumping the ship rather than admit to having been selected by Lowe to row a lifeboat in which he stood for nine hours 'with the water up to his knees' before he was picked up.[54] His telegram to the Racquets Association was suitably brief and made no mention of the sinking: 'Match postponed; return next week.'[55]

Journalists even claimed that a number of the more cowardly men had dressed as women in order to save themselves. Such charges carried the implication that surviving men lacked true manliness. In particular, three cardsharps were singled out as having elaborately disguised themselves as women in order to save themselves:

> Doc Owen therefore got hold of a steward who, it is alleged, had been paid to keep the identity of the gamblers secret during the voyage, and, giving him a roll of bank notes, got him to furnish women's clothing and hats. Dressed in these clothes, the three men hurried to the deck and leaped into a lifeboat filled with women just as it was being lowered.[56]

Owen was not even on board.

Identifying professional cardsharps as cowards who saved themselves by disguising themselves as women was moral outrage against how they earned a living duping innocent victims rather than based on the characters or actions of the men concerned. There were warnings issued to passengers against professional gamblers. Indeed, it was expected that *Titanic* with its first-class complement of hard-drinking, card-playing men would offer easy prey and 'from various hotel detectives it was learned that at least a half-dozen well-known gamblers had left New York three weeks ago with the intention of returning on the *Titanic*' but 'some of them were unable to obtain cabin accommodations and are still in England'. It was said that one man 'had engaged return passage on the *Titanic*, but that he did not sail and was still on the other side. I don't believe it, however, because the chance of pickings on the initial trip would have been too tempting.' Another Broadway hustler did not consider making the journey because 'I am not a good sailor. I always get seasick and two experiences have been enough for me.'[57] The three most notorious gamblers aboard, George Brereton, Charles H. Romaine and Harry Homer, all survived, unlike many of the men they had preyed upon, making them easy targets of accusations of despicable behaviour. Ironically, one of their more infamous brethren, a forger and conman, who was not actually on board, was reported to have expiated previous sins by manly behaviour at the end: 'Jay Yates, gambler, confidence man and fugitive from justice, known to the police and in sporting circles as J.M. Rogers, went down with the *Titanic* after assisting many women aboard lifeboats.'[58]

William Sloper, a Connecticut stockbroker, was another of the men accused of having disguised himself as a woman in order to save his life. Described as 'a cur in human shape, today the most despicable human being in all the world', it was reported that he had rushed to his stateroom to don a skirt, hat, and veil.[59] At the time of the collision, he had been playing cards with the actress Dorothy Gibson, her mother and Frederick Seward. After helping the ladies into a lifeboat, Sloper and Seward were allowed to join them at the insistence of Dorothy Gibson. Sloper later stressed that other passengers were hesitant about joining them and that his party sat there for 'about ten minutes looking up into the rim of the faces of the passengers looking down at us trying to make up their minds to get in with us'. About nineteen passengers joined them and only when it was obvious that no more were coming forward was the order given to lower the boat.[60] A Chicago newspaper reported: 'resolved to die after having done his utmost to aid in placing the women and children of the *Titanic* aboard the lifeboats, councilman William T. Sloper, clad in a white night robe, was himself taken for a woman and thrust into one of the last lifeboats lowered away.'[61] It was perhaps to make it clear that he was not wearing anything in which he could be mistaken for a woman, whether by design or not, that Sloper described what he was actually wearing. Although his steward had laid out his dinner suit and a dress shirt for him, he had used it being Sunday night as an excuse for not changing into evening dress but was wearing a brand new heavy woollen suit made for him by a London tailor. He had added a sweater and thick winter overcoat to keep warm on deck. He took his turn with rowing and soon found that 'with my life preserver I was cumbersomely dressed' and 'a few minutes of pulling an oar in the lifeboat threw me into a dripping perspiration'. He gave his overcoat to Dorothy Gibson, who was not so warmly dressed, and later to Billy Carter, referred to by Sloper as William Dalton, who 'was standing in the lifeboat in his dinner suit with no overcoat or hat' when that boat came alongside Sloper's.[62] Evidence of being dressed and behaving like a gentleman was important to Sloper in shaking off any doubts about his manliness.

Daniel Buckley, from Cork, and Edward Ryan, from Tipperary, were perhaps the only men for whom there is evidence that they may have been confused with a woman which ensured their survival. Ryan openly admitted in a letter to his parents, which they happily showed to the *Cork Examiner*, that:

> I had a towel round my neck. I just threw this over my head and left it hang in the back. I wore my waterproof overcoat. I then walked very stiff past the officers, who had declared they'd shoot the first man that dare pass out. They didn't notice me. They thought I was a woman. I grasped a girl who was standing by in despair, and jumped with her thirty feet into the boat.[63]

Aged 21, Buckley had first become alarmed when he had woken to find water in his four-berth cabin in third class, but his roommates had laughed at him and told him to 'get back into bed. You are not in Ireland now.' He had struggled to reach the boat deck through various barriers, having followed instructions to get on deck, only to find himself the only person without a lifebelt until a first-class passenger gave him one and helped the frightened young lad to put it on. He was standing by a lifeboat when a group of male passengers, firemen and sailors jumped in and Buckley decided to take his 'chance with them' only for the men to be ordered out by two officers. The distraught Buckley stayed where he was, and 'I was crying', but he was again saved by the kindness of another first-class passenger who 'had thrown her shawl over me, and she told me to stay in there'. Covered by a shawl he remained unnoticed while the officers fired warning shots to force the other men from the boat.[64] He believed that it was Mrs Astor who 'saved him by throwing a cloak over him that made him look like a girl', though she was actually in a different lifeboat.[65] His true identity was to be discovered when Harold Lowe was transferring survivors between lifeboats and 'I found the Italian. He came aft and had a shawl over his head, and I suppose he had skirts. Anyhow, I pulled the shawl off his face and saw he was a man.'[66] For Lowe, the young Irishman was a foreigner to be dismissed like all other nationalities and races as an 'Italian'.

Buckley was not the only frightened young man to receive the sympathy of the women in the lifeboats. Charlotte Collyer saw 'a young lad, hardly more than a schoolboy, a pink-cheeked lad, almost small enough to be counted as a child' standing close to the rail with 'his eyes fixed piteously on the officer'. When he finally realised that he was being left behind to die, the boy jumped into the boat and crawled under a seat, where Mrs Collyer and another woman tried to hide him under their skirts 'to give the poor lad a chance'. Despite begging for his life, and pleading that he would not take up much room, the boy was threatened by the officer with the words, 'I give you just ten seconds to get back on to that ship before I blow your brains out.' When the boy continued to beg for his life, the officer changed his tone and urged him to 'for God's sake, be a man! We've got women and children to save.' The boy silently crawled back onto the deck and lay face down. The women in the lifeboat were also sobbing whilst Mrs Collyer's daughter Marjorie took the hand of the officer and said, 'Oh Mr Man, don't shoot – please don't shoot the poor man.'[67]

Less sympathetic were attitudes towards Alfred Nourney from Cologne, whose expensive and expansive wardrobe and lordly airs had enabled him to travel with the fake title of Baron Alfred von Drachstedt and upgrade his ticket for a small fee from second to first class; he had attempted to ingratiate himself with his fellow passengers with his false nobility. He had then proved himself to be less than a gentleman by making sure that he was one of the first into a lifeboat and then behaving boorishly towards the ladies in the boat. Rather than assist with the rowing, he had sat back and 'smoked an obnoxious pipe incessantly and refused to pull an oar'.[68] He also amused himself with firing his pistol in the air to attract attention to the boat.[69] He was later quick to claim for the extensive wardrobe and jewellery he had lost on the ship, complaining that he was now destitute without means or clothing having changed from his evening dress to a more practical sweater, vest and life preserver before finding a way to save his life.[70] Safe on board *Carpathia*, he again put his own convenience and comfort first in appropriating a stack of blankets to make himself a warm and comfortable bed on deck whilst other survivors were shivering with cold for want of a blanket. Margaret Hays, who had asked him to give up his 'nice warm bed', took two of his blankets and told him, 'You were saved and women and children went down with the ship.' No longer so suave without his expensive new clothes or the opportunity to wallow in luxury, he made himself so unpopular that 'some wanted to throw him overboard'.[71]

A variation on the idea of men dressing as women in order to secure a place on a lifeboat was a report that wealthy playboy and banker Thomas Cardeza, travelling with his mother, had 'through bribery of a sailor obtained two uniforms, one of which he donned, while he gave the other to his secretary'.[72] It was alleged that he had confessed this in a letter to his wife. He himself was to tell reporters that he and his valet had been allowed to board the boat in which his mother Charlotte Cardeza and her maid Annie Ward were seated when there were no women waiting to board and first male passengers then crew were allowed to board.[73] Friends of the Cardezas claimed that he was only allowed to board because his mother refused to leave without her son, who had been ill and had gone to Europe to recuperate.[74] However, Cardeza's ill health would not explain why his valet Gustave Lesueur was needed to tend him as well as his mother and her maid. Cardeza also claimed that 'I caught a piece of the wreckage when the vessel sank. We tried to paddle it with pieces of wood. I don't remember much that happened after we were thrown into the water, except that I was picked up,' offering a more heroically active account of his own survival than one of having passively got into a boat with his mother and attendants.[75]

Many men claimed to have jumped into departing lifeboats at the last minute having seen that the boats were not full, but only after they had helped women and children to safety. Dulwich College science master Lawrence Beesley jumped into a lifeboat when:

the call for ladies was repeated twice again, but apparently there were none to be found. Just then one of the crew looked up and saw me looking over. 'Any ladies on your deck?' he said. 'No,' I replied. 'Then you had better jump.' I sat on the edge of the deck with my feet over, threw the dressing-gown (which I had carried on my arm all of the time) into the boat, dropped, and fell in the boat near the stern.[76]

Surgeon Henry Frauenthal and his lawyer brother Isaac both jumped into a lifeboat, claiming that there were no women passengers left. Annie Stengel remembered the incident differently, reporting that 'as the boat was being lowered, four men deliberately jumped into it. One of them was a Hebrew doctor, another was his brother. This was done at the risk of the lives of all of us in the boat.' She also alleged that Henry Frauenthal had struck both her and a child as he landed in the boat, knocking her unconscious and dislocating two of her ribs.[77]

Hugh Woolner was more careful to control the narrative of his own survival. The son of sculptor Thomas Woolner and himself a Cambridge graduate, he did not wish to be seen in a less than heroic light, especially when his reputation had already suffered from being declared a bankrupt. In his account of his experience, he stressed that he had helped Helen Candee, whom he had danced attendance on during the voyage, to put on her lifebelt and escorted her to a lifeboat before helping to fill other boats. He and Mauritz Håkan Björnström-Steffansson, another of the men who had formed Mrs Candee's coterie, even forcibly ejected from a boat some men from steerage and helped some 'foreign' women to take their place. He was determined to distance himself from such men both in terms of social status and nationality so that no one could accuse him of unmanly behaviour. He had then turned to his friend with the words 'there is nothing more to be done here' and 'this is getting rather a tight corner'. Both men then saw one of the collapsible lifeboats being lowered and noticed that there would be space in it for them. Björnström-Steffansson tumbled into the bow of the boat, but Woolner's descent was even less graceful as he bounced off the gunwale and fell backwards. Clinging by his fingers to the gunwale and with his legs dangling in the water, he was pulled into the boat by Björnström-Steffansson. Both men had then taken their turn at rowing the boat away from the sinking ship.[78] One of Woolner's friends later emphasised that 'Woolner had come on deck in his evening clothes. He had plenty of time to change to warmer and more comfortable clothing but did not think there would be any need and simply threw on a fur overcoat,' showing how at first there had been little sense of alarm and urgency but also suggesting that when he did realise the danger, Woolner had acted to save others rather than make himself more comfortable in more practical clothing.[79] Woolner himself emphasised that 'I did what a man could'.[80]

Archibald Gracie was similarly keen to assert his masculinity and superiority over the 'weak and helpless' by ascribing his own survival to his own athleticism, self-reliance, physical strength and quick thinking. After first fulfilling his duty towards others by helping women and children into the boats that he also helped launch, he was pulled down with the ship twice, only to be blasted to the surface by an explosion of hot gas and boiling water. In surviving this he had in his own estimation gone down with the ship like the other men whose lives were lost but had survived through good luck and his own strength. In this way, he justified his own survival by having shown no less courage than the men who died. He was also to have no respect for any man who survived by stowing away or jumping into the lifeboats, nor for those who had chosen to take a place when offered it. These men were unmanly in contrast to his own conduct.[81] The only redemption in his interpretation was for men like him to have jumped from the ship and swum to safety.

Middle-aged Yorkshire landowner Algernon Barkworth later claimed that his decision to try his luck in the water was because he had learned to swim at Eton. He was afraid to dive because the water was full of steamer chairs and other debris, but instead simply climbed onto the rail and stepped off into the ocean. Plunging some 30 feet, Barkworth afterwards said:

> I cannot recall that I had any sensations as I went down, but when I struck the water it seemed terrifically cold. I went under, and I must have had my mouth open at the time. For I came up, spitting out salt water.

He was then hit on the nose by a plank, which helped keep him afloat until he could swim to a capsized boat. Some of the other men huddled together on the capsized raft died but 'the death of these two men didn't seem to make any particular impression upon any of us.' Barkworth later befriended another young survivor, William Mellors, a 19-year-old former valet, who had been hit by a wave that had swept him against a stanchion, injuring his ankle. Mellors' other foot was frozen and Barkworth took it upon himself to look after the young man on *Carpathia* and then to help him find him work.[82]

Seventeen-year-old Jack Thayer had also made it to the same collapsible as Barkworth. He had jumped alongside an acquaintance he had made the previous evening. Thayer was dining alone, as his parents were guests at the Widener dinner party, when he was approached by 29-year-old Milton Long, who asked him for a match to light a cigarette. Thayer, who didn't smoke, offered him the container of matches, but 'he looked lonely, sitting all alone, and I was lonely, so I pulled my chair up to his table and asked if I might join him.' They later met again on deck and Long asked, 'Do you mind if I stick with you?' Having lost sight of Jack Thayer's parents, the two young men considered trying for a lifeboat that was being lowered, but amidst the crowds 'pushing and shoving wildly' gave up on the idea as 'we thought it best not to try to get in it, as we thought it would never reach the water right side up, but it did.' Then, like gentlemen, they shook hands and wished each other good luck. Thayer then straddled the rail and Long put his legs over the rail. Hanging over the side and clinging to the rail, Long then asked, 'You're coming, boy, aren't you?' before sliding down the side. Thayer never 'saw Long again. I am afraid that the few seconds elapsing between our going meant the difference between being sucked into the deck below, as I believe he was, or pushed out by the backwash.' Thayer himself was 'pushed out and then sucked down'. He felt as if 'the shock of the water took the breath out of my lungs'.[83]

Another survivor who swam to the comparative safety of an upturned collapsible was George Rheims, travelling on business with Joseph Loring, his brother-in-law. Only when all the boats had left did he consider jumping, after standing around for several hours in his lifebelt watching the loading of the boats. His brother-in-law was reluctant to jump so, after shaking hands with him, Rheims had leaped alone over the side of the boat and claimed to have swum for a quarter of an hour until he reached a boat where 'the people were in the water up to their knees. Seven of them died during the night. Only those who stood all the time remained alive.'[84]

Stories of how Robert Daniel, a 27-year-old Philadelphia banker, escaped from the ship are full of contradictions that suggest that the charming Virginia-born Daniel was clinging on to his image as a chivalrous southern gentleman while entertaining and winning over the journalists he courted. He seems to have spent much of his time on *Titanic* cultivating useful contacts and charming their wives, including Archie Butt, Clarence Moore, Archibald Gracie, Isidor and Ida Straus, the Thayer family, businessmen Howard Case, Percival White, Walter Clark and Duane Williams, tennis player Richard Norris Williams, and Charles Hays, whom he met in the Turkish bath.[85] Despite having only made acquaintance with Moore and Butt on the day they sailed, he referred to Moore as 'one of the most genial and charming men I had ever known'[86] and Butt as 'one of the finest fellows I ever knew'.[87] He was ready for bed when *Titanic* struck the iceberg but went on deck to find out what had happened, then went back to bed.[88] In another newspaper interview, he claimed that 'I was in my cabin dictating to the stenograph when the ship struck the berg' and 'I went on dictating until somebody knocked at my door and cried out that the ship was sinking.'[89] Dressed in his nightclothes and dressing gown and with his father's watch around his neck, he went on deck and claimed to have jumped the ship as it went down, leaving behind his clothes, money and prized French bulldog, Gamin de Pycombe.[90] Jack Thayer remembered seeing Daniel:

> come through the door out onto the deck with a full bottle of Gordon's Gin. He put it to his mouth and practically drained it. 'If ever I get out of this alive,' I thought, 'there is one man I will never see again.'[91]

It was not the gentlemanly image Robert Daniel wanted to project of himself. Rather he wanted to be known for having heroically plunged into the water and 'I lashed the water in an effort to get away from the *Titanic*.'[92] One newspaper reported that he was dragged aboard a lifeboat manned by an apprentice member of the crew who was 'too young to handle such a situation', leaving it to Daniel to claim that he 'took charge and began quieting the women'.[93]

Perhaps one of the most honest interviews he gave was when he admitted to a reporter, 'I can't tell you what happened – I hardly know myself.'[94]

Whether from the exposure or from the bottle of gin he was alleged to have downed, Robert Daniel was unconscious when picked up by *Carpathia*. Wearing only a red nightshirt or pyjamas under his dressing gown, or even 'picked up naked from the ice-cold water and almost perished from exposure', according to some of the newspaper interviews that he gave,[95] he was assumed to be a third-class passenger and woke to find himself sharing a bunk with a sailor.[96] Without the distinction and social status afforded by his smart clothing, all of it lost with the sinking, Daniel could not immediately be identified as a gentleman. Once conscious and able to identify himself, he was quickly transferred to join his fellow survivors from first class. The ship's doctor, Árpád Lengyel, who was treating the third-class survivors, loaned him a suit, which was good quality but ill-fitting, yet a better reflection of his class status.[97] In his borrowed clothes, he circulated among his fellow survivors from first class and it was even alleged that he had helped with the ship's wireless transmissions.[98] He was later to tell some reporters that his only contact with Bruce Ismay was on *Titanic*,[99] but told others that Ismay was 'terribly cut up',[100] whilst also insisting that 'what Mr. Ismay said to me, I must treat as confidential'.[101] Whilst he may not have been so intimate with the prominent men he liked to name drop, he undoubtedly used his considerable charm to console the many women who had lost their husbands, being praised by Virginia Clark for being 'such a comfort to everybody'.[102] Among them was Eloise Smith, whom he was to marry in 1914.[103] When he landed in New York, he shed his customary debonair manner and instead of the doctor's suit wore a borrowed dilapidated derby hat, 'a pair of trousers large enough for a giant, a blue shirt he had bought from the *Carpathia*'s barber and he had no coat, only an old shawl', which with the cuts and bruises on his face made him look like an heroic man who had suffered greatly and lost everything. Despite his usual readiness to speak to the press and promote his own role, he 'was so overcome that he had to be led to a rail where he rested himself for a few moments' and asked the reporters to 'let me smoke a cigarette before we go on'. However, one reporter, seeing beyond his charisma and ready gift for storytelling, had some reservations about him and snidely commented, 'Mr. Daniel seemed little the worse for his experience, and in the afternoon entertained a score or more of his friends at the Waldorf.'[104]

Charges of cowardice and bad behaviour were most publicly made against Bruce Ismay and the Duff-Gordons, who were seen as having betrayed their class and country by saving themselves without a thought for others. Lady Duff-Gordon certainly courted publicity. As the owner of Maison Lucile, she was a fashionable couturier with shops in London, Paris and New York, and a client list that included Queen Mary when she was still Duchess of York, Queen Ena of Spain and Margot Asquith. Her husband Cosmo, a notable fencer, had organised the British fencing team at the 1908 Olympic Games. When they gave evidence at the British inquiry on the sinking, the only passengers to be called, she cut a fashionably striking figure dressed in black with a cloak faced with purple and the gallery was packed with society figures, including Margot Asquith, Lady St Helier, Lady Middleton, the Duchess of Wellington, Prince Albert of Schleswig-Holstein and the Russian ambassador. The ladies in the gallery expressed sympathy for Sir Cosmo by applauding his mention of the cries of the drowning and were there to support his wife, who was keen to repudiate everything she had said in an article published immediately after her arrival in New York.[105] Despite asserting to one newspaper that 'the adventures of the night are horrible beyond description' and that 'it is impossible to paint a word picture that would be vivid enough and which would give all the details and incidences of heroism and cowardice, of self-sacrifice and cowardice',[106] she had been more forthcoming to another in signing an article on her own experiences for the *New York American*, which was widely reprinted in other newspapers. In it she admitted to having said that 'we might as well take the boat; it will be only a pleasure cruise until morning' and repeated a jocular remark from a passenger that 'you will get your death of cold out there in the ice'. She also described hearing shots and dwelt in particular on 'an awful chorus of shrieks' from the drowning which lasted an hour until 'the last cry was that of a man calling "My God! My God!" He cried monotonously in a dull, hopeless way.'[107] She was to deny having heard any of this at the Inquiry, said she had been 'pitched' into a lifeboat rather than chose to board one and claimed that the article 'is rather inventive. A man wrote it from what he thought he heard me saying.'[108] Bizarrely, the man who she claimed had ghostwritten the article she signed was her journalist friend, Abraham Merritt, who had come to supper with her at her New York hotel immediately after she arrived on land. In her memoirs, she reiterated many of the details from the article she had dismissed as having nothing to do with her. By this time, the conduct of the Duff-Gordons had come in for criticism and she was obviously intent on deflecting any blame that may have arisen from what now seemed her misguided initial grab for publicity.

Had the Duff-Gordons only been one of a number of couples who had escaped on a lifeboat, aspersions of cowardice might have been directed at Sir Cosmo as they were at other male survivors, but what made his offence worse was that there were very few passengers in the boat and that the only women on it were Lucy Duff-Gordon and her secretary, Laura Francatelli. Despite having a capacity of forty, the lifeboat only held twelve people when it was launched. The Duff-Gordon party was joined by two American men, Charles Stengel and Abraham Salomon. The others were all members of the crew. By no stretch of the imagination could it be described as 'women and children first'. Instead, lifeboat 1 was dubbed 'the millionaires' boat' or 'the money boat'.[109]

Leading Fireman Charles Hendrickson asked whether they ought to go back to help the people swimming in the water but Lady Duff-Gordon was concerned that they might be swamped by people trying to get on board and it was agreed that it would be too dangerous to go back. Instead, at Stengel's suggestion they headed off towards a light, ignoring the cries for help. When questioned at the British inquiry, the couple were careful to deny having heard any cries after the initial sinking. Lady Duff-Gordon pleaded seasickness as an explanation for not being aware of much during their escape.[110] They did not wish to be shown as heartless. Not only would it be bad for business but it would compromise Sir Cosmo's status as a gentleman. Lord Mersey accepted that 'the members of the crew might have made some attempt to save the people in the water, and that such an attempt would probably have been successful', but he did not believe that Duff-Gordon had prevented any such rescue though he pointed out that 'if he had encouraged the men to return to the position where the *Titanic* had foundered they probably would have made an effort to do so and could have saved some lives.'[111] There had been a failure of the leadership expected of a man from his class.

They were not the only lifeboat passengers to refuse to turn back to pick up any survivors, but there were accusations that Duff-Gordon had bribed the crew not to go back. When Fireman Robert Pusey told Duff-Gordon that the men had lost all their kit, and would not get paid from the moment of the sinking, he offered to pay each of them £5 in compensation and as a thank you for their rescue work. This remark on what the crew had lost had been prompted by Lady Duff-Gordon tactlessly commiserating with Miss Francatelli on the loss of her clothes: 'Just fancy, you actually left your nightdress behind you!'[112] The offer of assistance might have been to placate the crew as much as it was to thank them. Henry Stengel corroborated the explanation given by the Duff-Gordons for their bounty to the crew. He said that:

> the men weren't working the way they ought to have done. Sir Cosmo Duff-Gordon said, 'You take care of us safely and I'll make you all a present.' Lady Gordon, who wasn't feeling well, added, 'I've quite some money myself.' Sir Cosmo then gave each one of the sailors a cigar and afterwards, on the *Carpathia*, an order on Coutt's Bank, London.[113]

The promised money was publicly presented to the men on *Carpathia* and Lady Duff-Gordon said to her husband that:

> some of the other survivors might have done the same thing for the men in their boats and raised a collection among themselves. Of course one could not expect the third-class passengers to do it but the first- and second-class could well afford it and it would only have been a small thing to do for these men who have lost far more by being shipwrecked than we have.[114]

It came as a shock when they were accused of having bribed the crew of the boat not to go back to pick up any survivors and saw headlines such as 'Baronet and Wife Row away from the Drowning' and 'Sir Cosmo Duff-Gordon Safe and Sound While Women Go Down on *Titanic*'. Naturally, none of the men who benefitted from the money admitted that it was a bribe, but the suspicion about his motives for being so generous dogged Duff-Gordon for the rest of his life. In many ways, the Duff-Gordons were vilified for not having behaved in ways that would have been expected of their social status.

Bruce Ismay was to become even more the upper-class villain than Duff-Gordon. His sin was that he had stepped into one of the last lifeboats to leave. This might have been forgivable had he not been chairman and managing director of the White Star Line. Many of his contemporaries believed that, like the captain, his role was to go down with the ship. Instead, he survived and was branded a coward. H.G. Wells saw him as merely representative of his class with its sense of entitlement:

> It fell to the lot of that tragic and unhappy gentleman, Mr. Bruce Ismay, to be aboard and to be caught by the urgent vacancy in the boat and the snare of the moment. No untried man dare say that he would have behaved better in his place. He escaped. He thought it natural to escape. His class thinks it was right and proper that he did escape. It is not the man I would criticise, but the manifest absence of any such sense of the supreme dignity of his position as would have sustained him in that crisis. He was a rich man and a ruling man, but in the test he was not a proud man.[115]

G.K. Chesterton was perhaps more sympathetic when he wrote that 'you will hunt poor Ismay from court to court, as if he were the only man that was saved'.[116] Nevertheless, Ismay was never forgiven for the sin of surviving.

Survivors and relatives of the victims of the wreck were particularly vituperative about Ismay. Eloise Smith, who lost her husband Lucian, complained:

> not only did J. Bruce Ismay, managing director of the White Star line, get into one of the first lifeboats to be launched, but he was escorted and assisted by several seamen, while the women had to tumble in and take care of themselves.[117]

Alfred Stead, brother of the journalist W.T. Stead, asked:

> Speaking of Mr. Ismay, by what right was he saved? He was higher in the White Star service than the captain of the *Titanic*. Why did he not

stick to the ship and share the fate of the victims of the line's faults and misfortunes? If he had been picked out of the water, one could excuse him – but it is said here that he took a place in a boat – a place which certainly belonged to some woman or man for whose life White Star had assumed responsibility.[118]

Barber August Weikman defended Ismay's conduct in entering a lifeboat, stating that 'there was no finer man on the boat than Ismay. He is a brick, a white man, and did not get a square deal in the papers.'[119] He not only praised Ismay but also claimed that he was 'literally thrown into the lifeboat by a seaman, who did not recognize him and thought he was interfering with his work'.[120] Jack Thayer later recalled, 'I saw Ismay, who had been assisting in the loading of the last boat, push his way into it. It was really every man for himself.'[121] Steward Edward Brown claimed that Ismay 'was calling out for the women and children first. He helped to get them into that boat and he went into it himself to receive the women and children.'[122] Bruce Ismay, however, insisted that he had only entered the boat as it was being lowered, but that there were no women or children on the deck at that time.

Although the surviving crew, more concerned about pay and future employment than the cowardice or bravery of the head of the White Star Line which had employed them, generally made no criticism of Ismay's action in entering a boat, there were suggestions that his role in directing the loading of the lifeboats was not altogether appreciated. Fifth Officer Harold Lowe, irritated because 'Mr. Ismay was overanxious and he was getting a trifle excited', even admitted that he told him, 'If you will get to hell out of that I shall be able to do something.' Ismay had ordered him to lower the boats more quickly, to which Lowe had replied, 'Do you want me to lower away quickly? You will have me drown the whole lot of them.'[123] Another report was that a man, not recognising him, had said, 'What are you interfering for? You get back out of the way,' and, even after he was warned that he was being rude to his employer, insisted, 'I don't care who he is, he's got to get back or go overboard. We can't be bothered with him and his orders now.'[124] Ismay's decisive action in helping women and children into the lifeboats, even if it was seen as interference with the work of the officers and crew, has been seen as a vindication of his later decision to save himself when he was aware that the ship would soon sink, but it also showed that by asserting his authority, he was not just a passenger. Lawyer Karl Behr was to stress this point when trying to establish a case for compensation from the White Star Line for steerage passengers. Behr successfully argued that Ismay could not claim to be on board solely as a passenger when he was giving orders for the launching of boats and that 'in effect he was the owner on board' and could have instructed the captain to slow the ship.[125]

There were two areas in particular where Ismay was deemed to be more culpable for the disaster rather than just demonstrating cowardice. He was accused of having cut corners to save money by insisting on fewer lifeboats than were necessary, though there is no evidence for this, and he was charged with having encouraged Captain Smith to increase the speed in order to arrive in New York earlier than scheduled. Mahala Douglas said that she and Emily Ryerson had seen Ismay reading a Marconigram warning of the ice ahead but, when asked whether the ship would slow down, he replied, 'No, we're going ahead at full speed.'[126] However, when questioned by reporters about the allegation that the ship was speeding to get ahead of schedule, Ismay denied this, and:

'Absolutely false,' replied Mr. Ismay with more animation than he showed at any time during the interview. 'I can speak for the White Star Line that such a proceeding is not the case, and that the *Titanic* at no time during her voyage had been at full speed.'[127]

He disingenuously denied having had any influence over Captain Smith and claimed to have enjoyed no more privileges than any other passenger in first class, despite Elizabeth Lines testifying that she overheard Ismay tell Smith that 'we will beat the *Olympic* and get into New York on Tuesday' in a conversation where 'it was Mr Ismay who did the talking.'[128]

Ismay's almost complete physical and emotional collapse after being rescued by *Carpathia* only underlined his perceived failure to act as a manly man and was taken as evidence of guilt. It was reported that his first words on being taken aboard were, 'For God's sake get me something to eat. I'm starved. I don't care what it costs or what it is, bring it to me.'[129] He was immediately given his own cabin from which he did not emerge until the ship reached New York. Second Officer Lightoller believed that Ismay was 'obsessed with the idea that he ought to have gone down with the ship because he found that women had gone down'.[130] Jack Thayer, whose father had been a friend of Ismay, saw him in that cabin, 'seated in his pyjamas, on his bunk, staring straight ahead, shaking like a leaf'. When Thayer told him 'he had a perfect right to take the last boat, he paid absolutely no attention and continued to look ahead with his fixed stare.'[131] Neurasthenia was seen as denoting a weak man and received little sympathy in one who was expected to have the emotional stamina of a gentleman. A committee made up of passengers demanded to see him and were reassured that 'the company would do all in its power to make a partial repayment for the suffering of the survivors' but could get nothing else from him.[132] Eloise Smith was angry that 'I know many women who slept on the floor in the smoking room while Mr. Ismay occupied the best room on the *Carpathia*, being in the centre of the boat, with every attention, and a sign on the door. "Please do not knock."'[133] Ismay was described after his death as:

> of striking personality and in any company arrested attention and dominated the scene. Those who knew him slightly found his personality overpowering and in consequence imagined him to be hard, but his friends knew this was but the outward veneer of a shy and highly sensitive nature.[134]

It was perhaps this personal aloofness that alienated many of his fellow passengers, while his intense dislike of publicity failed to win over the 'yellow press' of the day, especially that of William Randolph Hearst, who dominated the American press as much as he seems to have disliked Ismay.

William Carter escaped in the same boat as Ismay and was to be lambasted as another coward, especially after his conduct at the sinking was evidenced in the divorce proceedings later brought against him by his wife Lucille, though she had defended him at the time. Carter had spent his evening drinking and playing cards in the Smoking Room, and when warned of the danger went to wake his wife and children. He was then said to have seen them aboard a lifeboat. Lucile Carter remarked, 'I kissed my husband good-bye and as he stood on the deck I went down the side of the lifeboat. There were no seamen there. It was for life or death. I took an oar and started to row.'[135] Obviously aware that men stood a better chance of getting a place in a lifeboat on the starboard side of the ship, Carter suggested to Harry Widener that they both head there to try for a boat but Widener said that he preferred to take his chance on the ship. When he saw Ismay enter collapsible boat C, Carter followed him. He later defended his own actions and those of Bruce Ismay in boarding a lifeboat in terms that betrayed a certain sense of entitlement that went with his wealth and social status, while claiming to have helped the women and children from third class:

> The statements which have been made about Mr. Ismay's conduct are an injustice to him. ... The women that were in the boat were from steerage, with their children. I guess there were about forty of them. Mr. Ismay and myself and several of the officers walked up and down the deck, crying 'Are there more women here?' We called for several minutes and got no answer. One of the officers then declared that if we wanted to we could get into the boat if we took the place of a seaman. He gave us this preference because we were among the first-class passengers. Mr. Ismay called again, and after we got no reply we got into the lifeboat. We took the oars and rowed with the two seamen.[136]

Lucile Carter was also defensive of any criticism of the supposed cowardice of her husband, who was 'much shaken by his experience and his face showed lines of suffering'. Billy Carter spoke of the horror of his experience, despite having had an easy time compared with other people, but must be shown to have suffered:

> Terrible, terrible. No pen can ever depict and no tongue can ever describe adequately the terrors of our experience. Everywhere was a cold, hopeless despair and grief in its most hellish forms. Some were dumb with horror; others beat their breasts like things crazed, and a few laughed hysterically and insanely.[137]

In turn, his wife emphasised the bravery and spirit of 'noble sacrifice' of her husband and his friends,[138] and, when writing to Ismay asking him to recommend their chauffeur's widow in Leicestershire for financial support from the *Titanic* Relief Fund, commented, 'The notoriety we all got and the dreadful things our press is allowed to say in this country is certainly revolting and makes us sometimes ashamed that we live here.'[139] She was relieved that press interest was dying down. However, it was noticed that they were 'the only Philadelphia family on the *Titanic* to be rescued without the loss of a member', and that they showed 'few effects of their experience'.[140] The marriage quickly broke down and Carter's behaviour on the *Titanic* was cited as desertion and grounds for divorce, though Lucile Carter's account was very different from what she had said in the aftermath of the sinking. Now she claimed:

> When the *Titanic* struck my husband came to me and said, 'Get up and dress yourself and the child.' I never saw him again until I was put aboard *Carpathia*. He was leaning over the rail as we climbed up from the boats to the deck, and all he had to say to me was, 'I have had a jolly good breakfast, but I never thought I would make it.'[141]

Popular opinion in 1912 was all too ready to condemn the cowardice and failings of the survivors whilst lauding the conduct of those men who lost their lives, dividing them into heroes and villains, saints and sinners. In reality, whilst there were some men who showed a spirit of self-sacrifice, many were complacent and thought themselves safer on the ship than in a lifeboat, others were in the wrong place when lifeboats were being boarded and some had no chance of a place in a boat unless they were to force their way onto one that was partly filled. For those who leapt into their sea, luck dictated whether or not they would make it. Past demeanours could be redeemed when so many 'people were able to die bravely though they had not been able to live bravely' and 'chivalrous things were done even by men who had not been chivalrous in their past lives, as well as by those who had always been so'.[142] Libertine and poet Wilfrid Scawn Blunt was less generous in his view that 'if any large number of human beings could be better spared than another, it would be just these American millionaires with their wealth and insolence', but generally past sins were seen as having been washed away by a watery grave.[143] Whilst only good could be said of the dead, survivors could not gain redemption for past demeanours so easily and had to live with the stigma of having survived.

The contemporary consensus about the *Titanic* was that chivalry had prevailed, and that even though 'there is no rule of the sea ... it is customary in cases of this kind for the women to be saved first'. Indeed, 'even the women in the steerage would have been taken off before the men passengers of the first and second cabin.'[144] Up to this time the more common view of who should survive a shipwreck was summed up by the observation made by a survivor from the German emigrant ship *Wilhelmsburg*, which sank in 1863, that 'in such a moment one has enough to do to think of himself, and has also enough to do to save himself.' His experience of 'thus cowering together in the boat, exposed to every sea which swept the vessel, sometimes lying on the dead, at other times packed between corpses, I awaited the dawn of day' was one that left little room for chivalry or altruism.[145] It had only been with the wreck of the troopship *Birkenhead* in 1852 that prominence had been given to the idea of 'women and children first' when men had stood back so that all the women on board could be saved.[146] Now, once again, the many tales of gallantry among the first- and second-class passengers on the *Titanic* perpetuated the belief in what constituted a perfect gentleman and seemed to go back to an immutable tradition, albeit a recent one, that was to be best articulated on *Titanic*. However, today, despite contemporary views of a man in 1912 that there was 'some moral duty upon him to wait on board until the vessel floundered', there would be more sympathy for and acceptance of Lord Mersey's verdict after the British inquiry into the shipwreck on Ismay saving himself by boarding a lifeboat, a verdict that would exonerate all the survivors from the stigma of cowardice: 'Had he not jumped in he would merely have added one more life, namely his own, to the number of those lost.'[147]

Chapter Four

Dutiful and Undaunted en Deshabille

The traditional role and expected behaviour of women was to be reinforced and challenged by the events of what certainly came to be seen as a night to remember for them. Male dominance and a sense of patriarchy was bolstered by the perceived deliberate self-sacrifice of the men who died in accordance with the principle of 'women and children first'. Bereaved widows accepted this picture to some extent as it validated the deaths of their husbands and sanctified their memories. Matania, in his *Women and Children First* illustration for *The Sphere*, showed how women were expected to behave: women being helped into the lifeboats by officers, the fashionable young woman's sad farewell from her dinner jacketed companion, the wife reluctant to leave her husband dressed in his pyjamas and exhorting her to be saved. However, not all women agreed with such an interpretation nor with their own reduction to the second-class status of weak women to reinforce the heroism of the chivalrous men.

Nevertheless, it was conservative views of the respective roles of strong men to protect and weak women to be protected that drove the narrative in the first reports of the sinking. A good wife was expected to obey her husband. Young cinematographer Daniel Marvin was determined to get his pregnant wife Mary into a lifeboat, so much so that:

> Dan grabbed me in his arms and knocked down men to get me into the boat. As I was put in the boat he cried 'It's alright, little girl, you go and I will stay a while. I'll put on a life preserver and jump off and follow your boat.' As our boat shoved off, he threw a kiss at me, and that is the last I saw of him.

Mary Marvin was given no choice about what she would do. Her husband decided for her.[1] Violet Asquith, daughter of the British prime minister, found the 'cruelty of the separations ... almost unbearable', especially that of 'one honeymooning couple of 18 and 19 torn from each other and the one drowned and the other saved'.[2] She was probably referring to newspaper reports about Daniel and Mary Marvin, although there were other couples of a similar age on honeymoon.

Lucian Smith, also on honeymoon like the Marvins, was perhaps more enlightened in telling his pregnant wife Eloise when she proved reluctant to leave without him that he 'never expected to ask you to obey, but this is one time you must; it is only a matter of form to have women and children first. The boat is thoroughly equipped, and everyone on her will be saved.' In a crisis, the couple had slipped despite themselves into the traditional role that the man must make the decision and the woman obey. Lucian Smith had been playing cards at the time of the collision with three Frenchmen, all of whom survived, unlike him, and had gone to wake his wife. When she heard the order to enter a lifeboat, Eloise, the independent-minded daughter of a Republican congressman, at first refused to join the ladies on A Deck without her husband but he had insisted that she follow the instructions of the officers. When nothing happened for a long time before the officers realised that boats could not be launched from there because the deck was enclosed by glass, she had ignored orders to return to the top deck, instead joining her husband in the gymnasium, where they passed the time chatting idly. When her turn came to leave the ship she was insistent that she would not go unless her husband could accompany her but Captain Smith completely ignored her when she went up to him to request that her husband should be allowed to go with her. An embarrassed Lucian Smith had said, 'Never mind, Captain, about that; I will see that she gets in the boat,' and told her she must obey him for once. His last words to her were, 'Keep your hands in your pockets. It is very cold weather.' She was adamant that 'I had not the least suspicion of the scarcity of lifeboats, or I never should have left my husband'.[3]

Many men were careful not to alarm their wives, instinctively seeing it as their role not only to protect them from harm but also to spare them from worrying. Emily Ryerson remembered that:

My husband joked with some of the women he knew, and I heard him
say, 'Don't you hear the band playing?' I begged him to let me stay with
him, but he said, 'You must obey orders. When they say, "Women and
children to the boats" you must go when your turn comes. I'll stay with
John Thayer. We will be all right. You take a boat going to New York.'[4]

Eloise Smith was reassured by her husband telling her that:

We are in the north and have struck an iceberg. It does not amount
to anything, but will probably delay us a day getting into New York.
However, as a matter of form, the captain has ordered all ladies on deck.

When he later told her that there was no danger and that everyone would be
rescued, Eloise 'felt some better then, because I had absolute confidence in what
he said'.[5] Walter Clark similarly gave his wife Virginia the impression that he
'felt no apprehension and fully expected to join me later'. Tyrell Cavendish also
reassured his wife that he would see her soon and everything would 'be alright
because the ship could not sink' despite the haste he had shown in waking her
up and giving her only time to put on a wrapper and one of his heavy overcoats
over her nightclothes. When his own corpse was later recovered he was more
properly dressed in a black striped flannel suit and with his gold cufflinks and
collar studs in place in his shirt and his watch engraved with the date of his
marriage in his fob pocket.[6] Julia Cavendish was 'prostrated by the loss of my
husband, but rejoice in the fact that my children are safe, having been left at
home'.[7] Charles Hays told his wife and daughter that the ship would stay 'afloat
for at least ten hours'. This optimism was perhaps not the best preparation for
the men's wives to face the reality of the loss of their husbands, but it was seen
as a way of protecting them and shielding them from the truth.

It was also seen as a husband's role to provide for his wife and spare her from
financial worries, though most women were more than capable of dealing with
such matters after they were widowed. Edith Pears, who, despite inheriting a
life interest in her husband's estate, was unable to continue living in the marital
home, Mevagissey in Isleworth, after the death of her husband as it was owned
by the family soap manufacturing firm he had worked for, claimed from the

Bank of England for £213 worth of notes lost on the *Titanic*, writing to the bank that her:

> husband had eight of the bank notes when he embarked. I had four which I cashed after I left the boat. The thirteenth I cannot account for. Husband used to carry bank notes in a brown leather case especially made to carry notes and he generally always had it on his person. I saw it several times after we sailed, including the morning of April 15th.[8]

She was fully aware of what money he had with him, although Thomas Pears had kept control over it while it was in his possession since financial matters were the preserve of the husband, not the wife. Although Tom Pears had made sure that his wife had some money on her, it was the assumption of many men that their wives should not be bothered with financial matters, which resulted in their widows arriving in New York without any immediate means of support that they could call upon.

Husbands were there to protect their wives and children, shielding them from all practical financial worries. Soon after the sinking, a newspaper reported that 'a wealthy businessman' had visited a 'well-known solicitor' the day before the sailing to ask him to agree to act as guardian to his two children for fear that 'my boys are not left in anyone's care supposing that something should happen' even though 'all this sounds very absurd and even my wife laughs at me'.[9] It is more than likely that this was Tyrell Cavendish, actually a 'gentleman of independent means' rather than a man of business. An experienced though careful traveller determined to provide for his family, he made out his will the day before setting out on his last journey. In it, he appointed his close friend MP and King's Counsel Norman Craig as guardian of his two sons should anything happen to him and his wife. Craig had been planning to accompany his friends on *Titanic* but cancelled his booking at the last minute and played golf instead. When interviewed by the newspapers, he did not know whether or not either of the Cavendishes had survived, though Julia Cavendish was among those rescued and she was to remain a widow for the rest of her life, bringing up her children and running a country estate as very much the matriarchal figure in the absence of their father.[10]

A practical and sensible wife was expected to be a helpmate to her husband. Theodore Roosevelt, the exemplar of rugged masculinity of his age, declared that:

> The man must be glad to do a man's work, to dare and endure, and to labor, to keep himself and to keep those dependent on him. The woman must be the housewife, the helpmeet of the homemaker, the wise and fearless mother of many children.[11]

Whilst upper-class society women were expected to act as hostesses and oversee households where the work was done by servants, middle-class and working-class women had a more down-to-earth role in running a household and supporting their husbands. Lillian Carter was described as the 'perfect complement of her husband' Ernest, vicar of the parish of St Jude in Whitechapel, though there was some suggestion that this 'man of moderate attainments, of which the most striking was his sincere modesty about the rest' relied heavily upon the skills of his wife in their charitable work. The daughter of the Christian Socialist Thomas Hughes, author of *Tom Brown's Schooldays*, Lillian Carter was imbued with a belief in social reform and the harnessing of 'the Christian faith as the instrument of progress', which led her to play a leading part in her husband's Bible studies groups at their vicarage in Commercial Street and in larger public meetings in support of temperance and home and foreign missions at the People's Palace.[12]

It was taken for granted that gentlemen would offer their protection to unaccompanied women for the duration of the voyage. Their role was to dine with them, attend concerts, escort them for walks on deck and generally make themselves agreeable companions. Margaret Brown and her friend Emma Bucknell were attended by Arthur Brewe, a Philadelphia physician interested in nervous diseases. Helen Churchill Candee, writer, decorator and divorcee, attracted a group of men to dance attendance upon her. She had been recommended to Archie Gracie by friends in England and he, together with his friend James Clinch Smith, sought her out. They were joined by Buffalo architect Edward Kent, who was to be entrusted with one of Mrs Candee's most valued possessions, an ivory and gold miniature portrait of her mother, when he escorted her to a lifeboat; this was returned to her when his body was recovered.[13] Edward Colley, an Anglo-Irish civil engineer and land surveyor in British Columbia who celebrated his thirty-seventh birthday on the morning of the sinking, was keen to offer his services as one of Mrs Candee's coterie as a means of making friends and combatting loneliness, since on first joining the ship he had written, 'How I wish someone I liked was on board but then nice people don't sit at tables for two unless they're engaged or married. I wonder my blue blood didn't tell me that?' An admirer of the plays of George Bernard Shaw, he had seen *Man and Superman* a few days before the sailing and had amused himself by spotting the celebrity passengers with a humorous take on them: 'our most distinguished passengers seem to be W.T. Stead, Astor, Oh and the Countess of Something, but her blood is only blue black. (Give me good red corpuscles, I seem to know more about them.)' He was perhaps the quietest of the group but always the genial 'roly-poly Irishman'.[14] Completing the group were Hugh Woolner, a discharged bankrupt eager to recover his fortune through the advantageous marriage he was to make to an American widow in August 1912, and Mauritz Håkan Björnström-Steffansson, the son of a Swedish wool pulp manufacturer who was also keen to meet influential friends and make his fortune. It was Woolner and Björnström-Steffansson who were to make sure that Mrs Candee got away safely.[15] Colonel Gracie had other ladies to attend to and escort to the boat deck – three sisters, Mrs E.D. Appleton, Mrs R.C. Cornell and Mrs John Murray Brown, all of them friends of his wife. He also took their friend Miss Edith Evans under his wing. They were returning from the funeral of another sister, and 'that they would have to pass through a still greater ordeal seemed impossible, and how little did I know of the responsibility I took upon myself for their safety'.[16]

The diffident and somewhat socially reclusive theological student Stuart Collett, who was later to be hazed and branded on his forehead in the shape of a cross with silver nitrate by other undergraduates at Denison University because he would not mix with his fellow students, became a reluctant chaperone to two young women, but it was that role that possibly saved his life. His aunt, who was seeing him off, pointed to Marion Wright, who was 'coming to New York to meet her lover', to suggest that he offer her his protection. Marion Wright, having been 'in this manner, as it were, put into my charge', in turn suggested that he should also act as a protector to her friend Kate Buss 'in order that I might not make love to her'. He made sure that both women got on deck and into lifeboats, then he noticed 'there were no more women to go and I asked the officer if there was any objection to my going in that boat. He said "No, get in" and I was the last one in.' Collett described the sinking as 'like the noise from a football field, not loud like a shout of victory, but hushed as though there was canvas over it'.[17]

An upper-class woman was expected to stay calm and dignified in such adversity, offering an example of good behaviour to her social inferiors. Emily Ryerson was mindful that 'my chief thought and that of everyone else was, I know, not to make a fuss and to do as we were told'.[18] Ruth Dodge later commented:

I think it is foolish to speak of the heroism displayed. There was none that I witnessed. It was merely a matter of waiting your turn for a lifeboat, and there was no keen anxiety to enter the boats because everybody had such confidence in that wretched ship.[19]

Clara Hays and Orian Davidson may have called out in vain their husbands' names whenever the lifeboat they were in approached another, 'but these brave women never lost courage'.[20]

There was a similar calmness and acceptance among women in third-class who refused to be parted from their husbands:

One young couple walked steadily up and down the boat deck throughout pretty well the whole of the proceedings. Once or twice the young chap asked if he could help. He was a tall, clean-bred Britisher, on his honeymoon I should say. The girl – she was little more – never made the slightest attempt to come towards the boats, much less be taken on board, although I looked towards her several times with a look of silent invitation, but no, she was not going to be parted from her man.[21]

This young couple has been identified with Neal McNamee, a branch provisions manager with Lipton's in Salisbury sailing to New York, where he was taking up a new post for his company, with his new wife Eileen.[22] John Bourke, a Mayo farmer emigrating with his new wife Kate and sister Mary, had tried to board a lifeboat, having found a ladder to the upper decks after they 'were held back by officers, who said things were not ready' only for John to be prevented from entering a boat. His wife and sister both refused to part from him: "'I'll not leave my husband," said Kate Bourke. "I'll not leave my brother," said Mary Bourke.'[23] These were similar to the sentiments of Sarah Chapman travelling in second class with a large group from Liskeard in Cornwall who, realising her husband would not be allowed to accompany her, said to a friend, '"Goodbye Mrs Richards, if John can't go, I won't go either" before stepping back and rejoining her husband.'[24] Praise was given to the way:

> these delicate women, these young brides, and American heiresses, and English emigrants, women made of the same clay as their sisters in all the streets of life ... subdued their fears and were quiet and calm in those awful hours ... there went up no shrieks of despair, no wild hysterical wailing, no madness of grief.[25]

It was the Darby and Joan devotion of one elderly well-known couple that was celebrated as an example of a husband and wife who were to be inseparable in death. Isidor Straus, co-owner of Macy's department store, a one-time Democratic Representative for New York and a noted philanthropist, and his wife Ida had been married for fifty years. They were returning from wintering in the south of France for the benefit of 67-year-old Straus's health. Ever the solicitous wife, Ida refused to leave him. Members of their family were aware that:

> Mrs. Straus had been at her husband's side continually from the moment that ill health affected him. It is possible she refused to realize the gravity of the situation, but even if she did understand it, I doubt if she could have been induced to leave him.[26]

Archibald Gracie had asked whether an exception could be made to the women and children only ruling in favour of allowing him into a boat, but Straus refused the concession to his age and infirmity. His wife gave her fur coat to her maid to keep her warm in the lifeboat and joined her husband, with the words, 'I will not be separated from my husband. As we have lived, so will we die, together.' The devotion of Isidor and Ida Straus was seen as an inspirational illustration of the sanctity of marriage compared with the rising divorce rate in American high society and the resultant breakdown of family life. Their faithfulness to each other was seen as a lesson that:

> in this day of frequent and scandalous divorces, when the marriage tie once held so sacred is all too lightly regarded, the wifely devotion and love of Mrs Straus for her partner of a lifetime stands out in noble contrast. The world needed a reminder that married love and devotion can not be cast off like a worn garment.[27]

The self-sacrifice of Ida Straus could also be seen as an assertion of equality in marriage in that she was the one who chose to stay with her husband, not out of obedience or deference but because it was what she herself had decided as the right thing for her to do. The directors of the Sanatorium for Hebrew Children, of which the couple had been patrons and benefactors, expressed the belief that 'the heroism of Isidor and Ida Straus in the terrible and overwhelming tragedy of the sea sheds a radiance upon mourning humanity' in recognition that they should both be seen as heroes of the disaster.[28]

The refusal of women to leave their husbands was not regarded as admirable by everyone, although there was simultaneously much criticism of wives who did survive and suggestions that 'perhaps some day these widows will explain how it happened that they allowed themselves to be torn away from their husbands instead of going down with them'.[29] Lucy Duff-Gordon 'could not comprehend the behaviour of the American wives who were leaving their husbands without a word of protest or regret, scarce of farewell'. The only way she could explain it was that 'they have brought the cult of chivalry to such a pitch in the States that it comes as second nature to their men to sacrifice themselves and to women to let them do it'.[30] She herself had no intention of being parted from her husband nor of not being saved. Wireless operator Harold Bride later told the Stirling Rotary Club that:

The *Titanic*'s first-class passengers were the first to give trouble. It was well-nigh impossible to persuade the women and children to leave the apparent safety of the liner for a little boat in mid-ocean. And to add to the difficulty many women refused to leave their husbands.[31]

Rather than being regarded as the perfect wives, these women were seen as weak in clinging to their husbands and making the work of the crew more difficult than it would have been otherwise. Those who obeyed their husbands' orders to leave the ship were less trouble.

Not only was a woman expected to be a dutiful wife, she also had a role as a mother, her femininity and softness contrasting with the masculine discipline of the father. It was a reminder of their maternal responsibilities that persuaded many women to enter a lifeboat without their husbands. Leila Meyer could only be coaxed into entering a lifeboat when her husband reminded her that their daughter at home in New York also needed her:

> I tried and tried to get Edgar to come into the lifeboat with me, and pleaded to be allowed to stay behind and wait until he could leave, he not caring to leave before all the women had been saved. Mr. Meyer finally persuaded me to leave, reminding me of our one-year-old child at home. I entered the lifeboat and watched until the *Titanic* sank, but only for a short time did I see my husband standing beside the rail and assisting other women into boats in which he might have been saved.[32]

The Meyers were only travelling on *Titanic* because they had just heard news of the death of Leila's father, Andrew Saks, who had built up the Saks chain of department stores. 'Recognized for his ability, but valued even more highly by those who came in contact with him for his gentle and pleasant personality and his manly and straightforward manner,' Edgar, a mechanical engineer who while a student at Cornell had developed a new method for measuring the velocity of flame propagation in gas engines, reasoned with his wife in the knowledge that maternal feelings would prevail over her loyalty to him.[33] He had remained cheerful during their parting but his wife realised that this and his show of energy was assumed. Ironically, when he was asked to write in

Lucille Duff-Gordon's autograph book and note down his 'madnesses ... he laughed as he said: "I have only one – to live," and wrote it down. In less than two hours after he was drowned.'[34]

The Ryersons were also hurrying home to attend a funeral, that of their eldest son who had been killed in a motoring accident. It was to be especially distressing for them when their surviving son John was refused a place on a lifeboat with his mother and sisters. It was only when his father, Arthur, insisted that 'of course that boy goes with his mother. He is only thirteen' that he was allowed on.[35] The officer in charge of loading the boat had then insisted that no other boys would be allowed to board. Only by putting a woman's hat on her 11-year-old son was Lucille Carter able to sneak her son William onto the lifeboat. It was reported that John Jacob Astor had saved an unnamed boy in that way.[36] It is possible that many of the crew, most of whom had begun working as young as 13, had a different idea of when childhood ended than did the parents of boys travelling in first class.[37] Certainly, a number of boys travelling in third class saw themselves as men and preferred to stay on the ship with their fathers rather than be seen as children under the care of their mothers. The three Asplund brothers, Filip, 14, Clarence, 10, and Carl, 8, 'clung to their father' Carl and were considered by their mother to be 'my three grown boys who smiled sweetly at me to the last'.[38] Similarly, 12-year-old James van Billiard and his 9-year-old brother 'refused to leave their father on the doomed ship and remained with him to the last'.[39]

Many mothers showed a determination to protect their small children and babies even if it meant sacrificing themselves. Bess Allison was distraught when she thought that she had lost her son in the confusion. Arthur Peuchen believed that:

> Mrs Allison could have gotten away in perfect safety, but somebody told her Mr Allison was in a boat being lowered on the opposite side of the deck, and with her little daughter she rushed away from the boat. Apparently she reached the other side to find that Mr Allison was not there.[40]

It was not only her stockbroker husband Hudson that she was searching for but also her baby son Trevor, who was actually safe in the hands of his nursemaid,

Alice Cleaver. Mrs Allison had become hysterical while waiting for her husband to find out what was happening after hearing of the collision and Alice Cleaver, while dressing the children, had to calm her. Hudson Allison seemed 'too dazed to speak' so Cleaver 'handed him some brandy and asked him to look after Mrs. Allison and Lorraine and I would keep Baby'. Alice Cleaver and the baby became separated from the Allisons. Bess Allison, worried about her son, became hysterical again and 'Mr. Allison had difficulty with her and I can only surmise that is how they lost their lives – as there was plenty of room in the lifeboats because people refused to leave thinking it was safer on the ship.'[41] Lorraine was the only first-class child to be lost with both her parents.[42]

There were many reports of small babies being thrust into the arms of women in the lifeboats by their mothers in a bid to save them. The assumption was that all women had maternal instincts and would protect a babe in arms, even one that was not their own. Stewardess Violet Jessop was disconcerted when Sixth Officer James Moody, having helped her into a lifeboat, dropped a bundle containing a baby onto her lap with the words, 'Here, Miss Jessop, look after this baby.' There was no sign of the mother until they were rescued by *Carpathia* some eight hours later:

> I was still clutching the baby against my hard cork lifebelt I was wearing when a woman leaped at me and grabbed the baby, and rushed off with it, it appeared that she put it down on the deck of the *Titanic* while she went off to fetch something, and when she came back the baby had gone. I was too frozen and numb to think it strange that this woman had not stopped to say 'thank you'.[43]

Other women related similar experiences, including Mary Marvin, herself pregnant, who was said to have had a 5-year-old 'brown-eyed waif shoved into her arms, whom she cared for both in the lifeboat and on *Carpathia* until she could hand the little French girl over to the chairman of the Women's Relief Committee in New York'.[44] Second-class passenger Mary Jewan 'found a baby in my possession without the least idea whom it belonged to' and was quite indifferent to the child's fate once it was taken on board *Carpathia* in a net and 'I never saw it again.'[45]

It was recognised by unmarried and childless women that mothers enjoyed a special status and must be saved for the welfare of their children. Edith Evans, one of the few women travelling in first class not to survive, gave up her place on an overcrowded lifeboat to Caroline Brown, who had children at home who would need her whereas Miss Evans was unmarried.[46] Her parting words were, 'I must be the one to go. You stay, you have children at home, I have nobody.'[47] Similarly, Lillian Carter, childless wife of a clergyman in the East End of London, took the attitude, alongside her husband, to 'let the mothers get to the boats first; you and I must see this out together'.[48] The role of the mother was vital for the breeding and raising of the next generation, safeguarding both their children's future and the continuance of the best elements of the human race. It did not go unnoticed that 'if we start to weigh the relative value of lives lost, some emigrant child saved from the wreck may be or beget a second Lincoln'.[49]

The closeness of the mother and child relationship could be seen among various passengers on *Titanic*. Eleanor Widener, in her desire to perpetuate his memory, showed a deeper sense of mourning for her son Harry than for her husband George. When planning her son's memorial, she wrote to his close friend and book dealer Rosenbach that:

> Over two years have gone since I lost him – and I am no more reconciled than I was at first and never will be again. All joy of living left me on April 15 1912. Forgive me for writing you like this but you knew Harry, and can understand my sorrow.

The first Christmas after his death, his mother continued the tradition of buying him fine first editions or giving him gifts of money to help him build up his book collection, and 'all his books were put in his room the same as each year, whilst we could not see him – I know he was with us'. Harry's own bond with his mother was reflected in the pleasure he had in pointing out the inscription on the frontispiece of his copy of Cowper's *Task* that had once belonged to Thackeray: 'A great point in a great man, a great love for his mother. A very fine and true portrait; could artist possibly choose a better position than the above? – W.M. Thackeray.' Widener would then reflect, 'Isn't that a lovely sentiment? And yet they say Thackeray was a cynic and a snob.'[50] On a humbler level, Cornish baker George Hocking from Penzance helped his mother and the other women they were travelling with into a lifeboat, kissed her and said, 'No mother, the men are good enough to stand back for you and I must do the same and let their wives and mothers go,' leaving his inconsolable mother calling out his name.[51] Fanny Maria Kelly, a Bloomsbury boarding house landlady, was travelling to New York in second class with her life savings of $8,000 to help her son Richard establish his own lunchroom business. The money was lost but newspapers reported her son's joy at his mother's survival: '"My mother is saved!" he cried while tears of joy streamed down his face. "I don't know whether she lost the money or not, and I don't care so long as I have her."'[52]

Not all women were such devoted mothers. Although Walter and Virginia Clark were said to have been returning home to be in time to celebrate their son's second birthday as befitted caring parents, Virginia was later to be accused of being an unfit mother by her husband's parents in a bitter custody battle for the child. Leaving the boy James Ross Clark with his grandparents in Los Angeles again, she had remarried in New York on 26 September 1912, only informing her mother and the Clarks by letter after the wedding and asking for her mother to escort her son to New York once she returned from honeymoon in Europe. Her new husband, John Tanner, was a divorcee who devoted his time to playing tennis and polo. James Ross Clark immediately sued for custody of his grandson and namesake, who had inherited $40,000 of his father's $78,000 estate.[53] He charged Virginia Tanner with having neglected her son and abandoned him without having adequately provided for his support and claimed to be 'at a loss to understand Mrs Tanner's actions in this matter. She was not irrational since the *Titanic* disaster so we cannot excuse her for that reason.'[54] However, it had been reported that when William Clark, her husband's cousin and close friend, escorted her home after her rescue, he had been concerned that 'she is in such a condition of mind and of physical collapse that we shall exercise the greatest care for her wellbeing' and that she needed 'careful attention by physicians to bring her back to health and greater comfort of mind than which she is now experiencing'.[55] Virginia Tanner denied having neglected her son and claimed to have given him the best of care.[56] Joint guardianship was later awarded to the mother and paternal grandparents, with each having custody for six months.[57]

Although in a patriarchal society childcare was very much seen as the responsibility of the mother, fathers too were to show their concern for the welfare of their children. Constance Willard told a story of a distraught father, 'a foreigner', holding out a bundle and begging, 'with tears running down his face', that she would take care of his child, with the words, 'O, please, kind lady, won't you save my little girl, my baby. For myself, it is no difference, but please take my little one.'[58] Shop assistant Edwy Arthur West from Truro made sure that his wife and daughter were safely in a lifeboat, then:

> returned to the cabin for a thermos of hot milk, and, finding the lifeboat let down he reached it by means of a rope, gave the flask to his wife Ada, and, with a farewell, returned to the deck of the ship.

For this thoughtful act he was acclaimed as being 'one of the least known of the *Titanic* heroes, but none will deny him the distinction of being one of the noblest'.[59]

Less noble was Michel Navratil, travelling under the alias of Louis Hoffman, who had kidnapped his sons, Michel and Edmond, from his estranged wife in Nice. He led his fellow passengers to believe that the children's mother was dead. Lawrence Beesley noticed him playing with the two boys, answering to Lolo and Momon, and that he was 'devoted to them, never absent from them'.[60] He found them places in a lifeboat, but the two boys were too young to tell other passengers anything about themselves and they were dubbed the '*Titanic* Orphans'. Margaret Hays, a young unmarried woman who could speak French, took charge of them once aboard *Carpathia* and temporarily offered them a home under the supervision of the Children's Aid Society, though her father was insistent that this was only a short-term measure and that if they could not be identified soon they would be put up for adoption, rather unsympathetically replying to a journalist's question about whether they might be identified by their tickets with, 'I have never travelled second cabin or steerage, so I don't know anything about such matters.' On hearing this, the reporter who had asked him the question later commented, 'Why can I never learn to keep my distance from the aristocracy of West End Avenue, even when it has given shelter to two charming, well-mannered little children of the second cabin?'[61]

Luckily, their mother recognised them from a newspaper photograph and was reunited with them.[62]

However, many of the cossetted women of first class were to prove themselves of stern metal when faced with adversity and to be the equal of their menfolk, though they were to be described in the press as 'plucky' rather than heroic so as not to compromise their femininity. Perhaps the most celebrated of them in her time was the Countess of Rothes. Travelling to join her husband, Norman Leslie, Earl of Rothes, who was on a business trip to Canada and the United States, Noël the Countess of Rothes had also confided to journalists who interviewed her before her departure that they were interested in buying an orange grove in California. With her as a companion was her cousin Gladys Cherry. The two women had been woken by a crash, and, going on deck to investigate, were told by Captain Smith to return to their cabins to put on their life jackets. With their maid, they entered a lifeboat where it soon became obvious that the seamen on board were not fully competent. Another passenger, Dr Alice Leader, said that 'the Countess is an excellent oarswoman and thoroughly at home on the water. She personally took command of our boat when it was found that the seamen who had been placed at the oars could not row skilfully.'[63] The countess herself claimed that 'I asked the seaman if he would care to have me take the tiller as I knew something about boats' and his response was, 'Certainly, lady.'[64] Thomas Jones, the able seaman in charge of the boat, remembered it all slightly differently: 'She had a lot to say, so I put her to steering the boat.'[65] He was also to say:

> I saw the way she was carrying herself, and I heard the quiet, determined way she spoke to the others, and I knew she was more of a man than any we had on board. And I put her in command.[66]

It should not have been surprising that she should have taken control as she was very much imbued with the principles of *noblesse oblige* and what she saw as the rightful role of the aristocracy in providing leadership. An active philanthropist, the countess patronised such charities as the Queen Victoria School, the Randolph Wemyss Memorial Hospital and the Chelsea Hospital for Women, the Princess Mary Scholarship at Cedars College for Blind Girls, the YMCA Bazaar, the

Children's Guild, the Deptford Fund and the Village Clubs Association. She formed a branch of the Red Cross at Leslie, Fife, near her husband's estate, and endowed it with three ambulances as well as receiving training in basic nursing skills and first aid herself, which became invaluable during the Great War when she served as a VAD at a hospital she set up in a wing of Leslie House and later at the Coulter Hospital in London. As the wife of a landowner, she took a prominent role in local charities. A staunch conservative opposed to socialism and Irish Home Rule, she also chaired local chapters of the Women's Unionist Association, a conservative society supporting votes for women. This charitable impulse and the prominent role she played in society gave her the authority and confidence to take the leadership on a lifeboat whilst not forgetting her duty to encourage and comfort women who lacked her emotional resilience. On *Carpathia*, continuing in her lady bountiful role, 'Her Ladyship helped to make clothes for the babies and became known amongst the crew as the plucky little countess.'[67]

In the lifeboat, the countess had taken charge of the tiller and steered for over an hour before handing over to her cousin Gladys. Meanwhile, 'several of the women took their place with the Countess at the oars, and rowed in turns, while the weak and unskilled stewards sat quietly at one end of the boat.' The countess saw it as her role to maintain morale since, 'the first impression I had as we left the ship was that, above all things, we mustn't lose our self-possession.' For her, 'the most terrible part of the whole thing was seeing the rows of portholes vanishing one by one.'[68] She wished to see if they could pick up any survivors but, for once, was overruled by other passengers and crew:

> Several of us wanted to row back and see if there was not some chance of rescuing anyone who had survived, but the majority in the boat argued that we had no right to risk their lives on the bare chance of finding anyone alive after the final plunge.[69]

Gladys Cherry, writing to Tom Jones, who had also wanted to search for survivors, bitterly regretted the failure to do something:

> The dreadful regret I shall always have, and I know you share with me, is that we ought to have gone back to see whom we could pick up; but

if you remember, there was only an American lady, my cousin, self and you who wanted to return. I could not hear the discussion very clearly, as I was at the tiller; but everyone forward and the three men refused; but I shall always remember your words: 'ladies, if any of us are saved, remember, I wanted to go back. I would rather drown with them than leave them.' You did all you could, and being my own countryman, I wanted to tell you this.[70]

When told by a stewardess on *Carpathia*, 'You have made yourself famous by rowing in the boat,' the countess's characteristic response was, 'I hope not. I have done nothing.'[71] Instead, she stressed the roles of Thomas Jones and steward Alfred Crawford for 'alternately cheering us with words of encouragement, then rowing doggedly'.[72] The other women too played a major part in their own survival, as Emma Bucknell acknowledged:

The plight of some of the women in our boat was pitiable. While some were fully dressed, others wore only their nightgowns and kimonos. The maid to the Countess of Rothes, who pulled one of the best oars in the boat, was dressed in this fashion, and her hair was streaming down her back and shoulders all the time we were in a little boat. The women would row until they would fall from exhaustion, their place being taken by another woman who would gently move aside the collapsed one and work in her place until exhaustion also overcame her.[73]

If the Countess of Rothes was the suitably aristocratic British heroine of the night, her American counterpart, Margaret Tobin Brown of Denver, came from a far more modest background. Also a socialite and philanthropist, she came from a humble Irish Catholic immigrant family but had married a Colorado gold miner, J.J. Brown, who made his fortune through his engineering ability in devising a timber-and-hay bale method to hold back the dolomite sand that had prevented miners from reaching the gold at the lower depths of the silver mine at which he was superintendent.[74] Her husband's newly acquired wealth enabled her to study language, literature and drama at the Carnegie Institute in New York. Having started her charitable activities with organising and working in soup kitchens in the mining town of Leadville, she was able to extend the scope of her philanthropy as her husband became wealthier. She fundraised to build the Cathedral of the Immaculate Conception in Denver and took an interest in the welfare of destitute children and the problem of juvenile delinquency. Working with the Denver Women's Club, she campaigned for the education of women and later worked with the Colorado Chapter of the National American Women's Suffrage Association for the right to vote. At the same time as she proved herself a tireless campaigner for social reform, she launched herself into society. Fluent in French, German, Italian and Russian, she indulged in her love of travel. She had joined the Astors in Egypt while in Europe visiting her daughter, a student at the Sorbonne, but was rushing back to New York when she heard that her grandson was seriously ill.[75]

What she remembered of the scenes on the deck as the lifeboats were lowered was that:

> The whole thing, was so formal that it was difficult for any a one to realize that it was a tragedy. Men and women stood in little groups and talked. Some laughed as the first boats went over the side. All the time the band was playing.[76]

She noticed that the boats were not full when they were launched and believed that 'the excessive loss of life came from gallantry carried to an extreme' and suggested that 'if the authorities put more lifeboats on this they must label them "for men" or they will never use them'.[77] She busied herself with helping other women into the boats, speaking in French to one woman who could not understand the instructions she had been given in English. She herself felt that she owed her life to two men who had acted as escorts for her during the voyage and were to the last keeping an eye on her, the department store buyers Edward P. Calderhead and James McGough, who 'practically threw me into the boat with the words, "you are going, too"'. The boat was lowered 'as gently as if it were a boat drill'. At this stage, 'it all seemed like a play, like a drama that was being enacted for entertainment. It did not seem real.'[78]

It was not long before this flamboyant, energetic and business-like woman took charge of the lifeboat. In order to keep warm she took an oar and helped with the rowing. Irritated by the pessimism of Robert Hichens, the quartermaster in charge of the boat, who moaned that they stood no chance of survival because they had no compass, food or drinking water, she 'told him to be still or he would go overboard. Then he was quiet. I rowed because I would have frozen to death. I made them all row. It saved their lives.'[79] Together with Helen Candee and Julia Cavendish, she argued for going back to save any survivors after the ship went down, but could not bully everyone else into agreeing with her, while Hichens told the women to row and not risk the boat being submerged by any of the survivors trying to clamber aboard.[80] As the sun came up, she marvelled that:

> The most wonderful dawn I have ever seen came upon us. I have just returned from Egypt. I have been all over the world, but I have never seen anything like this. First the grey and then the flood of light. Then the sun came up in a ball of red fire.[81]

However inspirational she may have been in a lifeboat cast away on the sea, it was her work with survivors on *Carpathia* that really sealed Brown's reputation. Her down-to-earth manner and language skills enabled her to communicate with immigrant survivors in steerage. She distributed blankets, offered advice and urged the wealthier passengers to donate money to help the less fortunate. This work she continued when everyone had disembarked in New York.[82]

She was early recognised as a heroine of the wreck. Reporters interviewing her commented that she was still in the clothes she had worn when leaving the *Titanic* and had not bothered to brush her hair since Sunday morning because 'there was work to do' and 'there were many women there whom I had to look out for'. It was reported that the women survivors had dubbed her 'Lady Margaret' and believed her to be 'the strength of them all'.[83] With her typical forthright humour, she was later to tell her daughter:

> After being brined, salted, and pickled in mid ocean I am now high and dry. I have had flowers, letters, telegrams, people until I am befuddled. They are petitioning Congress to give me a medal ... If I must call a

specialist to examine my head it is due to the title of Heroine of the Titanic.[84]

She saw nothing special in her actions since 'I simply did what was to be done'.

Margaret Brown was a strong exponent of women's rights and she was not a lone voice among women on the ship. Edith and Elsie Bowerman were both suffragettes. The widow of a Hastings property landlord, Edith Bowerman Chibnall had formed a branch of the Women's Tax Emancipation League and actively campaigned for the vote for women. Her daughter, educated at Girton College, Cambridge, where she had studied medieval and modern languages, joined the Women's Social and Political Union at Cambridge. During the Great War, she was to work as an orderly with Dr Elsie Inglis for the Scottish Women's Hospitals, going out to Russia with an all-women's unit. She was later to act as Christabel Pankhurst's election agent for the Women's Party in the 1918 general election when women over 30 could vote, and was to qualify as a barrister in 1924. A dedicated conservative and snobbish in attitude, she believed it was her mission to encourage individual responsibility and enterprise whilst opposing socialism and communism as secretary of the Women's Guild of Empire. Despite their strong opinions, the two women seem to have kept a low profile during their rescue from *Titanic*, though Elsie did comment that 'to pull an oar in the midst of the Atlantic in April with ice-bergs floating about, is a strange experience'. The Women's Social and Political Union, however, did celebrate the survival of these two women who were 'very enthusiastic workers in the cause'.[85]

An exception to the calmness and fortitude of most of the women from first class was the hysterical conduct of 22-year-old María Josefa Pérez de Soto y Vallejo, the spoiled daughter of the financier Manuel Pérez de Soto, President of the Madrid Provincial Council, enjoying an extended seventeen-month honeymoon across Europe with her equally wealthy and well-connected husband, Victor Peñasco, visiting Monte Carlo, Biarritz, Vienna, Paris and London. The attractive young couple stayed in the most luxurious hotels, ate in the finest restaurants and spent extravagantly on jewellery and fine clothes, which they both enjoyed showing off on visits to the opera and the theatre, gambling at the casino and eating in the fashionable restaurants they liked to patronise and be admired in. The cost of their grandiose honeymoon was said to be a lavish 290,000 pesetas. They enjoyed life and new experiences to the full and had travelled on the Orient Express before deciding on a whim while dining at Maxim's in Paris, excited by brochures they had recently picked up, to go on the maiden voyage of the *Titanic* and then stay at the Plaza Hotel in New York simply because it seemed a romantic thing to do. Peñasco's valet, Eulogio, was left behind in the luxurious Hotel Majestic, their base in Paris, to send pre-written postcards, telling of visits to Versailles, Notre Dame, the Louvre and the Opera Garnier, to Victor's mother, Purificación Castellana, to prevent her from worrying about them as she had warned them against taking ocean voyages while on their honeymoon.[86] In this, they showed an immaturity that went with the self-indulgence they relished. Meanwhile, the two 'lovebirds', as one fellow passenger described them, enjoyed their short time on the ill-fated liner, the focus of attention with their eye-catching elegant appearance. Fellow passenger Helen Bishop remembered them as 'just like little canaries. They were so loving, and were having such a happy honeymoon that everyone on the *Titanic* became interested in them.'[87]

Victor Peñasco was protective of his wife and showed perhaps more fortitude and dignity than her, and a greater acceptance of reality, when their idyll was abruptly ended. His behaviour was seen as worthy of a manly man taking on responsibility despite the flamboyance of his style and as an expiation of his hedonism. Whereas Victor must be seen as a hero, his wife could be allowed to show womanly weakness and immaturity. At the moment of the fateful collision with the iceberg, Peñasco was undressing for bed after dinner followed by late night socialising with two Uruguayan passengers, Francisco Mauro Severiano Carraú and José Pedro Carraú-Esteves, young men of a similar age to the couple with whom they could speak Spanish. Hearing a loud bang, he donned his dinner jacket once again to go on deck to find out what had happened and then returned to escort his wife, with only a shawl and lifebelt over her nightgown, and her maid, to a lifeboat, briefly returning to their cabin to collect the jewellery she had left there and was distraught at the thought of losing. His clinging young wife was reluctant to board a lifeboat without her husband, but he left her in the custody of the Countess of Rothes in a lifeboat, which he was not allowed to board. The other women in the lifeboat almost had to drag his

Women and Children First by Fortunino Matania, a representation of true manliness. (*Wikicommons, public domain*)

'The Great Titanic Disaster', a photo montage centred on Captain Smith, the wireless operator and the lifeboats, images of negligence or duty? (*Library of Congress, LC-USZ62-61940*)

The airy drawing office of Harland & Wolff, where the sleek *Titanic* was designed under the supervision of Thomas Andrews and Roderick Chisholm, both lost with the Guarantee Group. *(Wikicommons, public domain)*

A marvel of modernism under construction. *(LC-USZ62-26743)*

A giant of modern technology whose propellers dwarfed the Harland & Wolff workers who built her. *(LC-USZ62-34781)*

The *Titanic* after her launch. *(LC-USZ62-56585)*

The Grand Staircase, the most recognisable emblem of the opulence of *Titanic* and a fitting backcloth for social display, although photographs of it come from *Olympic*. (LC-USZ62-26812)

The feminine and refined atmosphere of the Veranda Café and Palm Court. (LC-USZ62-116095)

An athletic man following the cult of keep fit was accommodated in the gymnasium, similar to the one on *Olympic*. (LC-USZ62-26823)

The Smoking Room, a bastion of masculinity, both its virtue and vices, identical to the room on *Olympic*. (LC-USZ62-26825)

The Great Promenade Deck, usually a scene of calm but one of confusion during the sinking. (LC-USZ62-116096)

Naval architect Thomas Andrews, the abstemious, clean-cut practical man of action. (Wikicommons, public domain)

Archie Butt, military aide to Presidents Roosevelt and Taft, the epitome of swaggering martial masculinity. (LC-USZ62-116070)

John Jacob Astor, 'the world's greatest monument to unearned income', tainted by the scandal of his divorce and marriage to the much younger Madeline, and in need of redemption. *(LC-USZ62-91221)*

Charles M. Hays, eulogised as a great entrepreneur though his railway empire was unstable.
(McCord Stewart Museum II-199189.0)

The successful businessman, athlete and clubman as the embodiment of Anglo-Saxon manliness, Thornton Davidson.
(McCord Stewart Museum II-186045)

The self-effacing scion of robber barons, Harry Widener was reincarnated as a new type of sensitive cultural hero. (*Wikicommons, public domain*)

Exquisitely tailored Victor Peñasco could pose as the gallant romantic lead, only for someone else's corpse to be purchased as proof of his death. (*Wikicommons, public domain*)

The *Denver Post* hired actors to reconstruct the alleged shootings of Italian passengers on *Titanic*, 19 April 1912. (*Library of Congress newspaper collection, public domain*)

Class and gender conflict was rife in the lifeboats. (LC-USZ62-93570)

The unsinkable Margaret Brown and Captain Rostron of *Carpathia*, both of whom saved lives and helped the survivors by their decisive leadership. (LC-USZ62-47788)

The plucky Countess of Rothes, a lady bountiful and the equal of any man. (*Wikicommons, public domain*)

Charlotte Collyer and her daughter, clutching a White Star blanket from the wreck, survived but her husband perished. (*LC-DIG-ggbain-19397*)

The Navratil orphans of the *Titanic*, abducted by their father and at first feared unidentifiable. (*LC-USZ62-56585*)

Lucy Duff-Gordon, the fashion designer and dutiful wife determined to survive alongside her husband and contemptuous of women who left their husbands to die. (*LC-USZ62-135822*)

Titanic survivors who came through their ordeal respectably dressed and without a scratch, George and Dorothy Harder with Sallie Beckwith on *Carpathia*. (LC-USZ62-56452)

Survivors on the deck of *Carpathia* were still distinguished by their social status whether wearing evening dress or dressing gown. (LC-USZ62-56453)

Stuart Collett, saved by his chivalry as an escort. (LC-USZ62-85391)

The heroic casualty Harold Bride, Marconi operator, whose feet were so badly frostbitten he had to be carried up a ramp. (LC-USZ62-85392)

Stewards Frederick Dent Ray, Andrew Cunningham and William Burke ready to justify their own survival at the American Inquiry in Washington, DC, 27 April 1912. (LC-DIG-hec-00940)

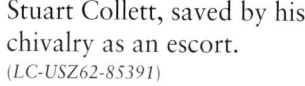

Men and women of all classes waiting for news at White Star Offices. *(LC-DIG-ggbain-10349)*

Journalists dominated the crowds waiting to greet survivors in New York. *(LC-USZ62-26635)*

Harold Cottam, Marconi operator on *Carpathia*, was overawed when questioned by the Senate Inquiry. *(LC-USZ62-68080)*

The guilty men? Bruce Ismay (far right) and White Star Line officials. *(LC-DIG-hec-00933)*

No mercy for Bruce Ismay under grilling during the Senate Inquiry at the Waldorf Astoria. (*LC-DIG-ds-13444*)

'Which? Fate or Economy in Lifeboats', a cartoon criticising the cause of the loss of life on such a large scale. (*LC-USZ62-121019*)

The corpses of the recovered victims were embalmed on *Minia* and the other rescue ships, but only first-class passengers enjoyed the luxury of a coffin. (*Wikicommons, public domain*)

The Women's Monument to the *Titanic* heroes in Washington, DC, an accolade to the ideal of the manly man. (*LC-DIG-ggbain-21094*)

The Congressional Medal presented to Captain Rostron by President Taft featured heroic images of the male victims. (*LC-DIG-hec-01690*)

wife away from her husband, who in the end threw her into their arms and asked them to look after her before returning to the other men standing on the deck. He then gallantly merged into the crowds on the deck so she would not follow him as he had seemed only too resigned to his fate when he had told her on parting that he hoped that her future life would be happy.[88] Without the support of her husband and having to face up to reality rather than the protected and self-indulgent dreamland she had hitherto enjoyed, she became hysterical and demanded the attention she had enjoyed in happier times.

As the ship went down, the Countess of Rothes was concerned when:

> Signora de Satode Peñasco began to scream for her husband. It was too horrible. I left the tiller to my cousin and slipped down beside her to be of what comfort I could. Poor woman! Her sobs tore our hearts and her moans were unspeakable in their sadness.[89]

The countess felt that she had to protect her from the full enormity of what was happening in order to calm her down and stop her upsetting the other women. The first sighting of the *Carpathia* raised false hopes in her that were soon dashed:

> The bride was full of joy in the belief that it was still the *Titanic*, and that her husband, consequently, was safe. When she was disillusioned her grief was something terrible to witness. She broke down and cried piteously, being quite inconsolable.[90]

Such a conspicuously open display of grief and raw emotion was put down to her being Spanish. It was perhaps more the reaction of a spoiled, rather immature woman for the first time deprived of the protection of an attentive husband, which for her was the normal relationship between the sexes.

Pepita Peñasco was not the only woman to show such signs of weakness as timidity, fear, hysteria and materialistic vanity. Ruth Dodge, whose husband was not in the same boat as her though he survived, was rather scornful of the women accompanied by their husbands who 'became hysterical – about what I don't know; they were missing none of their people. I was trying to keep baby from realization of what was happening, but when these women shrieked he would begin crying and asking, "Where's papa?"' It was said that many of them had become overwrought confined to a lifeboat and had refused to return to save men and women floundering in the sea. Ruth Dodge found this particularly upsetting and 'I told them, "how do I know, you have your husbands with you, but my husband may be one of those who are crying."' Her pleas were in vain as the other passengers argued that:

> If we got back where the people were struggling, some of the steerage passengers, crazed with fear and the cold, might capsize the boat struggling to get in, or might force the officers to overload so we would all go down.[91]

It was claimed that some of the widows 'mourned gems more than husbands', being more concerned about the loss of their jewellery and clothes than the fate of their spouses.[92] Lifeboats were described as having 'drifted away with weak and vain and frivolous, worthless and hapless women and little children'.[93] This self-centeredness and dependency on men was contrasted strongly with the self-sacrifice and altruism of the 'heroes of the sea' who had 'met death with calm intrepidity that the weaker ones might be saved'.[94]

> Without any distinction of rank or wealth or strength, the men stood aside. There was no wild fight for life, in which the stronger gained an ignoble victory. The ancient law of the sea, 'women and children first' was maintained with perfect courage by more than a thousand men ... In the words of the Prime Minister, 'the best traditions of the sea' were observed.[95]

Male sacrifices on behalf of women were seen as normal, instinctual and part of the unalterable order of society:

> At such moments, what man gives a thought to the 'war of the sexes'? In the face of a calamity, men are still men, and women are still women ... In the hour of mourning ... it is a healing thought that the old

chivalrous cry of English seamen 'women and children first!' rang from deck to deck.[96]

Ella White had a more pragmatic approach to men sacrificing themselves for their wives by remaining on the sinking ship while their wives went off in flimsy lifeboats manned only by inexperienced and inept crew members:

> I never saw a finer body of men in my life than the men passengers on this ship – athletes and men of sense – and if they had been permitted to enter these lifeboats with their families, the boats would have been properly manned and many more lives saved, instead of allowing stewards to get in the boats and save their lives under the pretence that they could row when they knew nothing about it.[97]

Mrs White's assumption was still that it was the role of the man to protect the woman. It was a view that was not to go unchallenged. The suffragette Laura Aberconway questioned whether or not the custom of women and children being saved first was not indeed a form of discrimination against men:

> This traditional custom is now carried out without the direct consent of the individual men who are thereby doomed to die, or of any wish expressed by women, who no doubt are almost equally deprived of choice … In loss at sea we claim our right to die for those we love, or share their doom.[98]

As an advocate of equality and women's rights, she argued that women should have been given the choice of whether or not to be saved but rather more unconventionally thought that men were so blinded by chivalry that it left them no choice if they wanted to be seen to behave in manly fashion.

Other feminist critics challenged the assumption that chivalry had proved effective in saving lives and declared that:

> while our papers were vaunting the chivalry of the men and claiming it as an argument against women's suffrage, almost half of the steerage

women and seven-tenths of the steerage children were lying dead at the bottom of the Atlantic.[99]

Others observed that whilst men gained honour and a swift death by behaving chivalrously in a shipwreck, their wives were left to face bereavement and economic hardship.[100] It was argued that now that 'men and women are comrades and co-workers' and wives were no longer 'helpless, loving, dutiful chattels', it was surely the time when 'women must have a chivalry of their own. Let us say, "the children first". In such a scenario, fathers as well as mothers would have priority over childless women.'[101] This was an extension of the prevalent eugenist view that it was right that women should be saved because of their role as mothers or potential mothers safeguarding the future of the human race since 'the race is carried on by children and women are needed to care for the children'.[102] In a time of concern about the differential birth rate and the physical deterioration of the race, the role of the mother was regarded as paramount. It was more revolutionary to raise the importance of fatherhood and put fathers ahead of 'the casual woman in distress'.[103]

Support for such a view came surprisingly from the Chinese Merchants Association of America, whose spokesman, Henry Moy Foi, declared that 'in China it would really have been a crime to take care of the women first'. It would have been the responsibility of Chinese sailors to make sure that the men had priority, followed by children, with women being left to the last. The rationale for this was that 'the men are the most valuable for the nation'. In contrast to the economic value of men, 'the average woman would be destitute without her husband'. Children were less likely than their widowed mothers to be a burden on the country because 'childless families can always be found to take care of them'.[104] In many ways, it supported arguments for the superiority of men, though from a different perspective from the usual one that the man's duty was to protect the weak, which gave him a moral advantage.

Opponents of women's suffrage used the tragedy to argue that 'the suffragettes in placing a plank in their platform abolishing the rule "women and children first" will probably make no headway so long as manhood shall endure'.[105] They argued that there was a clear distinction between the roles of men and women shown by the men putting the weaker women and children ahead of their own salvation and the acquiescence of the women assuming a dependent role in all of this, and that 'if men and women are to be rivals, can she expect such chivalrous protection as the women of the *Titanic* received?'[106] Winston Churchill, the First Lord of the Admiralty, considered that:

> The strict observance of the great traditions of the sea towards women and children reflects nothing but honour upon our civilisation. Even I hope it may mollify some of the young unmarried lady teachers who are so bitter in their sex antagonism, and think men so base and vile.[107]

More bluntly, it was suggested by one man that 'when a woman talks women's rights, she be answered with the word *Titanic*, nothing more – just *Titanic*'.[108]

The controversial pathologist Sir Almroth Wright, dubbed by fellow members of the medical profession as 'Sir Almost Wright' and 'Sir Always Wrong', used the example of the sinking of the *Titanic* to back up his misogynistic argument in his *The Unexpurgated Case against Woman Suffrage* that women were inferior to men and thus psychologically and medically unfit to have the vote. It was his belief that men had a superior ethical code by which:

> in all times of crisis he may be counted upon to apply the principles of communal morality which have been handed down in the race. The *Titanic* disaster, for example, showed in a conspicuous manner that the ordinary man will, 'letting his own life go,' obey the communal law which lays it upon him, when involved in a catastrophe, to save first the women and children.

By contrast, a woman confined her altruism to family, sexual partners and close friends rather than humanity in general, which limited her judgment on political issues, an extreme opinion that Wright typically failed to back up by examples from the *Titanic* or elsewhere.[109] Although Wright liked to portray himself as a profound and original thinker, his ideas were far from unique to him and were common in the press of the day, which stressed the rights of wealthy men to rule because they were unafraid to sacrifice themselves for the greater good:

> Those who are saved are not the strong and able-bodied but the weak and the dependent – not the grasping millionaire from the private suite on the promenade deck, clutching a roll of banknotes, or the lusty shellback from the fore-peak, wielding the sheath-knife plucked from his leather belt, but the defenceless wives and sisters and children, from the saloon and steerage alike ... Thus is our civilisation vindicated; ... thus does man prove his fitness to be the master of things, because he is master of himself; thus is 'death swallowed up in victory'.[110]

Suffragettes countered such arguments with the suggestion that if women had had the vote and could influence laws, the disaster of the *Titanic* might never have happened:

> Some people think that the grievous tragedy of the 'Titanic' supplies a reason why women should not have the vote. On the contrary, it supplies one of the strongest reasons ever heard of why they should have it. ... Because the law allows it, the *Titanic*, in order to make a record and save a few hours, followed a dangerous, and, as it proved, a fatal northerly course, instead of a longer and more southerly course. Because the law allows it, she was equipped with a hideously inadequate number of lifeboats ... A terrible sacrifice this, made with full legal sanction, to the essentially masculine passion for record breaking and money-making at any and every cost![111]

They also argued that women would also deal with social injustices ashore since 'the chivalry shown to a few hundred women on the *Titanic* does not alter the fact that in New York City, 150,000 people, largely women and children, have to sleep in dark rooms with no windows'.[112] Nor did it go unremarked that many of the heroes of the *Titanic* were actually responsible for much of this social injustice and were resolutely opposed to women having the vote or of being in a position to remedy them:

> Most of those men, no doubt, stubbornly opposed the idea of the rights of women in participation in government affairs, exploited them in

industry, voted for the white slave pen, sent the daughter to the street, the son to the army, the husband to tramp the streets for a job.[113]

Although often relegated to a subservient, secondary place by the chivalry of the men in accounts of the sinking of the *Titanic*, the importance of the role of women was even recognised at the time by the *New York Times*:

> Oftentimes it has been written that out of each great moment of history some man has emerged as master of the situation, some one hand and mind that has controlled where others held back. From verified statements and from circumstances explained by others the work of the women makes them the central figures in the great sea tragedy.[114]

The norms of society at the time meant that the heroism of women was often perceived in terms of their obedience to their husbands and their quiet dignity in the face of a catastrophe, but women played an active role in the fight for survival and their actions raised questions and arguments relevant to the progress of the rights of women and equality.

Chapter Five

Class, Prejudice and Conflict

As a floating microcosm of Edwardian society, *Titanic* reflected the attitudes, prejudices and social divisions of a highly stratified age. Yet it would be a mistake to see class division in simplistic terms of first, second and third classes on the ship corresponding to upper, middle and working classes. Both at sea and ashore there were overlaps between the classes, grey areas in regard to status and sharp divisions. Social stratification was not always clearly defined.

The wealthy families and passengers in first class tended to gravitate towards each other in line with previous social connections and common business interests. Even as the ship went down many of them congregated together along the rail although by this stage there was little future advantage in them sticking together. Especially prominent was the Philadelphia social and business circle surrounding George and Eleanor Widener. Peter Arrell Browne Widener, the son of a mason and himself once a butcher's boy, had founded the family fortune through supplying mutton to the Union Army during the American Civil War and then investing the profit in public transportation as founding partner in the Philadelphia Traction Company. He had then helped to found US Steel and the American Tobacco Company. He also had substantial holdings in Standard Oil and the International Mercantile Marine Company, parent company of the White Star Line. A die-hard Republican, he supported the US Steel Corporation suppression of labour organisations in its plants after a bitter strike in 1901.[1] His son George Dunton Widener took over the running of the Philadelphia Traction Company, overseeing the development of cable and electric streetcar operations. He also served as a director of the Philadelphia Traction Co., Land Title Bank and Trust Co., Electric Storage Co., and Portland Cement Co. He married Eleanor Elkins, daughter of a transport magnate, the partner of his father, with whom he had two sons and a daughter. The patriarchal Peter Widener had built an imposing mansion, Lynnewood Hall, as a home for himself, his two sons and grandchildren, and for his art collections, which included works by Raphael, Vermeer, Rembrandt, El Greco, Manet, Corot, Renoir and Degas now in the National Gallery, Washington. His grandson, the bibliophile Harry, once remarked that 'we are a family of collectors. My grandfather collects paintings; my mother collects silver and porcelains, Uncle Joe collects everything, and I, books.'[2] Yet this vast wealth and veneer of culture could not buy social acceptance among the more established families of Philadelphia 'dedicated to the principles of snobbery'. Nor was an elitist Harvard education enough to protect Harry from the snobbish sneers of Sir Sidney Colvin, Slade Professor of Fine Arts at the University of Cambridge and a friend of Robert Louis Stevenson, when the eminent man of letters commented of that 'curious' young man that 'one seemed to see visible in his features the hereditary acuteness of a money-making and rather low-bred stock at issue, or at any rate in imperfect combination, with an amiable character and a very genuine love of letters'.[3]

With their new money, the Wideners were more interested in cultivating fellow industrial magnates rather than worrying about social snubs and the lack of invitations to prestigious balls in Philadelphia. They had the wealth and prominence to create their own social circles which could be just as elitist as the ones from which they themselves were excluded. The dinner party in the à la carte restaurant hosted by the Wideners and attended by Captain Smith on the eve of the sinking has come to epitomise the doomed glamour of the ship. It was a select gathering. The star catch, in addition to the captain, was presidential aide Archie Butt. Although his close friend, the distinguished artist Frank Millet, had become close to Harry Widener, staying up late at night to share their love of their alma mater Harvard, Millet was not invited. Instead, the other guests were business associates and friends from Philadelphia, John Borland Thayer, vice-president of the Pennsylvania Railroad, and his socialite wife Marian, and William and Lucille Carter, whose fortune was based on anthracite coal mining. It was meant to be a glittering social occasion, though other diners observed a lack of gaiety among the guests and that Captain Smith had left at the earliest opportunity.[4]

Other less prominent but still wealthy passengers had toured Europe together before boarding *Titanic* or had met during their travels. Travelling together were three Canadian businessmen who described themselves as 'the three musketeers', realtor Thomson Beattie, his best friend, Union Bank President Thomas McCaffry, and John Hugo Ross, the son of Arthur Wellington Ross, the Liberal-Conservative Member of Parliament for the Manitoba riding of Lisgar. They were returning from cruising the Nile and travels through Italy and Greece in the company of fellow Winnipeg businessman and land speculator Mark Fortune, his wife Mary, son Charles and daughters Alice, Ethel and Mabel. All the men from this group of travelling companions were to lose their lives, only the women in the Fortune family surviving. Although described as 'of such as retiring disposition that little was known of him except by his most intimate friends', Beattie was a keen sportsman and 'almost inseparable' from McCaffry, whom he was said to resemble in appearance and manner. Ross was suffering from dysentery when he boarded the ship and was effectively confined to his cabin. It was here that his close-knit group of friends proved invaluable in keeping an eye on him, though when they told him the ship had struck an iceberg and that he should get dressed, Ross was said to have dismissed the warnings and told them 'it will take more than an iceberg to get me off this ship'.[5]

This close group of friends and travelling companions also had strong links with other wealthy Canadians on the ship, including Charles Hays, Thornton Davidson, Harry Molson, Hudson Allison and Arthur Peuchen. For Arthur Peuchen, once he was safely on *Carpathia*:

> then came the sad part of it all. I had ten personal friends, Canadians, on the *Titanic*. I began the search for them and I saw Mrs. Hays and the Allison's nurse and baby. I went to look for Hugo Ross, Mr. Hays, Mr. Davidson and Mr. Molson. But I was the only Canadian man on that boat. I kept going around the deck, but couldn't find them.[6]

These men not only had shared business interests but were members of the same social circuits and clubs. Their wives socialised with each other. Peuchen and Molson were business associates, with Molson holding a directorate in one of Peuchen's companies. Indeed, Peuchen had persuaded him to extend his stay in England so they could travel home together on *Titanic*. Allison and Davidson were Montreal stockbrokers, though Davidson was the more thrusting and prominent of the two men. Thornton Davidson and Harry Molson were both members of the Royal St Lawrence Yacht, St James, Montreal Hunt, and Montreal Jockey clubs but whereas Molson was wealthy enough to be very much the hedonistic playboy, his younger fellow clubman was always conscious of potential business links that might be made. They shared with Arthur Peuchen and Hugo Ross a passion for sailing. By contrast with his brash son-in-law for whom business contacts and social contacts were closely connected, Charles Hays's 'devotion to work left him with little time for social pleasures, and he was reported to have had few intimate friends, but public organizations and charitable institutions knew him as a generous supporter'.[7]

Shared business and commercial interests similarly brought a group of department store buyers together in first class who would have had little or nothing in common with the wealthiest social groupings. These five men, all of a similar age in their late thirties or early forties, dined together on the last night and signed the menu with their names and addresses as a souvenir. Edward Calderhead of New York City, James McGough from Philadelphia, and John Irwin Flynn of Brooklyn all worked as buyers for Gimbel's department stores. Spencer Silverthorne from St Louis was a buyer for Nugent's department store. These men shared two adjacent cabins. Dining with them was George Graham, a sales manager and chief buyer for Eaton's department store in Winnipeg, having previously been head of the crockery and fine china division of the store in Toronto. Graham was the only one of these five men not to survive, though the autographed menu card was saved in the dinner jacket pocket of one of the surviving buyers.[8]

Shipboard friendships seem to have been easily formed though may not have lasted for more than the duration of the voyage. Lawrence Beesley, a Christian Scientist and science schoolmaster at Dulwich College, found enough in common with Ernest Carter, an Anglican clergyman working in an East End parish, to discuss:

> the relative merits of his university – Oxford – with mine – Cambridge – as world-wide educational agencies, the opportunities at each for the formation of character apart from mere education as such, and ... the

lack of sufficiently qualified men to take up the work of the Church of England.[9]

He also described other second-class passengers making new acquaintances:

> Close beside me – so near that I cannot avoid hearing scraps of their conversation – are two American ladies, both dressed in white, young, probably friends only: one has been to India and is returning by way of England, the other is a school-teacher in America, a graceful girl with a distinguished air heightened by a pair of pince-nez. Engaged in conversation with them is a gentleman whom I subsequently identified from a photograph as a well-known resident of Cambridge, Massachusetts, genial, polished, and with a courtly air towards the two ladies, whom he has known but a few hours; from time to time as they talk, a child acquaintance breaks in on their conversation and insists on their taking notice of a large doll clasped in her arms.[10]

Whereas wealth may have been a unifying factor among first-class passengers, second class was more diverse. As well as teachers, clergymen of all denominations, shopkeepers, clerks, engineers and farmers, there were miners, glassblowers and workmen. Erik Collander was the technical director of a Helsinki paper mill, Hull Botsford was an architect specialising in railway architecture, Denzil Jarvis was the manager of an engineering firm and Ernst Sjöstedt was a metallurgist, all of whom were well educated and wealthy enough to have travelled first class.[11] By contrast, Franz Pulbaum was a 27-year-old machinist who had emigrated from Bremen in 1907 and was returning to New York from a visit home and a stay in the French capital to inspect the mechanical rides at the Luna Park amusement park in Coney Island. In his cabin trunk, recovered from the ocean in 1993, among other personal possessions including a striped grey tie, a newly purchased pair of silk socks still attached to each other at the toe and a German-English dictionary, was a completed and signed declaration of his intention to become a United States citizen, an ambition destined never to be realised.[12] Whilst valets and ladies' maids were usually accommodated in first class so as to be readily available to attend their employers, chauffeurs, such as Hudson Allison's 19-year-old driver George Swane, last remembered for a vigorous pillow fight with his cabin mates on the night of the sinking, were often accommodated in second class. Edwin Wheeler, footman and valet to George Vanderbilt, was only on board to accompany his master's luggage as the Vanderbilts had cancelled their booking for the voyage and travelled on an earlier crossing on *Olympic* but had sent their luggage on the *Titanic* as originally planned.[13] Philip Stokes was a bricklayer from Catford and Charles Whillems was a glassblower from Forest Gate.[14] Harry Rogers was a 19-year-old waiter from Tavistock, 'a smart and steady young fellow' who 'intended to turn his hand to anything that came along'.[15]

Some of the passengers in second class could have fitted into first class socially, but there were others who might have found third class more congenial. Joseph Fynney, a wealthy unmarried Liverpool rubber merchant, could have afforded and easily fitted into first class. He was a frequent traveller to Canada to visit members of his family now living there and on most of his voyages was accompanied by a male companion chosen from among the juvenile delinquents he tried to reform and redeem through his local parish church, where he was said to take a particular interest 'in connection with the Young Men's Club and matters appertaining to the welfare of boys and young men'.[16] His neighbours were suspicious of, and complained about, the noise from the late night visits he received from these young men in whose welfare he took such an absorbing interest, though his family remembered on his gravestone that 'his delight was in doing good'. Whilst Fynney would have been more than acceptable in first class, his companion on *Titanic*, apprentice barrel maker William Gaskell, would have felt uncomfortably out of place and might even have felt more at home in third.[17]

Lawrence Beesley was aware of a second-class passenger whose husband was travelling in steerage:

Another interesting man was travelling steerage, but had placed his wife in the second cabin: he would climb the stairs leading from the steerage to the second deck and talk affectionately with his wife across the low gate which separated them. I never saw him after the collision, but I think his wife was on the *Carpathia*. Whether they ever saw each other on the Sunday night is very doubtful: he would not at first be allowed on the second-class deck, and if he were, the chances of seeing his wife in the darkness and the crowd would be very small, indeed.[18]

This story of an unnamed couple reflects the segregation of the classes on the ship with no movement between the two just as much as it shows the grey areas of status in which those travelling in one class might have just as easily fitted into another. Hans Givard, a much travelled Danish farmer who made the trip annually home to Denmark from the United States or Argentina, wherever he was working at the time, was travelling with two friends, blacksmith Martin Ponesell and dairy worker Einar Windeløv, but only Givard and Ponesell could afford to travel in second class and Windeløv was relegated to third class until he could hope to rejoin his friends at the end of the voyage.[19]

Other groups of second-class passengers were able to stay together for the duration of the voyage, enjoying the company of familiar friends and also the same amenities, among them a number of groups from Cornwall. Butcher's boy Percy Bailey was originally booked to travel on *Oceanic* but had transferred to *Titanic* to make the journey with his friends, baker George Hocking and builder Harry Cotterill, all of whom had attended the primitive Methodist Sunday School in Penzance and were travelling to Akron, Ohio. With them were Hocking's mother, two sisters and two nephews.[20] En route, they met with other Cornish emigrants 'at St. Erith bound for the same place as we are going so we are a big family altogether'.[21]

There was no official mixing allowed between classes nor any contact beyond distant views from the decks of passengers in other classes. For the poorest of the emigrants in third class, what they saw of the public rooms and even cabins enjoyed by their social superiors as they passed through them in search of the lifeboats came as a revelation and revealed the very great material gaps between the classes. Anna Kincaid and another girl with her were 'quite awed at the splendour' of the first-class dining room, which Anna described as 'the banquet hall', where 'the tables were so beautifully set and all the furniture, and everything about this huge room was out of the world to both of us'. She later confessed that 'we even thought of going in and helping ourselves, but decided we might have to pay, so didn't'.[22] Similar thoughts crossed the mind of Swedish socialist August Wennerström when he and two girls were scavenging for lifebelts and they entered a stateroom where they found 'magnificent suits, clothing thrown all over, on a table were jewels and diamonds, and on other tables champagne'. He was tempted by such lavish and hastily abandoned trappings of wealth were it not that, with the ship about to sink, 'money and wealth are death things and of no value to you when you are face to face with death'.[23]

Third-class passengers were even more diverse in origin than in the other two classes. It is estimated that 118 of them were English, Scottish and Welsh, 113 Irish, 104 Swedish, 79 Lebanese, 55 Finish, 43 American, 35 Bulgarian, 25 Norwegian, 22 Belgian, 12 Armenian, 8 Chinese, 7 Danish, 5 French, 4 Italian, 4 Greek, 4 German, 4 Swiss and 3 Portuguese. There were 44 subjects of the Austro-Hungarian Emperor, many of them Croatian, and 18 subjects of the Russian Tsar, many of them from Poland and the Baltic countries. They included farmers, farm labourers, foresters, miners, engineers, printers, builders, bricklayers, plumbers, carpenters, potters, tailors, bakers, salesmen, cooks, barmen, waiters, domestic servants, jewellers and chemists.[24] Even among travellers from the same country, there could be great differences. Most of the Irish emigrants were Roman Catholic, but standing out amongst them was 31-year-old general labourer Thomas Rowan Morrow, the Presbyterian former Master of the Drumlough Loyal Orange Lodge and a vocal opponent of Home Rule who may have shared the same social class of his countrymen but had very different views.[25]

With people of so many diverse backgrounds in third class, there were many people who did not really fit in with the others and had not found people of a similar background with whom to socialise. Lawrence Beesley, looking down from second class at the lower deck, observed one man who seemed completely isolated and remote from his fellows:

Standing aloof from all of them, generally on the raised stern deck above the 'playing field,' was a man of about twenty to twenty-four years of age, well-dressed, always gloved and nicely groomed, and obviously quite out of place among his fellow-passengers: he never looked happy all the time. I watched him, and classified him at hazard as the man who had been a failure in some way at home and had received the proverbial shilling plus third-class fare to America: he did not look resolute enough or happy enough to be working out his own problem.[26]

In contrast to the misery of that particular passenger was the optimism of many emigrants intent on bettering themselves when they reached their final destination. It was the desire to make a good impression in a new country in a new suit that led to two young men transferring to the ship. Two bantamweight boxers in their early twenties from the Rhondda Valley were on their way to take part in a series of prize fighting competitions to be held over the following twelve months arranged by sports promoter Frank Torreyson. Leslie Williams was a colliery blacksmith and Dai Bowen a coal miner, but for both of them boxing offered an escape from the mines of South Wales. They were originally booked to travel on *Lusitania* but were delayed because Williams, afraid that new clothes would be more expensive in America, was waiting for a local tailor to complete a suit for which he had been measured for his travels and instead were booked on *Titanic*. Despite promising to 'make good use of the gym on board, so they ought to be fit to hold their own on the other side', opportunities for them to practise their boxing skills would have been limited as the gymnasium was only for first-class passengers.[27] Neither man survived but Williams's body was recovered wearing a blue serge suit.[28] There is no way of knowing whether or not this was the fateful suit that had delayed his journey nor indeed whether or not he ever got to cut a dash in the new clothes he was so determined to take to America with him. He was buried at sea, his few personal possessions retrieved from his pockets were returned to his wife and his sea-stained clothing was destroyed. Even after death, he was destined to be separated from the prized new suit that had been so unlucky for both him and his friend.

Although both young pugilists were described by those who knew them well as 'steady and unassuming' and 'above the average in skill', Leslie Williams was remembered differently by second-class survivor Edward Beane, a newly married bricklayer from Norwich, who saw him among the third-class male passengers who had to be held back at gunpoint from rushing the lifeboats, though Beane got his first name wrong. Beane claimed to have survived by jumping overboard and swimming for hours until picked up by the very same lifeboat in which he had seen his wife off, though he was also to allege that he had been picked up by a different boat altogether, but was scathing about third-class men, many of a similar background to his own, who had the same will to survive, and was sensitive as one of the few men to survive from second-class that he needed to defend himself from charges of cowardice, justify his own survival and distinguish himself from the masses.[29] He recalled, 'I saw Charles Williams, the prize fighter coming over for a tag match, drop back when the rifle fire scorched his fingers for over eagerness. He was a big brute of a man, too.'[30] Beane's recollection perhaps owed far more to snobbery than any reality.

It was a form of snobbery that led one crew member to grudgingly welcome Irish passengers because 'at least this lot spoke English'.[31] The number of different languages spoken in third class was a barrier to effective communication in an emergency. Even in first class, not all passengers were fluent English speakers. The modish Victor Peñasco may have honed his knowledge of English in order to communicate his sartorial preferences to his tailors, but his wife Pepita and her maid Fermina did not understand much English. As a result, the young couple sought the company of fellow native Spanish speakers when socialising on the ship. The Countess of Rothes, not a Spanish speaker, used Italian or French to communicate with them when Peñasco was trying to persuade his wife to board a lifeboat without him, and once aboard, Pepita's lack of comprehension of the language shared by her fellow passengers may have contributed to her sense of isolation and hysteria at being separated from her husband.[32] For many passengers in steerage the confusion and fear resulting from their lack of understanding of English was to result in more than a hysterical reaction to their isolation. It could lead to their deaths.[33]

Lucy Duff-Gordon noticed one survivor on *Carpathia*, a shabbily dressed old woman with a shawl over her head who had somehow been 'dumped down on the first-class deck' and who could not make herself understood. All attempts to speak to her in English, French, German or Italian were equally unintelligible to her. Finally, two Russian-speaking passengers from steerage were found who could understand her and 'listen to her sad story' of how she had lost her husband, four children, brother, sister-in-law and their children with whom she was emigrating from Russia to the United States.[34]

In an emergency, clear instructions about what to do were essential, especially when the escape route was not obvious to passengers in third class. There was only one third-class steward acting as the ship's interpreter. German-born Ludwig Müller, fresh from a similar posting on *Olympic*, was responsible for interpreting for over 700 passengers. It is not known which languages he spoke but it is unlikely that he was familiar with all the different languages spoken on board. During the evacuation of the third-class passengers, his role was crucial in giving them instructions on the route that they should take to the boat deck and the promise of safety. Charles Joughlin, the Chief Baker, saw 'the interpreter passing the people along that way, but there was a difficulty in getting them along because some of the foreign third-class passengers were bringing their baggage and their children along'.[35] This caused some confusion and 'hampered the interpreter and the men who were helping him, because they could not prevail on the people to leave their luggage'.[36] In the absence of any orders about what he should do, Müller took upon himself the responsibility of 'getting all his people from forward aft' and onto E Deck.[37]

It was the responsibility of the third-class stewards to rouse the women passengers and give them guidance, but this was not carried out as comprehensively as it might have been.[38] Ben Pickard remembered that 'the only warning given to steerage passengers after the collision was that we were ordered to take our lifebelts and go on deck'.[39] Marian Assaf, returning to her home in Ottawa after a visit to her native Syria, was reassured by the stewards that 'everything was alright' but she and some of her fellow passengers 'began to think that they were not telling us the truth and that we might be sinking'.[40] Abraham Hyman from Manchester was similarly told that there was nothing to worry about and to 'just keep calm'.[41]

In the absence of clear instructions that all third-class passengers could understand, many passengers in third class did not realise the danger that they were in. Some of them refused to put on their life jackets because 'they did not believe the ship was hurt in any way'.[42] Some of the women when guided through the third- and second-class parts of the ship preferred to return to their cabins when they found the boat deck cold and saw the lifeboats being lowered away, since 'they preferred to remain on the ship rather than be tossed about on the water like a cockleshell'.[43] At first, the men in third class were not allowed near the boat deck, and were forbidden from accompanying the women and children. Many women refused to leave their husbands and were also reluctant to abandon their luggage.[44]

It was not easy for passengers from third class to find their way to the boat decks, which were in the first- and second-class areas of the ship. They could only be accessed from third class by a maze of ladders and passageways.[45] The layout of the ship was considered so complicated that it had taken First Officer Lightoller a fortnight to navigate them easily. For bewildered passengers in the midst of an evacuation it was an almost impossible task, especially if they were hampered by attempting to save their luggage. Surprisingly, third-class passengers remained calm and orderly as they heaved their luggage through the ship with them and 'you would think they were landing on the tender taking their baggage to New York'.[46] The British inquiry into the wreck, chaired by Lord Mersey, concluded that poor emigrants would be reluctant to leave behind their possessions because they 'would certainly be carrying all they possessed with them ... more probably than a person whose property was not all in the vessel'.[47]

The difficulty of finding an easy way to the boat decks was made even harder by the physical barriers that prevented the different classes from mingling. American immigration legislation insisted on the physical separation of steerage passengers from other classes, ostensibly to prevent the spread of infection. Laura Cribb escaped up a stairway normally only accessible to employees, but her father, who had been a butler in New York and knew many of the stewards on *Titanic*, used his personal contacts to gain privileged permission to use those stairs.[48] Anna Kincaid found her way blocked because 'the stairway was closed' and was only able to proceed when three young Swedes showed her an emergency staircase. It was not until later that the main stairway was opened and 'until then there was no help of any kind accorded to third-class passengers' and it was 'only in the very last desperate moments that third-class passengers were given any chance to reach safety'. Anna Kincaid was convinced that this was not the result of any discrimination but because 'those in charge were sure that the ship would be saved and I suppose did not think it best to have more people above than necessary'.[49] Margaret Kelly, another Irish passenger, was less charitable to the ship's crew, whom she accused of having 'fastened the doors and companionways', giving the excuse that 'they wanted to keep the air down there so the vessel would stay up longer', which meant 'certain death to all who remained below. And while the sailors were beating back the steerage passengers, lifeboats were pulling away, some of them not half filled.'[50]

Daniel Buckley did not think that there was any conscious policy of keeping the men in third class below deck nor any attempt to stop them from leaving their part of the ship. Yet he also observed that 'they tried to keep us down at first on our steerage deck. They did not want us to go up to first class at all.' After a passenger attempted to break free, members of the crew locked the gate but it was broken open and third-class passengers were able to get onto the boat deck. Once there, with all classes milling around the lifeboats, Buckley believed 'they had as much chance as the first- and second-class passengers'.[51] Ben Pickard, a Polish leatherworker, testified that 'the steerage passengers were not prevented from getting up to the upper decks by anybody, or by closed doors, or anything else'. He himself escaped by going through a door into second class and then into first, ignoring the sign that 'second-class passengers have no right to penetrate there'. His personal experience was that 'nobody was prevented from going up'.[52] The British inquiry chaired by Lord Mersey concluded that there was no discrimination made between women and children from different classes in loading the lifeboats and that there was no truth in the charges that 'the first- and second-class passengers were given precedence in getting places in the boats', yet fewer from steerage survived even if 'they were not unfairly treated'.[53]

Racial prejudices and tensions came into focus in the aftermath of the sinking. Whereas casual racism may have been ingrained in people at the time, it was to be forcibly expressed and revealed in the ugliest of terms. The *New York Times* deplored that 'disorderly conduct, and there was enough to cause bloodshed, occurred among the steerage passengers. Some of the men were determined to save their own precious lives, in spite of the orders to let the women and children go first.'[54] Charlotte Collyer did not have much sympathy for a man, 'an Italian, I think', who had injured a child when he tried to jump into a boat, and almost gloated that:

> As we shot down toward the sea, I caught a last glimpse of this coward. He was in the hands of about a dozen men of the second cabin. They

were driving their fists into his face, and he was bleeding from the nose and mouth.⁵⁵

Chief Steward John Hardy was irritated by 'Syrians in the bottom of the boat, third-class passengers, chattering the whole night in their strange language'.⁵⁶ Cornelia Adams complained of cowardly men who had snaked into the lifeboats and dismissed them as Chinese and Armenian.⁵⁷

Although there were no black crew members there were invented stories of black men behaving badly, which betrayed an undercurrent of racism whatever the truth may be. Wireless operator Harold Bride witnessed:

> a fireman or coal trimmer gently relieving Mr. Phillips of his lifebelt. There immediately followed a general scrimmage with the three of us. I regret to say that we left too hurriedly to take the man in question with us, and without a doubt he sank with the ship in the Marconi cabin as we left him.⁵⁸

In his evidence to the British inquiry, Bride stated that Phillips had hit the man, while he himself held him down,⁵⁹ though in an interview with the *New York Times* he had claimed credit for striking the stoker and 'I hope I finished him'.⁶⁰ Very soon the story was embellished by the popular press. The man was depicted as 'a grimy stoker of gigantic proportions' who was shot, rather than hit, by Bride.⁶¹ The story was then embroidered further, with an added racial dimension:

> When the second wireless man came into the boxlike room to tell his companion what the situation was, he found a negro stoker creeping up behind the operator and saw him raise a knife over his head. He said afterwards – he was among those rescued – that he realized at once that the negro intended to kill the operator in order to take his life-belt from him. The second operator pulled out his revolver and shot the negro dead. 'What was the trouble?' asked the operator. 'That negro was going to kill you and steal your life-belt,' the second man replied. 'Thanks, old man,' said the operator … The wireless operator and the body of the negro who tried to steal his belt went down together.⁶²

Class prejudice was also shown in the assumption that the man was a fireman, trimmer or stoker who could not be expected to behave like a gentleman. Yet, an early newspaper version of the story suggested that Phillips's assailants were very different in status from the crew, with the *Washington Times* reporting that:

> Wireless Operator Jack Phillips did not desert his post when the *Titanic* sank, but was torn from the key by a party of fear-crazed first cabin passengers, who assaulted him in an effort to take from him a big life belt he wore.[63]

The only black man actually aboard *Titanic* was travelling as a second-class passenger with his family rather than in steerage, to which modern-day assumptions about colour prejudice in 1912 would have consigned them. Joseph Philippe Lemercier Laroche, nephew of the president of Haiti, Cincinnatus Leconte, was a highly educated engineer returning to Haiti to take up a post as a mathematics teacher with his French wife Juliette and mixed-race daughters, Simone and Juliette. He had found it difficult to find work in France because of racial discrimination and decided that his education and family connections would enable him to better provide for his family in Haiti. The Laroches were separated in the confusion of the sinking and Juliette and her daughter Simone were pushed into a lifeboat, from which:

> In the midst of the crush, I caught a glimpse of my husband, who, both arms outstretched above the crowd, was holding our younger daughter. He was trying to shield her from all the pushing, he was struggling with the crewmen, and was showing them the little girl, to try to convince them that she had been separated from me, her mother.

Eventually, mother and child were reunited and the last words she heard above the din from her husband were, 'I'll see you soon, my darling! There'll be room for everyone, go with the lifeboats. Look after our little girls. See you soon!'[64]

There was a general prejudice shown against Italians by the British and American passengers and crew, who often just assumed that any bad behaviour by passengers in third class must be by Italians, although there were only four Italian men actually travelling in third class, of whom only one survived. The steward George Crowe described a rush for the boats by 'various men passengers, probably Italians or some foreign nationality other than English or American'. Cecil Fitzpatrick, the engineers' mess steward, reported that 'an officer had shot a "Dago"' trying to jump into a boat and that there were 'crews of foreigners hanging round the lifeboat ready to leap, but they cowered when they saw one of their number shot dead'.[65] Hugh Woolner referred to having pulled men, 'probably third-class passengers', by their legs and feet to stop them from climbing into a boat so that 'a bunch of women – I think Italians and foreigners' could be hoisted up and in, though he considered that the women he had helped to have had 'not much spring in them at all'.[66] Arthur Peuchen was contemptuous about a stowaway who 'was an Italian by birth, I should think' with a 'broken wrist or arm, and he was of no use to us to row'. Significantly, he differentiated the man from American-born Italians who presumably had been civilised to an extent by their country of birth, but on the whole they were all considered much the same.[67] Fifth Officer Lowe used strong language that betrayed his prejudices against Italians in particular and foreigners as a whole. He was contemptuous of an alleged Italian sneaking into a boat dressed as a woman. He justified his firing of a pistol by the feral behaviour of Italian third-class passengers:

> Coming down past the open decks, I saw a lot of Italians, Latin people, all along the ship's rails – understand, it was open – and they were all glaring, more or less like wild beasts, ready to spring. That's why I yelled to look out, and let go, bang, right along the ship's side.[68]

Such intemperate language at the Senate enquiry was enough to raise a protest from the Italian ambassador to the United States and Lowe was forced to retract his statement and instead refer to 'immigrants belonging to the Latin races'.[69]

This prejudice against Italians was widespread at the time and cowardly panic of Italian passengers in a shipwreck was something of a cliché. Lowe would have agreed with criticisms of the behaviour of Italian passengers during the 1891 sinking of *Utopia*, where 'the Italians were thrown into a state of complete and cowardly panic' and 'the only instances of manliness occurred among the people in the rigging' whilst 'the majority of the Italians, however behaved more like beasts than like reasoning men'.[70] It was claimed that 'the lower class of emigrants from Southern Europe cannot be trusted with knives and pistols at any time' and that 'the officers and crew were powerless to cope with the horde of Italians who fought for the boats' during the wreck of *Sirio* in 1906.[71] Such aspersions were resented by Italian-Americans such as Vincent Lattarulo, who responded that 'when it is asserted that the Italian emigrants acted as savages and bloodthirsty men, killing everybody, having no respect for age or sex, abandoning even their dear ones, and simply aiming at their own salvation', this was a slur on 'a people that rightly claims to have been, and to still be, the most civilized and humane of all peoples', and that what should be remembered is 'how deep is the sentiment of brotherhood in the Italian, to what extent the idea of altruism is inculcated in his character, and, above all, how great is the ascendancy the woman … has over the heart and life of the average Italian man, in whatever stage of society he may be'.[72]

Lowe was just as contemptuous of the Japanese as he was of Italians and the Latin race in general. Charlotte Collyer claimed that he was not keen to save a man seen floating on a door on the grounds that 'what's the use? He's dead, likely, and if he isn't there's others better worth saving than a Jap.' He had then decided to investigate further only to discover that the man he had thought to be a corpse was actually still alive and willingly took a turn at rowing. Once again, Lowe was to revise his racist assumptions, though more readily than he had been towards Italians, and muttered, 'By Jove! I'm ashamed of what I said about the little blighter. I'd save the likes of him six times over if I got the chance.' Archibald Gracie was to describe the Japanese passenger as 'plucky' and 'surprisingly self-possessed and uncowardly'.[73]

It was a time of concern about a perceived 'yellow peril'. Mrs Fortune and her three daughters were unhappy at having to share a boat with 'a Chinaman, an Italian stoker, and a man dressed in woman's clothing', only one of whom was able to row. The Chinese were depicted as cowards with no concern for anything but their own survival and totally lacking in any sense of chivalry:

When the revised list of survivors was made up at the White Star Line office yesterday it became known that among those saved from the *Titanic* were six of eight Chinamen who were among the steerage passengers on the big liner. It seems that they climbed into one of the lifeboats without anybody making objection, despite the fact that many of the women in the steerage of the *Titanic* went down with the ship.[74]

Closely allied to racial and class bias was religious prejudice. The elegantly dressed and worldly young multimillionaire Victor Peñasco may have been seen kneeling in prayer, but most of the men and women receiving spiritual consolation from the Catholic priests on deck in the last hours came from humbler third-class backgrounds. Their Christianity was perceived as inferior by committed Protestants who dominated in first class. Archibald Gracie, when he was pulled to safety in a lifeboat, could barely conceal his prejudices against the crew, especially one man whom he characterised as 'uncouth, a Roman Catholic seaman' but changed his opinion when the seaman asked everyone their religion and then proposed that they should all recite the Lord's Prayer as an appeal to God acceptable to Roman Catholics, Episcopalians, Presbyterians and Methodists, all of whom were represented among the men on the lifeboat.[75]

A form of muscular Christianity was indeed linked with the heroism of first-class men in particular, who were said to have demonstrated that 'in spite of our apparently frivolous ways, our moral and physical courage, our Godliness is as virile as ever in the history of humanity'.[76] This was exemplified by Gracie, who ascribed his personal survival and 'providential deliverance' to a 'God given physical strength and courage'.[77] Protestant preachers praised the men who faced death 'with unflinching courage, with the calmness of perfect submission and hope inspired by faith'.[78] Such faith was lauded in young men such as Edward Dorkings, a 19-year-old third-class passenger who jumped off the ship and swam to a lifeboat after he and two other boys had first 'knelt and prayed'.[79]

There were fears that religion was becoming too much the preserve of women and that there was a great need to revive masculine interest in religion. The Men and Religion Forward Movement was founded in 1911 'to bring business methods into religion, and to work for the attainment of moral ends with the same energy, concentration and common-sense that are used in the making of a great fortune'. The pioneer of investigative journalism and social reformer W.T. Stead was travelling on *Titanic* to address a Men and Religion Forward meeting on 'World Peace' in Carnegie Hall, New York.[80] Notorious for his crusade against child prostitution and his prison sentence for having bought a child in order to reveal the 'white slave trade', Stead was a convinced pacifist, nominated unsuccessfully for the Nobel Peace Prize, but his obsession with spiritualism was to tarnish his reputation. Nevertheless, his friend and fellow social reformer Bramwell Booth could declare that he was 'great on better laws and generous government; he hated war, and struggled for the liberty of small peoples, but he knew that neither laws nor Governments nor liberty can support the human spirit – and he said so. "Only the living God can hold up a living soul"' – a view that the son of the founder of the Salvation Army could share with Stead's own sensationalist brand of muscular Christianity.[81]

Self-sacrifice and virile Christianity were even more likely to be equated with social status and class:

> A multi-millionaire and a man from steerage stand side by side. Each has an equal place and chance, and yet they are not equal. Cowards and heroes are there. The issue of the hour reveals them. The trappings of life are swept away – men are equal, character abides, men are unequal. Thus they meet God.[82]

Even men 'who until their last moment had never known a spiritual thought ... were glorified in death'.[83] Harry Widener's cenotaph in Laurel Hill Cemetery, Philadelphia, was appropriately inscribed with a line from the penitential Psalm 130, *De Profundis*, 'Out of the deep have I called unto thee'. However, this religious superiority was confined to Protestantism and its manly exponents, not those with different religious affiliations, since 'evidently Anglo Saxon civilisation, under the influence of Protestant Christianity, has developed a different fibre from Latin civilisation'.[84]

Anti-Catholicism was ingrained in Montreal stockbroker Thornton Davidson, from a fiercely Protestant family. His elder brother Shirley, an ice hockey player for Montreal Victorias, had died in 1907 in a sailing accident with his fiancée, Aileen Hingston, daughter of a surgeon and senator, despite being as experienced a yachtsman as his younger brother. It was suspected that they had died in a suicide pact because the young man's father, Sir Charles Peers Davidson, Chief Justice of the Quebec Supreme Court, had refused to allow them to marry when he learned that the girl was a Roman Catholic. The Davidsons were United Empire Loyalists and staunch Episcopalians. The wealthy Baxter family were not welcomed in the higher echelons of Protestant Montreal society because of their Roman Catholic background and there is no record of any interaction with the Hays and Davidsons on *Titanic*. Thornton Davidson may have been the consummate clubman, but belonging to the right clubs meant not mixing with the wrong class of person or members of a different faith.

If Roman Catholicism was an obstacle to full social acceptance, being Jewish was even less acceptable. Although a number of wealthy Jewish men and women were travelling in first class and mixing socially with their fellow millionaires, anti-Semitism was close to the surface. Benjamin Foreman, a young New York businessman returning from a textile buying trip, was waiting in a queue for a table allocation in the first-class restaurant. Ahead of him was Eleanor Cassebeer, who was complaining about how long a Jewish passenger was taking to arrange his seating assignment, and whispered to Foreman, 'I hope I don't get next to that Jew.' Ben Foreman made no comment but when he later met with Mrs Cassebeer and she asked him if he would like to take a walk with her on the promenade deck, he remarked, 'You don't want to walk with me. You said you didn't like Jews and I'm one too.' However, after this unpropitious beginning and after Foreman had pointed out that as with all groups of people there were good and bad Jews and character depended on the individual, they became 'shipboard friends'.[85]

Anti-Semitism was perhaps less apparent in British royal and aristocratic circles than in the United States. Edward VII had counted a number of wealthy Jewish financiers among his close acquaintances and Lord Roseberry, a former prime minister, had married a Rothschild daughter. Julia Cavendish, whilst very much part of English society and a practising Anglican after her marriage, was the daughter of Henry Siegel, a German-born Jewish entrepreneur who had built up a successful chain of department stores. In 1906 she met 'an

Englishman of interest', Tyrell William Cavendish, at a ball in London and he was said to have proposed to her within a week and then followed her back to America to woo her. The *Charlotte News* of North Carolina snidely commented that 'the engagement was the result of mutual love at first sight and that Miss Siegel's money had nothing to do with it'. Despite admitting that Cavendish was personally popular and belonged to a good set, the newspaper could not resist commenting that Julia Siegel was not without other suitors and that:

> though her fiancé is not exactly what we term a parti, he will, when his expectations mature, be fairly well off in his own right. But the dowry Miss Siegel will bring him will make it easier for him to wait until he comes into his own.[86]

Henry Siegel was 'at first opposed to an engagement, but not to the young Englishman, as the extreme youth of his daughter was the only objection'.[87] His daughter was under 20 and his potential son-in-law was 31. Tyrell Cavendish was the great-grandson of Baron Waterpark and distantly related to the Dukes of Devonshire, but there was also a scandal in the family since his father had died a lunatic in Cheadle Royal Lunatic Asylum. In marrying a wealthy American bride, Cavendish was following in the path of several aristocratic families such as that of the Duke of Marlborough. His wife, whom he married in December 1906, was well able to adjust to life in an English country house as the wife of a country gentleman deeply interested in politics and devoted to shooting and fishing since she had been privately educated in Europe and her stepsister had recently married the Italian Count Carlo Dentice di Frasso. Presentation at court to Edward VII and Queen Alexandra was merely a matter of course for her. A wealthy young wife with the right social skills was perfect for a man of social status with political ambitions, regardless of her origins.[88]

The other side of the racist and class assumptions brought to the fore by reactions to the disaster was the sense of superiority felt by the British and American men and women on board. Archibald Gracie admired the courage of men who shared his own heritage and race: 'The coolness, courage, and sense of duty that I here witnessed made me thankful to God and proud of my

Anglo-Saxon race that gave this perfect and superb exhibition of self-control at this hour of severest trial.'[89]

Old Harrovian and aspiring Tory politician Tyrell Cavendish, who actually came from an aristocratic family, was eulogised as 'an English noble gentleman, unselfish and heroic to the last'.[90] Governess Elizabeth Shutes, meanwhile, praised 'the brave American man ... our American manhood'[91] and Helen Candee looked on them as 'God's noblemen'.[92] However, these were first- and second-class passengers whose exemplary conduct contrasted with that of foreigners in steerage. They were lauded for the 'Christian knightliness which seeks not its own, but the good of others'.[93] It was declared that 'one great fact stands out against the black background of the *Titanic*'s disaster as the stars stand in their radiance against the dark of the midnight sky – the American man's tenderness and care of his women and children'.[94] It was even claimed that in asserting authority over lower-class men and foreigners, the heroes of first class demonstrated that 'manhood met brutehood undaunted ... and honest fists faced iron bars, winning at last the battle for death with honor'.[95]

An unnamed crew member claimed that one of the officers had decreed 'British first' and '"a British life above all others" was the word that went around'. The journalist to whom he told this story commented, 'this, of course, did not discriminate against Americans, but it encouraged forcing back into the water Portuguese (even the women), Italians and other foreigners to save people who cried for help in English.'[96] There was a nobler interpretation to this mood which was just as jingoist but stressed the display of British values rather than discriminating in favour of fellow countrymen. James Johnstone, steward in the first-class dining room, claimed that the order to show a stiff upper lip came directly from Captain Smith and that was to be the rallying call of the crew's response to handling the disaster:

> When the first signal was given to lower the boats, some of the crew pressed forward. It was then that the rallying cry came through the megaphone from the bridge, 'Be British, my men.' It was Captain Smith's voice. Every man obeyed the command and faced death calmly. They knew that there was no hope and as the big, strong English seamen assisted the women and children into the boats they gave no sign that

they realized that Captain Smith's words 'Be British,' had sealed their fate. They remained at their posts and died like men.[97]

William Lygon, Earl Beauchamp, First Commissioner of Works in Herbert Asquith's Cabinet, patriotically found much to praise in the 'heroism and self-sacrifice' of British men on *Titanic* despite being a radical Liberal who supported housing reform, industrial safety legislation, workmen's compensation and a minimum wage for coal miners. He was thrilled that:

> They were ordinary common or garden members of the Anglo-Saxon race. It makes one proud to think that there were so many men ready to face death quietly and in a self-sacrificing spirit, making way for the women and children to be rescued. Not only does it make us proud of our race, but it makes us sure that there is a great destiny reserved in the world still for the Anglo-Saxon race.[98]

Even more important than belonging to a perceived superior Anglo-Saxon race was being a member of the elite:

> Outstanding in the *Titanic* disaster is the heroism that gives the lie to the croak of decay in the human race. The Anglo-Saxon may yet boast that his sons are fit to rule the earth so long as men choose death with the courage they must have displayed when the great liner crashed into the mountains of ice, and the aftermath brought his final test.[99]

Washington Dodge, City Tax Assessor for San Francisco, showed a fear of the lower classes when he recalled that 'when the steerage passengers came up many of them had knives, revolvers and clubs and sought to fight their way to the two unlaunched, collapsible boats. Many of these were shot by the officers', compared with the way in which 'the first-cabin men and women behaved with great heroism', in his prejudiced view.[100] For him, 'the panic was in the steerage, and it was that portion of the ship that the shooting was made necessary.' His wife similarly saw only the noble behaviour of her own class and remembered that 'from the upper rails heroic husbands and fathers were waving and throwing kisses to their womenfolk in the receding lifeboats'.[101]

Yet there was also a recognition that men from a lower social standing could also possess finer qualities. Lawrence Beesley asked the question:

> Major Butt and Colonel Astor and Mr Straus died as brave men died, but did not John Brown and Wilhelm Klein and Karl Johanssen? And yet they are not chronicled, and no newspaper has columns on their self-sacrifice and personal courage. But we know these things were true and we can bear testimony now to every brave man who perished in the steerage, even if we knew not his name.[102]

An example of a humble hero demonstrating the chivalry and fortitude of his social superiors was Olaus Abelseth who, after ensuring the safety of the two girls travelling under his protection, gave up the chance of using his experience as a sailor to take up a place in another lifeboat to stay with his brother-in-law, cousin and friend who had said to him, 'Let us stay here together.' He was the only one of the three who could swim and was saved when he reached a collapsible boat, where the other 'men did not try to push me off and they did not do anything for me to get on', other than to say 'don't capsize the boat'.[103] The 51-year-old tailor Johan Lundahl was as accepting of his fate as any gentleman in first class when he told his socialist friend August Wennerström, 'Goodbye, friend, I'm too old to fight the Atlantic,' before making himself comfortable in the third-class smoking room.[104] Wennerström himself watched 'with eyes wide open' as the last boats left and felt strangely detached as if he were in the audience of a 'wonderful dramatic play'.[105] Edwin Lundström was only too aware of the calmness and dignity he saw among his fellow third-class passengers and remarked, 'I was surrounded by young Swedes, who all seemed willing to die after they had placed their wives and sisters and babies in the boats,' and was to think of 'those brave young men who were drowned'.[106]

Progressives and socialists were critical of the capitalist elites who dominated society and who were immortalised for their bravery in the wake of the loss of *Titanic*. The American socialist John Reed compared the *Titanic* to a society 'built and bossed by a few colossi bestriding the multitude' but one that was threatened by a working class that could potentially 'crystallize overnight, massive and unrelenting'.[107] American progressives could not accept that the 'millionaires' aboard were anything but 'hardened to the consistency of the metal in which they deal'.[108] Such views challenged the assumptions that their heroism and sense of chivalry on *Titanic* had vindicated the economic dominance of the industrial magnates at a time when muckraker journalists were hypercritical of how many of them had created their fortunes. In asserting their sense of *noblesse oblige*, the upper classes were marking out their superiority over the lower classes:

> The man with a hundred million dollars stood aside and made room for his wife's serving maid. The man who has swayed continents with his pen gave place to a woman from the steerage. The railroad magnate remained on the sinking ship that a babe in arms might have his place in the lifeboat.[109]

At the same time, other critics saw a direct causal link between the lifestyle of the wealthy and the lack of sufficient lifeboats when criticising the 'rich men' who could not forego 'all the comforts and luxuries' they were accustomed to 'even for the few days of the crossing'.[110] As a result of such greed, 'fourteen or fifteen hundred lives were sacrificed to the god of ambition, business, greed and speed'. As a result of such materialism, 'the richest men of the earth along with the poorest [were] swallowed up in one gulp of old ocean, regardless of their worldly holdings or their learning.'[111] The New York Presbyterian preacher Charles Parkhurst thundered from the pulpit against the wanton pursuit of luxury that led to the disaster:

> The picture which presents itself before my eyes is that of the glassy, glaring eyes of the victims, staring meaninglessly at the gilded furnishings of this sunken palace of the sea; dead helplessness wrapped in precious luxury; jewels valued in seven figures becoming the strange playthings of the queer creatures that sport in the dark depths. Everything for existence, nothing for life. Grand men, charming women, beautiful

babies, all becoming horrible in the midst of the glittering splendor of a $10,000,000 casket.[112]

The progressive muckraking journalist William Allen White despaired that once the tragedy of *Titanic* was no longer so topical, the world would resume its 'mad chase after wealth and pleasure',[113] whilst the hack writer Marshall Everett lamented the 'human sacrifices made to the god of commercial greed'.[114]

Significantly, questions about the economic impact of the simultaneous deaths of so many of these industrial tycoons were asked in the press almost as soon as the loss of the ship was known, bolstering the claims of the critics of capitalism that money meant more than the lives of the poor. The combined wealth of the richest men to have perished made more prominent headlines than the number of individual deaths, with seven millionaires representing £91 million between them.[115] There was concern that 'it will be a long time before the insurance industry knows the extent of the loss which it has sustained'. Whilst there was no question about the amount for which the ship itself was insured, there were also expected to be claims for the lost cargo and for life policies taken out by the wealthiest passengers, which meant that 'insurers will now have to meet the heaviest individual loss ever sustained'. Lloyd's insurance underwriter Christopher Head took out a policy on the eve of the voyage, insuring his life for £25,000 'against ocean accidents', yet property could be more valued than lives. One American passenger had insured her pearls for £100,000. Another had a necklace worth £80,000 but her policy stipulated that she must wear it at all times when travelling, and to the relief of her insurers, she and her necklace had survived.[116] The *Toronto Star* wryly commented of the relatives and friends waiting for news of survivors and victims that 'when your friend is a millionaire you don't have to cry long for the truth. The financial significance of deaths gains recognition where the emotional goes unheeded.'[117]

The perceived depreciation of value to society from the loss of leaders of industry, seen as sacrificing themselves through a sense of *noblesse oblige* on their part, was questioned as being misplaced and having no rational justification:

Certainly, it was not a case of the survival of the fittest. There were men lost that the city and the country needed and there are widows who speak no language that you or I can understand, and who will inevitably become public charges. They did not ask why, nor if any helpless poor creature was worth saving. The maxims of commerce were forgotten. There was no question of buying cheap and selling dear. They sold themselves for naught; they gave their lives away. Such a sacrifice cannot be justified on any economic ground.[118]

The nobility of the men was assumed and goes unchallenged but their sacrifice was seen as wrong in terms of monetary value and lost potential. It was not only the loss of business activity and moguls that was seen as wasteful when:

the disease-bitten child, whose life is less than worthless, goes to safety with the rest of the steerage riff-raff, while the handler of great affairs, the men who direct the destinies of hundreds and thousands of workers, the learned men whose talents are dedicated to the cure of physical afflictions, writers whose words are as burning lamps in troubled darkness, and whose energies have uplifted humanity, stand unprotestingly aside.[119]

Even the progressive politician Louis Post, who later served as undersecretary of labor in Woodrow Wilson's administration, whilst linking 'the beneficiaries of privilege ... selfishly indifferent to the heart sickening perennial tragedies of our industrial life' with 'those of their own class who went down with the *Titanic*', conceded that 'the children of privilege on that doomed vessel' had proved themselves to be 'as democratic and as brave as any'. All they had lacked was the 'imagination' that should have revealed to them the consequences of their ruthless pursuit of wealth and made them aware of their social responsibilities to their brothers.[120]

The radical response was to challenge the widespread idealisation of the wealthy and to link them with the ills of modern capitalist society. The labour activist Mary Harris, one of the founders of the Industrial Workers of the World and popularly known as Mother Jones, could find nothing in mitigation of the conduct of leaders of business and industry either on *Titanic* or in their general attacks on the working classes in defence of their own privilege when addressing striking miners in West Virginia:

> The big guns wanted to save themselves, and the fellows that were guiding below took up a club and said we will save our people. And then the papers came out and said those millionaires tried to save the women. Oh, Lord, why don't they give up their millions if they want to save the women and children? Why do they rob them of home, why do they rob millions of women to fill the hell holes of capitalism?[121]

The humbler passengers and crew were now the ones holding back the selfish and entitled wealthy and, whereas 'the daily press has immortalized the multi-millionaires as men of heroic mould', it was actually 'the common men who made up the crew of the *Titanic* who kept back the patrician mob who yearned to seek safety in the lifeboats'.[122] It was an attempt to rewrite the popular myth into an alternative narrative stressing the heroism in steerage that equally played on class consciousness to make a political point, here denouncing rather than defending capitalism. Whilst criticism was made of individual greed such as that of J.P. Morgan, an owner of the White Star Line, of whom it was said 'the *Titanic* was driven on lest Morgan might have to economize in his fleet of private yachts', [123] the problem was actually that *Titanic* epitomised 'the contempt for human life which under capitalism inspired and presided over her creation'.[124]

Ben Tillett, general secretary of the Dock, Wharf, Riverside and General Workers' Union, expressed 'sincere condolences to the bereaved relatives of the third-class passengers' and 'sincere regret to the relatives of the Crew, who were drowned' in a letter to the Board of Trade but criticised the class bias revealed by the sinking of *Titanic*:

> We also offer our strongest protest against the wanton and callous disregard of human life and the vicious class antagonism shown in the practical forbidding of the saving of the lives of the third-class passengers. The refusal to permit other than the first-class passengers to be saved by the boats, is in our opinion a disgrace to our common civilisation.

He went on to express the hope that:

> We trust the saving of so many first-class passengers' lives will not deaden the solicitude of the Government for the lives of those who belong to the wage earning classes, and call upon the members of the Labour Party to force upon the Government the necessity of proper protection to the lives of all mariners and all passengers, irrespective of class and grade.[125]

Tillett was criticised for the intemperance of his language and there were calls for him to apologise for his insults to 'those brave first-class passengers who so heroically sacrificed their lives irrespective of class', and there were demands that 'the sooner the workmen select different men for their leaders the sooner will their needs be granted. Such men as these are not worthy to be called Englishmen.'[126]

However, Tillett's was a view supported by H.G. Wells, who believed that there was a growing distrust between the social classes as workers became increasingly aware of economic inequalities thrown into relief by the wreck of the *Titanic*, in which the poor in third class died disproportionately. He used the inequality of wealth represented by the millionaires on the doomed ship to attack 'the muddle of the present social situation' where:

> with our whole social order in danger, our legislature is busy over the trivial little affairs of the Welsh Established Church, whose endowment probably is not equal to the fortune of any one of half a dozen *Titanic* passengers or a tithe of the probable loss of another strike among the miners.

To him it illustrated 'the incompetence of the upper class in modern society' and their failure to provide for the welfare of the working class:

> It was the penetrating comment of chance upon our entire social system. Beneath a surface of magnificent efficiency was – slapdash. The ship was not even equipped to save its third-class passengers; they placed

themselves on board with an infinite confidence in the care that was to be taken of them, and most of their women and children went down with the cry of those who find themselves cheated out of life.[127]

Social inequality in all its complexity had been cruelly accentuated by the disaster.

Chapter Six

Heroes or Incompetents

The crew of *Titanic* enjoyed an ambivalent reputation in the immediate aftermath of the sinking. Hailed by some as the true heroes of the disaster, this body of men was at the same time blamed for the sinking and condemned for their bad behaviour as the ship went down. The ship's officers, in particular, were seen as heroes or cowards. In Britain, they were lauded for their courage and fortitude as part of a venerable British maritime tradition. Lord Mersey had nothing but praise for their conduct in his conclusions to the British inquiry into the sinking:

> The evidence satisfies me that the officers did their work very well, and without any thought of themselves. Captain Smith, the master, Mr Wilde, the chief officer, Mr Murdoch, the first officer and Mr Moody, the sixth officer, all went down with the ship while performing their duties; the others, with the exception of Mr Lightoller, took charge of the boats, and thus were saved. Mr Lightoller was swept off the deck as the vessel went down, and was subsequently picked up.[1]

It was very little different from the first American reports of the sinking praising the captain, officers and crew of the *Titanic* for displaying 'unexampled bravery in the face of the most appalling marine catastrophe' in which they 'heroically stuck to their posts to the end, encouraging, directing and assisting' passengers as 'they worked like Trojans while death, sure and swift, stared them in the face'.[2] The conclusions of the Senate Inquiry were very different and more critical of the ship's officers:

> Among the passengers were many strong men who had been accustomed to command, whose lives had marked every avenue of endeavour, and

whose business experience and military training especially fitted them for such an emergency. These were rudely silenced and forbidden to speak, as was the president of this company, by junior officers, a few of whom, I regret to say, availed themselves of the first opportunity to leave the ship.[3]

Once again, the assumption was that the business leaders and millionaires knew more than the professional sailors and their superior status meant that they should be listened to and obeyed. The Imperial Merchant Service Guild responded to the chairman of the inquiry, Senator William Alden Smith, that 'without a shred of evidence or a particle of truth, you accuse officers of the British mercantile marine of despicable cowardice' and asserted that 'in the midst of an appalling emergency perfect discipline prevailed, which was worthy of the best traditions of the British mercantile marine' and that 'the four officers who left the ship in charge of the four boats did so acting upon definite instructions from their superior officers'.[4] With similar condemnation of the officers, but with a different political perspective from those who thought they should have deferred to their social superiors, the *Daily Herald* argued that only the 'poor stokers' of the *Titanic* looked after passengers' interests – the officer class had neglected them: 'as usual, the "common man" came in to save the situation that the expert had bungled.'[5]

Inevitably, there were strict divisions and class distinctions in the tightly ordered society of a great ocean liner. A sense of social hierarchy as rigid as that in the wider world was also inherent in the way that the crew of *Titanic* was organised. At the top was the captain supported by the seven ship's officers. There were three departments: Deck, Engine and Victualling. The 73-strong Deck Department included the ship's officers, 2 surgeons, 7 quartermasters, 2 masters-of-arms, a boatswain, 5 look-outs, 2 carpenters, 2 window cleaners, 2 mess stewards, a lamp trimmer, a storekeeper, and 29 able seamen. In the Engine Department were 13 leading firemen, 162 firemen, 72 trimmers and 33 greasers. Hidden away from the passengers, they worked four-hour-long shifts twice a day, firing and stoking the furnaces. The Victualling or Stewards' Department was the largest, with 431 employed by the White Star Line, and the most visible to passengers, including a matron, stewards, cooks, bakers, plate washers, linen pressers, a masseuse, a stenographer, and boots employed to polish shoes. Also on the ship's books were 2 Marconi operators, 5 postal clerks and 68 à la carte restaurant staff who were employed by the Marconi Company, the General Post Office and the restauranteur Gaspare Gatti.[6] Travelling as second-class passengers and not part of the Stewards' Department were the ship's musicians.[7]

Also travelling as passengers were the men making up the Harland & Wolff Guarantee Group, led by Thomas Andrews. Their role was to make sure that everything was working efficiently and to report on any improvements that could be made to the ship once its maiden voyage was completed and in designing future ships. It was considered an honour for these men to be chosen for the task. As chief draughtsman working on both *Olympic* and *Titanic*, Roderick Chisholm was said to be the one person who 'knew more about the two liners than any other man'.[8] He also designed the lifeboats, but was not to take advantage of them.[9] The men were allocated accommodation according to their status within the company. Andrews, Chisholm and the assistant manager of the Electrical Department, William Parr, were given accommodation in first class. The other men, comprising a foreman fitter, a fitter, and apprentice fitter, joiner, plumber and electrician, were travelling as second-class passengers, though all nine men were to work closely together with access to all parts of the ship. They were kept constantly busy and Andrews would retire each evening to his cabin to mark up his plans of the ship and make notes for future improvements. Although his table companion in the dining room Mrs Cassebeer claimed that Andrews frequently told her over dinner that 'the steamer had been started before it was finished, but even though it should be cut in three parts, it would still float',[10] the man himself had written to his wife the day before leaving Southampton that 'the *Titanic* is now about complete and will I think do the old Firm credit tomorrow when we sail'.[11] It was a pride shared with his team. It may have been an elite group but all nine men were to go down with the ship.

In contrast to James Bruce Ismay, Thomas Andrews was to be remembered as one of the quiet heroes of the *Titanic*, 'heroic unto death thinking only of the safety of others'.[12] Horace Plunkett believed that it was his skill as an engineer that made him so remarkable and could have fitted him for a wider role. However, there is no evidence that Andrews ever had any ambitions to enter public life, though he was a committed Unionist and a strong Unitarian: 'his mastery over complicated mechanical problems – his power to use materials and to organise bodies of men in their use would not, I believe, have failed him if he had come to deal with the mechanics of the nation.'[13] It was not enough that he should have been competent in his own field, but must be seen as a loss to the greater good of the world. It was a eulogy to the expert that Andrews undoubtedly was. The nephew of Lord Pirrie, owner of Harland & Wolff, he had worked his way up through the firm from premium apprentice to become chief designer, naval architect and managing director. On *Titanic* he was remembered by the stewardess Mary Sloan as the person everyone went to if problems needed to be sorted out:

> He made you feel on the ship that all was right. It was good to hear his laugh and have him near you. If anything went wrong it was always to Mr. Andrews one went. Even when a fan stuck in a stateroom, one would say, 'wait for Mr. Andrews, he'll soon see to it,' and you would find him settling even the little quarrels that arose between ourselves. Nothing came amiss to him, nothing at all. And he was always the same, a nod and a smile or a hearty word whenever he saw you and no matter what he was at.[14]

In accounts of the sinking, he was always remembered as a reassuring presence, 'here, there and everywhere, looking after everybody, telling the women to put on lifebelts, telling the stewardesses to hurry the women up to the boats, all about everywhere, thinking of everyone but himself'.[15]

Dressed in his working clothes and bareheaded, Tommy Andrews tried to calm the passengers but also urged them to put on their life jackets, even reprimanding Mary Sloan and other stewardesses for not setting an example by not wearing theirs, and then giving them the order 'Ladies, you must get in at once. There is not a minute to lose. You cannot pick and choose your boat. Don't hesitate. Get in, get in!'[16] He was seen helping to load the lifeboats, going onto the bridge to speak to the captain, inspecting the flooding in the mail room and squash court, speaking to the engineers, firemen and trimmers below, and throwing deckchairs overboard to people floundering in the ocean. A steward towards the end saw him in the Smoking Room with his arms folded over his breast and his life jacket on a table. When asked 'Aren't you going to have a try for it, Mr. Andrews?' he made no reply but 'just stood like one stunned'.[17] This has come to be the iconic image of Andrews, stoically and resignedly meeting his end. A tall, good-looking, likeable man with a quiet unassuming manner and puritanical tastes who abstained from tobacco and strong alcohol, Andrews made the ideal and admirable heroic figure for his age.[18] Despite his being noted for always being highly active, the image of him standing in quiet contemplation almost had a religious dimension and enhanced his heroic stature for posterity.

Musicians in the ship's orchestra have been eulogised like Andrews for their stoical and public-spirited behaviour right up until the moment the ship went down. They were not employed by the White Star Line but were contracted through a Liverpool-based booking agency, C.W. & F.N. Black, which specialised in placing musicians on ocean liners. Wallace Hartley, who had performed with the Huddersfield Philharmonic Orchestra, had played the violin on Cunard liners RMS *Lucania*, RMS *Lusitania* and RMS *Mauretania*, before his assignment as bandleader on *Titanic*. His body was later recovered with his violin strapped to his back and he was to be given a public funeral worthy of a matinée idol, attended by 40,000 people, and hailed as 'Colne's hero, Britain's hero, the world's hero' by his many admirers in his home town of Colne in Lancashire.[19] Pianist William Brailey and French cellist Roger Bricoux had played together as musicians on *Carpathia*. Georges Krins had won first prize with distinction for the violin at the Conservatoire Royal de Musique in Liège, then played at the Ritz and Café Français in London. Fred Clarke was a well-known concert bass violinist in his native Scotland, but this was his first booking on a ship, and he had joked, 'Well, you know it would be just my luck to go down with the ship. I've kept away from it so long it might finish me on this trip.'[20] Cellist Percy Taylor was also a newcomer as a ship musician. John Hume had been a violinist on five liners, including *Carmania* as bandmaster, *Majestic*, *California*, *Megantic* and *Olympic* at the time of its collision with the warship *Hawke* in 1911, as had cellist Wesley Woodward. After the sinking, his family received a letter from the agency requesting the payment of 14s 7d for alterations to his uniform to sew on a badge and buttons with the White Star logo. This piece of meanness was condemned by the British Amalgamated Musicians' Union, of which the men were all members, which published the letter in its journal without any further comment considered necessary.[21] Accomplished musicians, all of them were to be remembered for their final performance.

Passengers stated that:

> from the moment the vessel struck, or as soon as the members of the orchestra could be collected, there was a steady round of lively airs. It did much to keep up the spirits of everyone and probably served as much as the efforts of the officers trying to prevent panic.[22]

Wallace Hartley, violinist and bandleader, was reputed to be 'a great believer in the power of music to prevent panic. I don't think he waited for orders,' according to fellow musicians who had played with him on other ships.[23] Although waltzes, polkas and the latest rag time tunes were played to keep spirits up, there were some commentators who believed that:

> Perhaps it was a poor choice of music. Beethoven would have been more sublime. Blowing hard into a cornet, flattening the keys of a piano, striving for exquisite pitch, avoiding flat notes all the time knowing that you are going to die in the black and icy waters – this is heroism at its most stirring.[24]

George Bernard Shaw, however, was to suggest that the band playing on and reassuring the passengers to prevent panic might actually have made them complacent and not fully aware of their peril, resulting in a greater loss of life:

> The Captain and officers were so afraid of a panic, that, although they knew the ship was sinking, they did not dare to tell the passengers so – especially the third-class passengers – and the band played Rag Time to reassure the passengers, who therefore, did not get into the boats and did not realize their situation until all the boats were gone and the ship was standing on her head before plunging to the bottom.[25]

The musicians were said to have played more solemn music to the end. Many survivors remembered the hymn 'Nearer My God to Thee', which was apparently a favourite of the Methodist Wallace Hartley. One Canadian musician believed that this hymn was appropriate since, 'I believe, knowing that they were doomed as the result of their own heroism, the members of the ship's orchestra thus commended their own souls to their God, giving expression to their petition in the notes of their instruments.'[26] Other passengers remembered other hymns, such as 'For Those in Peril on the Sea' and 'Lead Kindly Light' being played. Marconi operator Harold Bride's last memory of the band was of them playing 'Autumn', a hymn found in American Episcopal hymnals with the conveniently appropriate line 'hold me up in mighty waters'.[27] It has also been suggested that Bride was actually referring to a piece of light music, 'Songe d'Automne', popular at the time. Whatever piece of music was played as the ship went down is of minor importance; what was significant was that the heroism of the musicians was lauded. Joseph Conrad was a dissenting voice when he reflected that:

> I who am not a sentimentalist, think it would have been finer if the band of the *Titanic* had been quietly saved, instead of being drowned while playing – whatever tune they were playing, the poor devils. I would rather they had been saved to support their families than to see their families supported by the magnificent generosity of the subscribers.[28]

The two Marconi operators have also been depicted as heroes of the disaster, though, unlike Andrews, they did not escape some criticism of their contribution to it. Nevertheless, their reputations were redeemed by their sense of duty in carrying on to the end. As employees of Marconi International Marine Communication Company, Jack Phillips and Harold Bride were primarily concerned with receiving and transmitting passenger messages, though they were expected to give priority to any operational messages for the captain. Jack Phillips, the senior of the two men, at the age of 25 had considerable experience with the new wireless technology, having trained with Marconi in 1906 and then worked as a Marconigram operator on several ocean liners – *Teutonic, Campania, Corsican, Pretorian, Victorian, Lusitania, Mauretania* and *Oceanic* – as well as a stint at the Marconi station at Clifden, Ireland. Despite his familiarity with the work, his failure to respond appropriately to incoming warnings of icebergs by sending them in good time to the bridge was to be a major factor in the disaster. The equipment had broken down on Sunday, 14 April and it took Phillips and Bride almost six hours to fix it by binding burnt leads with rubber tape, leading to a backlog of passengers' private messages waiting to be transmitted via the Cape Race transmitting station. When a warning of the ice was received from *Mesaba*, an exhausted Phillips, concerned more with getting through the rather more personal but less important messages that had built up, did not pay it much attention: 'I just put the message under a paper weight at my elbow, just until I squared up what I was doing before sending it to the Bridge.' Lightoller considered:

> that delay proved fatal and was the main contributory cause to the loss of that magnificent ship and hundreds of lives. Had I as Officer of the Watch, or the Captain, become aware of the peril lying so close ahead and not instantly slowed down or stopped, we should have been guilty of culpable and criminal negligence.[29]

A later warning from *Californian* was also not sent directly to the bridge, though earlier warnings had been seen by the captain. Phillips, desperately trying to deal with the backlog of private messages and annoyed at the interruption, had responded to the rather informal message of 'Say, old man, we are stopped and surrounded by ice' that he had received from Cyril Evans, the operator on *Californian*, with a brusque 'Shut up, shut up, I am busy; I am working Cape Race.'[30]

Yet, Phillips, rather than being criticised for negligence has been seen as one of the heroes of the night for his devotion to duty. Bride was about to relieve Phillips when Captain Smith ordered them to be on standby to send out a distress signal, soon followed by an order to send out the emergency signal CDQ in Morse code. Bride also jokingly told Phillips to 'Send SOS, it's the new call, and it may be your last chance to send it.'[31] Despite the mythology, *Titanic* was not the first ship to use the signal. SOS had been in use since 1908, but this was a high-profile use of it long to be remembered in the popular imagination. Phillips and Bride continued to work after the captain told them that they could stand down: 'Men you have done your full duty. You can do no more. Abandon your cabin. Now it is every man for himself.' Phillips, though, continued at his post. He was annoyed by a message from the *Frankfurt* in response to his distress calls asking 'What's up, old man?' According to Bride's report to the Marconi Company, Phillips, clearly 'under a great strain', had rudely replied, 'You fool, stdb [standby] and keep out.'[32] By now, the power for the wireless was run down and water was coming into the 'Marconi Shack'. It was at this point that a stoker attempted to steal Phillips's life jacket and the two men overpowered him before heading for the lifeboats. Bride survived and, despite badly frozen and crushed feet, helped Harold Cottam, the *Carpathia* Marconigram operator, to deal with the messages being sent. Phillips did not survive but was memorialised with a massive Arts and Crafts style cloister and garden, raised by public subscription and the largest of all *Titanic* memorials to an individual, at his native Godalming. Bride cemented his epic status when he wrote:

> He was a brave man. I learned to love him that night and I suddenly felt a great reverence to see him standing there sticking to his work while everybody else was raging about. I will never live to forget the work of Phillips during the last awful fifteen minutes.[33]

By contrast, the role of the post office workers tends to be neglected despite accounts of those men continuing to carry out their duties against the odds and above what could be expected of them. They were not in the public eye on board the ship and they were simply carrying out their duties, though their attempts to save the mail as the post room was flooded went beyond what could be expected of them. Boxhall, the officer to be summoned to see the flooding in the mail room, said that the three American and two English clerks were 'carrying registered parcels and letters from the mailing room on deck E up to deck C, from which they thought it might be carried off and saved'. Even when it became apparent that the ship was sinking, 'they only worked more quickly and enlisted the services of the stewards still left aboard to aid them that the work might be hastened'. It was averred that:

Not once did they waver or blanch from their duty. No one can say that they attempted to get into the lifeboats or thought of themselves for a single instant. They stuck to that which their governments had entrusted to their care, and with it they died.[34]

As no sacks of post were saved, their devotion to duty was futile.

The fate of the restaurant staff, not given the choice of whether or not to sacrifice their lives nor the opportunity to help save others, was shameful. In many ways, they were victims of cultural prejudice since most of them were the despised Italians. They were also not seen as part of the crew. Gaspare Gatti, better known as Luigi, was an Italian-born London restauranteur who had recruited his staff from some of the finest restaurants in London. Most of them were Italian, some of them immigrants to Little Italy based around Holborn and Soho, but there were also French, Swiss, Belgian, Dutch, Spanish and English among them. To the rest of the crew they would all have been dismissed as 'foreign' or 'Italian'. This was to prove fatal for them. One man and two women cashiers were the only members of the restaurant to survive. The other men were prevented from leaving their quarters to go to the boat deck. Keeping them forcibly below deck was effectively manslaughter in the moral if not strictly legal sense. Kitchen clerk Paul Achille Maurice Germain Maugé and chef Pierre Roussillon were only able to get past the stewards because they were respectably dressed like passengers:

> Two or three stewards were there, and would not let us go. I was dressed and the chef was too. He was not in his working dress; he was just like me. I asked the stewards to pass. I said I was the secretary to the chef, and the stewards said, 'Pass along, get away.' So the other cooks were obliged to stay on the deck there; they could not go up. That is where they die.

Maugé had 'earlier been told by a steward "Oh, there is no danger; it is better you go to sleep."' He had gone back to sleep but later, hearing an alarm bell signal, had tried to get on deck only to be sent back to his cabin. It was only when he came fully and correctly dressed in his suit that he was allowed to proceed, unlike his fellow restaurant staff, whose clothing showed their true status. He saved himself by leaping into a lifeboat and 'I did ask the chef to jump many times, but the chef was too fat I must say – too big, you know. He could not jump.' Once safe in a boat, Maugé did call out to the chef to *'Sautez'* but could not hear his reply as a man told him to 'shut up' and 'a man from the *Titanic* tried to get me off to take my seat'.[35] Whether it was because he was recognised as one of the staff of the à la carte restaurant who should give up his seat place to his betters or, as a Frenchman, was seen as a foreigner, Maugé was still being discriminated against. His colleagues, lacking the status conferred by a respectably smart suit, were all to die.

The restaurant staff and stewards, conscious of the need to provide good service if they were to hope for generous tips from the wealthier passengers, often built up close personal relationships with the people they served. Archibald Gracie's bedroom steward Charles Cullen was ready to wake him early in the morning 'to get ready for the engagements I had made before breakfast for the game of racquets, work in the gymnasium and the swim that was to follow'. He was also among the stewards assisting both men and women passengers in adjusting their life jackets and insisted that Gracie return to his stateroom for his, which he then securely fastened on him.[36] Henry Etches served Thomas Andrews with tea and fruit at seven o'clock every morning then would next see him when he was dressing for dinner at quarter to seven in the evening, a time Etches considered late for dressing. His valeting duties also extended to seeing to Andrews's wardrobe; in particular, he remembered 'he had a suit, and I have seen that suit thrown on the bed when he had taken it off', a blue suit Andrews wore to visit the Engine Room and which he wore during the sinking. The steward was still on duty when Andrews was late in going to bed.[37] Etches was also entrusted by Benjamin Guggenheim, another of his charges, with passing on his last message to his wife. He had roused Guggenheim and his secretary or valet Victor Giglio and helped them to get ready, adjusting the lifebelt on Guggenheim until it fitted him comfortably and putting a sweater on over it, only to return later to find the two men had changed into evening dress.[38] Such a high level of personal service was expected to be rewarded well at the end of the voyage. Bedroom steward Richard Geddes despaired that 'there won't be much to be made on the outward journey but it won't matter so long as we get something good on the homeward one', a journey he was fated not to make.[39] Saloon steward Jack Stagg similarly complained to his wife:

> It's been nothing but work all day long but I can tell you nothing as regards what people I have for nothing will be settled until we leave Queenstown tomorrow, anyway we have only 317 first and if I should be lucky enough to get a table at all it won't possibly be more than two that I have, still one must not grumble for there will be plenty without any.[40]

Trusted by the passengers they served, the stewards were to play an important role in preventing panic, though they may have equally encouraged a sense of complacency that discouraged many of the passengers from entering the lifeboats that were early to leave. Despite having seen for himself the mail clerks 'wet to their knees' and the trunk room filled with water, Norman Chambers, a New York engineer who thought the ship's bulkheads made her unsinkable, agreed 'personally' with his steward's advice that there was no danger and to go back to bed with his wife.[41] Lady Duff-Gordon was told by her steward to 'wrap up warmly, for you may have a little trip for an hour or so in one of our lifeboats'.[42] Steward Andrew Cunningham, whilst reassuring the passengers, found himself helping stockbroker John Bradley Cumings to find his overcoat, showing Walter Miller Clark where to locate his lifebelt and instructing William Stead on how to fasten his lifebelt. Virginia Clark and Florence Cumings were in the same lifeboat as Cunningham and continued to treat him as their personal steward, with Mrs Cumings peremptorily instructing him to collect the names of everyone in the lifeboat.[43] Sisters Elizabeth Eustis and Martha Stephenson were not so reassured when their steward came down to close the porthole and, 'I asked him if the order had been given to close all the ports, but he said "no, it's only cold, go to bed; it's nothing at all."' The two women, having seen a man pull his shoes into his cabin from the passageway, decided to get dressed despite the advice of their steward. The two women were concerned enough about him to look in vain for their steward, John Penrose, on *Carpathia* but were 'confident that his belief after thirty years at sea, that nothing could sink the *Titanic*, made him stick close to the decks'. Penrose could also be a stickler for the regulations. Tennis player Richard Norris Williams was to be threatened by that same steward for having damaged White Star property by breaking open a door to rescue a man trapped in his cabin: 'the steward was most indignant and threatened to have him arrested for defacing the beautiful ship.'[44] Emma Bucknell noticed that whilst denying there was any danger, the steward gave away his true feelings as 'while his voice was calm and he delivered his message easily, his face belied the confidence of his words, expressing the fear he had in his mind'.[45]

Whilst most passengers only knew their own bedroom and dining room stewards, who gave them personalised service, there were some members of the Victualling Department known to them more generally. Thomas McCawley, the gymnasium steward, was a familiar figure to all first-class passengers, a:

> sturdy little man in white flannels and with his broad English accent! With what tireless enthusiasm he showed us the many mechanical devices under his charge and urged us to take advantage of the opportunity of using them, going through the motions of bicycle racing, rowing, boxing, camel and horseback riding.[46]

Despite Gracie remembering him as having a broad English accent, he was actually Scottish. While the passengers were waiting to board lifeboats, he kept them amused using the equipment in the gymnasium. Frederick Wright, the squash racquets attendant and coach, a 'clean-cut, typical young Englishman', was last seen by Archie Gracie on the staircase as Gracie asked him, 'Hadn't we better cancel that appointment for tomorrow morning?'[47] Lawrence Beesley took especial notice of one of the lift attendants, 'a bright-eyed, handsome boy, with a love for the sea and the games on deck and the view over the ocean – and he did not get any of them.' This particular boy had remarked to Beesley, 'My! I wish I could go out there sometimes!' when he saw a game of deck quoits in progress.

> [Beesley] wished he could, too, and made a jesting offer to take charge of his lift for an hour while he went out to watch the game; but he smilingly shook his head and dropped down in answer to an imperative ring from below.[48]

His schoolmasterly if not indeed fatherly concern for the lad was echoed by the chief bathroom steward, Samuel Rule, who said that he 'kept a special lookout for the lift-boys and bell-boys. Little lads they were. If I had seen any of them, I would have bundled them in the boats with the women.'[49]

It was a predominantly male crew. The stewardesses were there to perform similar duties to the male stewards but only for the women passengers, especially those travelling alone without a husband in attendance. They were to be treated as women rather than crew when it came to the loading of the lifeboats, though they were to be ordered into the lifeboats 'first to show some women it was safe'.[50] Ismay told one stewardess to jump into a lifeboat and when she said that 'I am only a stewardess' replied, 'Never mind, you are a woman, take your place.'[51] In many ways, Annie Caton, one of the Turkish bath attendants, was treated more like a woman passenger when:

> one officer calmly stopped me, took my lifebelt, and turned it, and tied it on me again, saying I had put it on wrongly. He patted me on the back, and told me not to be alarmed as they were only putting us in the lifeboats as a precaution.[52]

Mary Sloan, like many of the male passengers who survived, was pushed into a boat though she had already decided that it was time to enter one, having earlier declined to enter a boat at the suggestion of a bellboy. She had taken her turn at rowing and was pleased that 'the women said I encouraged them'.[53] Most of the women crew members survived though not all. Lucy Snape, a second-class stewardess, 'shook hands with her passengers as they got in but would not get in a boat herself', whilst Catherine Wallis, 'a nervous little woman', the steerage matron, locked herself in her cabin after seeing off her charges and remarked, 'I am going to stay where I am safe.'[54]

Whilst the stewards and other members of the Victualling Department were the most visible to the passengers both throughout the voyage and during the evacuation, the role of the engineers, stokers and trimmers was just as vital to the welfare of those travellers. Charlotte Collyer recounted a lurid and perhaps exaggerated picture of how the appearance of an injured stoker fleeing from the boiler room to the deck had made her realise the seriousness of the situation facing her:

> Suddenly there was a commotion near one of the gangways and we saw a stoker come climbing up from below. He stopped a few feet away from us. All the fingers of one hand had been cut off. Blood was running from the stumps and blood was spattered over his face and over his clothes. The red marks showed very clearly against the coal dust with which he was covered. I went over and spoke to him. I asked him if there was any danger. 'Danger,' he screamed at the top of his voice, 'I should say so! It's hell down below, look at me. The boat will sink in ten minutes.'[55]

George Kemish, a fireman, was more restrained in his account of conditions below where engineers were busy adjusting valves and carpenters were taking soundings. One of the engineers slipped and broke his leg only to be abandoned in the pump room. Meanwhile, there was much amusement about members of the crew packing their bags and moving them to the recreation deck when their quarters were flooded.[56] A greaser, Alfred White, fortunately escaped because he was sent on deck to report back to the engine room on the situation only to find himself unable to return below.[57]

Above all, it was for their handling of the evacuation of the ship and performance in the lifeboats that the quality and performance of officers and crew was to be judged. It was an area in which many of them were to prove inadequate, and which would reveal some of the deficiencies of *Titanic* regarding safety and competence.

Inevitably, most attention was focused on the conduct of the captain, who had overall responsibility for everything aboard ship and for the safety of the passengers. Edward Smith was a veteran of the White Star Line and approaching an honourable retirement when he took charge of *Titanic* for her maiden voyage. He was appreciated by his passengers for his affability and geniality as much as for any faith in his seamanship:

> Distinction and a somewhat patriarchal demeanour were conferred upon him by his carefully trimmed white beard. Captain Smith by

reason of his sociability was a great man amongst the passengers. He was very well read, had a great knowledge of the world, and was an excellent narrator of a fund of excellent stories.[58]

His attendance at a dinner party organised by Eleanor Widener on the eve of the sinking has come in for criticism and he was accused of having overindulged in alcohol, which may have made him unfit to assume command in an emergency. Mrs Widener and Marian Thayer, who were both actually present at the dinner, testified to his sobriety and that he had not drunk alcohol that evening. Mrs Thayer stated that:

> I noticed that the captain never took any alcoholic liquor of any kind at any meal. I do not remember hearing, during the dinner on Sunday night, any mention made by any person of ice being in the neighbourhood, or that we might expect to see ice, as Mr. Widener, Major Butt, and I were deeply engrossed in conversation on other subjects during the entire time of the dinner.[59]

If *Titanic* sank because of poor navigation, as the official inquiries into the wreck concluded, the responsibility was that of the captain. He was found to have neglected the ice warnings and failed to reduce speed. However, maintaining speed in an ice field was accepted practice at that time and:

> Several captains of Atlantic liners said that in similar circumstances to the *Titanic* disaster they would have continued their course and speed. Captain Pritchard, who formerly commanded the *Mauritania*, said he should only slacken speed if the weather conditions were unfavourable.[60]

What perhaps aggravated the danger was that William Murdoch, the officer of the watch, had reversed the engines and swerved the bows. It was thought that if the ship had been struck by the bow, it might have stayed afloat. Lord Mersey exonerated Smith from the charge of negligence in going too fast through an ice field with the judgement that:

It is, in my opinion, impossible to fix Captain Smith with blame. It is, however, to be hoped that the last has been heard of the practice and that for the future it will be abandoned for what we now know to be more prudent and wiser measures.[61]

Where Smith was more negligent was in not impressing the urgency of the situation on his crew and allowing the lifeboats to be launched below full capacity. There he proved more indecisive than he should. He also failed to communicate with his officers. His 'women and children' command was not fully explained and was open to differing interpretations from a literal interpretation that condemned men to die to a more humane and sensible policy of allowing male passengers to board lifeboats if there were no women to take the places. William Alden Smith condemned him since 'indifference to danger was one of the direct and contributing causes of this unnecessary tragedy, while his own willingness to die was the expiating evidence of his fitness to live'. Nevertheless, Arthur Peuchen remembered him as 'doing everything in his power to get women in these boats, and to see that they were lowered properly. I thought he was doing his duty in regard to the lowering of the boats.'[62] Lightoller remembered him as:

> one of the ablest Skippers on the Atlantic, and accusations of recklessness, carelessness, not taking due precautions, or driving his ship at too high a speed, were absolutely, and utterly unfounded; but the armchair complaint is a very common disease, and generally accepted as one of the necessary evils from which the sea-farer is condemned to suffer.[63]

It was important that Smith should be portrayed as going down with his ship in the best maritime tradition. Robert Daniel's account of this was almost a classic depiction of how the captain of a sinking ship should die:

> I saw Captain Smith on the bridge. My eyes seemingly clung to him. The deck from which I had leapt was immersed. The water had risen slowly, and was now to the floor of the bridge. Then it was to Captain Smith's waist. I saw him no more. He died a hero.[64]

Smith had earlier told his men, 'Well, boys, do your best for the women and children, and look out for yourselves,' before walking back to the bridge.[65] There were also reported sightings of him saving children as the ship went down. This was a contrast with charges that Smith had shot himself when he realised that his ship was going down, a rumour paralleled to suggestions that First Officer Murdoch had also shot himself, but Captain Rostron of *Carpathia* robustly rebutted such claims about Smith and stated, 'I have it from the lips of members of his crew who tried to save his life that he did not commit suicide. He stuck to the ship until he was washed from the bridge.'[66]

George Bernard Shaw was critical of the idea that:

> Though all the men must be heroes, the Captain must be a super-hero, a magnificent seaman, cool, brave, delighting in death and danger, and a living guarantee that the wreck was nobody's fault, but, on the contrary, a triumph of British navigation.

He went on to question whether Edward Smith deserved some of the adulation that he had received in the British popular press:

> Such a man Captain Smith was enthusiastically proclaimed on the day when it was reported (and actually believed, apparently) that he had shot himself on the bridge, or shot the first officer, or been shot by the first officer, or shot anyhow, to bring the curtain down effectively. Writers who had never heard of Captain Smith to that hour wrote of him as they would hardly write of Nelson. The one thing positively known was that Captain Smith had lost his ship by deliberately and knowingly steaming into an icefield at the highest speed he had coal for. He paid the penalty; so did most of those for whose lives he was responsible. Had he brought them and the ship safely to land, nobody would have taken the smallest notice of him.[67]

The efficiency of the ship was not improved by a last-minute reshuffle among the senior officers. Henry Wilde was reassigned from *Olympic* to serve as chief officer with the resultant demotion of William Murdoch to first officer and

Herbert Lightoller to second officer, whilst David Blair, who had served as second officer on the positioning voyage from Belfast to Southampton, left the ship. This put both Murdoch and Lightoller 'out of our stride' and caused some initial confusion until all the men concerned could settle into their new roles.[68] In his haste to leave the ship, Blair accidentally took with him the key to the crow's nest locker in which the binoculars reserved for the lookouts were kept. Had the lookouts had binoculars and seen the iceberg earlier, it is unlikely that they could have averted the collision but it added to the atmosphere of inefficiency and unpreparedness.

In the absence of regular lifeboat drills, the crew were not altogether familiar with the procedures for evacuating the ship. They were not a Board of Trade requirement and, although the White Star Line may have scheduled them for each Sunday morning, they were not a customary feature for the crew. George Cavell, a trimmer on the *Adriatic*, *Oceanic*, *Olympic* and *Titanic*, testified to the American inquiry into the sinking of the *Titanic* that in his eighteen months at sea, 'the only boat drill as I ever had was when we went to New York, on Sunday morning'.[69] Unaccustomed to operating the lifeboats, the officers were also afraid that if they filled the boats to capacity, the davits and tackle for them might buckle. They were very aware of a recent capsizing in the English Channel of a lifeboat in which nine people had drowned and did not know that Harland & Wolff had tested a lifeboat on *Olympic* to show that it could bear the weight of sixty-five people without buckling or strain while being raised or lowered. Second Officer Charles Lightoller, in particular, was said by an able seaman, John Poingdestre, to be 'frightened of the falls', and only forty-two women were placed into a boat designed for sixty-five.[70] Others left half empty.

Many of the passengers were also reluctant to commit themselves to the dangers of the lifeboats, and at first, 'there was practically no excitement on the part of anyone during this time, the majority seeming to think that the big boat could not sink altogether, and that it was better to stay on the steamer than trust to the lifeboats', according to Imanita Shelley. Mrs Shelley was far from impressed by the lack of equipment on the lifeboats when eventually she did board one, for:

> there was none in her boat except four oars and a mast, which latter was useless; there was no water nor any food; that there was neither

compass nor binnacle light nor any kind of lantern; that on questioning occupants of other lifeboats they told her the same story – lack of food, water, compass, and lights, and that several boats had no oars or only two or three.[71]

The *Titanic* actually had more lifeboats than was legally required of it when it struck the iceberg. Instead of the sixteen lifeboats the ship's tonnage required her to carry, there were fourteen lifeboats, four Engelhardt boats with collapsible canvas sides, and two cutters. This gave it a lifeboat capacity of 1,178, yet the ship was certified to carry 3,547 passengers and crew. In this it was no worse than most other ships of the time, even the best equipped of which, *La Provence*, only had lifeboats for 82 per cent of those on board. Lifeboats were seen as cluttering the decks and as being almost redundant at a time when 'the ships are built nowadays to be practically unsinkable, and each ship is supposed to be a lifeboat in itself', according to Arthur Rostron, captain of the *Carpathia*, who was instrumental in the rescue of survivors from the doomed liner.[72] Indeed, Alfred Chalmers of the Board of Trade considered that too many lifeboats might have led to an even greater loss of life than the 1,498 lost, 'for the simple reason that, knowing they had so many boats to trust to, they probably sent the first lot away not fully loaded', and that:

> I do not want to criticise the Officers or the Master of the ship at all, but I assume it is probable that that may have been the case; whereas if they had had fewer boats they would have taken good care that they utilised them to the fullest extent.[73]

William Sowden Sim, a captain in the United States Navy, was much more realistic when he commented after the sinking of the *Titanic* that:

> The truth of the matter is that in case any large passenger steamship sinks, by reason of collision or other fatal damage to her floatability, more than half of her passengers are doomed to death, even in fair weather, and in case there is a bit of a sea running none of the loaded boats can long remain afloat, even if they succeed in getting safely away from the side, and one

more will be added to the long list of 'the ships that never return.' Most people accept this condition as one of the inevitable perils of the sea, but I believe it can be shown that the terrible loss of life occasioned by such disasters as overtook the *Bourgogne* and the *Titanic* and many other ships can be avoided or at least greatly minimized. Moreover, it can be shown that the steamship owners are fully aware of the danger to their passengers; that the laws on the subject of life-saving appliances are wholly inadequate; that the steamship companies comply with the law, though they oppose any changes therein, and that they decline to adopt improved appliances; because there is no public demand for them, the demand being for high schedule speed and luxurious conditions of travel.[74]

The fate of the *Titanic* was of great concern to the crew of *Olympic*, who went on strike to fight for safety improvements. Additional collapsible lifeboats had been loaded on *Olympic* for her scheduled sailing from Southampton to New York on 24 April 1912 but the boiler room crew went on strike because they considered them to be substandard. Once the immediate issue of the safety of the lifeboats had been resolved, the strikers had refused to return to their duties unless White Star dismissed those members of the crew who had not joined the strike. A replacement crew was then found but many of the 'loyal men' now joined the strikers because the substitutes were deemed too inexperienced and posed greater risks than inferior lifeboats. The voyage was cancelled and on 4 May 1912, the fifty-three crew members from *Olympic* who deserted on 25 April were charged at Portsmouth Police Court with refusing to obey the captain's orders only for the charges to be dismissed because they had been 'unnerved' by the *Titanic* disaster.[75] The National Sailors' and Firemen's Union felt emboldened to demand the right to inspect life-saving equipment on all steamers and to insist on the employment of qualified seamen who would be capable of acting efficiently in an emergency.[76] The United Mineworkers' Union in America sympathised with the strikers on *Olympic* for being 'enclosed for days and nights in a stuffy, heated room some fifty feet below the waterline' and referred to the horrifying experience of the firemen, trimmers and greasers on *Titanic* who had an unenviable fate 'even if accompanied by a band playing 'Nearer My God to Thee''.[77]

It was not just White Star crew who had concerns. Following the sinking of the *Titanic*, there was a general demand that there should be sufficient numbers of lifeboats for everyone on board a passenger ship. The first international conference on safety at sea was held in London in January 1914 and attended by representatives of thirteen countries. It adopted the International Convention for the Safety of Life at Sea, which stated that 'at no moment of its voyage may a ship have on board a total number of persons more than that for whom accommodation is provided in lifeboats (and the pontoon lifeboats) on board'. The convention was to enter into force in July 1915, but with the outbreak of the First World War in Europe in August 1914, it was never formally ratified.[78]

The insufficient number of lifeboats and the failure of the officers to ensure that they were fully loaded was not the only inadequacy of the evacuation procedure to be so starkly revealed. The crew chosen to man them were not considered fit for the job by the passengers saved in them. Ella White was especially indignant about their conduct and capabilities:

Before we cut loose from the ship two of the seamen with us – the men, I should say; I do not call them seamen; I think they were dining-room stewards – before we were cut loose from the ship they took out cigarettes and lighted them on an occasion like that! That is one thing that we saw. All of those men escaped under the pretence of being oarsmen. The man who rowed me took his oar and rowed all over the boat, in every direction. I said to him, 'why don't you put the oar in the oarlock?' He said, 'do you put it in that hole?' I said 'certainly.' He said, 'I never had an oar in my hand before.' I spoke to the other man and he said; 'I have never had an oar in my hand before, but I think I can row.' Those were the men that we were put to sea with at night – with all these magnificent fellows left on board, who would have been such a protection to us.[79]

It was little wonder that the Countess of Rothes took charge of the boat, working alongside Able Seaman Thomas Jones, who actually knew what he was doing, unlike Steward Alfred Crawford and Able Seaman Charles Pascoe, who not only could not row and 'knew nothing about the handling of a boat' but continually challenged the authority of Jones, telling him, 'If you don't stop talking through that hole in your face there will be one less in the boat.'[80]

There was even greater conflict, much of it with connotations of class and gender on the boat of which Margaret Brown was to wrest control from Quartermaster Robert Hichens. Major Peuchen, who had been allowed into the boat because of his yachting experience, adopted a passive role for which he was later criticised, recognising that Hichens was a disagreeable man who would brook no disagreement and with whom 'it is no use you arguing with that man, at all. It is best not to discuss matters with him.' Hichens had insisted to Peuchen that he was in charge, not the gallant major, and ordered him to row. When opposition rose against Hichens, 'the rebellion was made by some of the married women that were leaving their husbands.' When they had urged him to return to try to save some of the victims they could hear crying for help, his callous response was, 'It is our lives now, not theirs.' Then, insensitive to many of the women in the lifeboat, including Julia Cavendish, Leila Meyer, Eloise Smith and Hélène Baxter, who had left husbands and sons on the ship, he had said, 'There was only a lot of stiffs there,' which caused much resentment.[81] He later told them that the *Carpathia* had not come to rescue the survivors but 'she is to pick up bodies'.[82] He annoyed the irrepressible Margaret Brown with his pessimism about their chances of survival until she told him 'to be still or he would go overboard'.[83] Eloise Smith condemned him as 'a lazy uncouth man, who had no respect for the ladies and who was a thorough coward'.[84] Unlike some of the other women she did not put his behaviour down to intoxication. Hichens rather clumsily and unconvincingly defended the charges made against him:

> Mrs Meyer was rather vexed with me in the boat and I spoke rather straight to her, and she accused me of wrapping myself up in the blankets in the boat, using bad language, and drinking all the whisky, which I deny, sir. I was standing to attention, exposed, steering the boat all night, which is a very cold billet. I would rather be pulling the boat than be steering. But I seen no one there to steer, so I thought, being in charge of the boat, it was the best way to steer myself, especially when I seen the ladies get very nervous with the nasty tumble on.[85]

Inevitably, questions were raised about why members of the crew had survived when passengers perished. Only 24 per cent of the crew, 212 men and women out of 885, actually survived but the perception was that the unworthiest of them had managed to save their own lives. The *New York Herald* declared, 'This country intends to find out why so many American lives were wasted by the incompetency of British seamen, and why women and children were sent to their deaths while so many British crew have been saved.'[86] Obviously some of them had been selected to man the lifeboats by the ship's officers, though little thought had been given as to whether the stewards had the necessary rowing skills. Others had jumped and reached a lifeboat like many male passengers. When asked 'how do you account for a large proportion of those in that lifeboat being members of your crew, and no male passengers?', Andrew Cunningham replied, 'Well, as far as I understand, when the boat left the ship's side there were only about three sailors in it, three men to man the boat; the rest were picked up out of the water.' Cunningham himself claimed to have thrown himself into the water and swum 'about three-quarters of a mile' from the ship to avoid the suction. He was hauled into a lifeboat.[87]

Perhaps some of the problems with the behaviour of the crew came from the way they were recruited at a time when many men in Southampton were desperate for work.[88] The national coal miners' strike for a minimum wage had resulted in a shortage of coal deliveries to the ports, compelling the shipping companies to lay up their ships and lay off crews. In Southampton, over 17,000 men were unemployed in April 1912. Although the miners' strike had been settled on 6 April, it would be some time before enough coal would be available for normal service to be resumed. In order for *Titanic*'s maiden voyage to go ahead as planned, coal was transferred from the holds of other White Star liners such as *Oceanic* and *Majestic*. Passenger bookings were also transferred from other ships whose voyages had been cancelled. There were also jobs now available and when recruitment began on 6 April, there was a rush of men desperate for work. The maiden voyage of *Titanic* was indeed seen as a salvation for many Southampton families since:

> During the coal strike many breadwinners were out of work, furniture was sold or pawned, and numerous families received notice to quit. Then

came the *Titanic*, and firemen, greasers and trimmers, who had known no work for weeks, eagerly joined the big ship to save their homes.[89]

Whereas the deck and engineer officers were directly recruited by the White Star Line, most of the trimmers, stokers, greasers and seamen were recruited through two unions, 228 men signing on with the British Seafarers' Union and 100 with the National Sailors' and Firemen's Union.[90] The British Seafarers' Union, only established in 1911, was essentially a 'Southampton Union' though it claimed that 'practically the whole of the seafarers of the *Titanic* are members of our union'.[91] Many of these men were described as 'strangers to the ship'.[92] Unused to the ways of the White Star Line and to the geography of the ship, they had little time to settle in.

Even the officers had difficulty in navigating around *Titanic*. Second Officer Lightoller admitted that it had taken him a while to familiarise himself with the ship, especially when:

> It is difficult to convey any idea of the size of a ship like the *Titanic*, when you could actually walk miles along decks and passages, covering different ground all the time. I was thoroughly familiar with pretty well every type of ship afloat, from a battleship and a barge, but it took me fourteen days before I could with confidence find my way from one part of that ship to another by the shortest route.

Three other officers had taken a day to find a gangway door that should have been obvious, and:

> No doubt with the help of a plan, it would have been fairly simple, but a sailor does not walk round with a plan in his pocket, he must carry his ship in his head, and in an emergency such as fire must be able to get where he wants by sheer instinct – certainly without a chance of getting lost on the way.[93]

Captain Smith was not even entirely familiar with his own ship and instructed one of the lifeboats to be filled from the promenade deck because it would be safer than from the open boat deck, seemingly unaware that the promenade deck was protected from the wind by glass windows known as Ismay screens. The passengers who had been sent down went back up the stairs they had just descended only to be called back when it was decided that it would be easier to remove the screens rather than haul the lifeboat back to the higher deck.[94] In the confusion of the sinking, the crew not knowing the best escape routes was hazardous.

However, several members of the crew had previously served on *Olympic* and other White Star ships, which should have given them greater familiarity with the procedures even though they were on a ship new to them.[95] John Marriott and his brother-in-law George Levett, both assistant pantrymen, had been on board *Olympic* at the time of its collision with *Hawke* in 1911. Marriott wrote to a friend:

> Don't you think it is a doomed ship? She lost one of her propeller blades this trip, and she's gone to Belfast for repairs again, so there has been something happening every trip. I think she is going down next trip. Really, I feel half scared to go on her next trip, but I think I will take a chance and do one more trip in her, and then stand by for the new boat *Titanic*. Perhaps that one might be more fortunate.

For Marriott and Levett, the decision to sign on for the new ship was to prove fatal.[96]

Harold Lowe commanded the only lifeboat to actively try to save victims in the water, though those efforts were belated and too cautious to be in any respect effective. He 'had to wait until the yells and shrieks had subsided – for the people to thin out – and then I deemed it safe for me to go amongst the wreckage.' He had managed to bring four other boats together and had roped them together for mutual protection. Now he transferred passengers from his lifeboat to the others and had asked for volunteers to go with him to the wreck. He had waited until the noise of the dying had quietened and there would be fewer people strong enough to try to make it onto the boat as 'it would not have been wise or safe for me to have gone there before, because the whole lot of us would have been swamped and then nobody would have been saved'. Unfortunately, they were only able to find four men still alive among the wreckage, but one of them, William Hoyt, died soon after being picked up. It struck Lowe as remarkable that 'to say, I did not see a single female body, not one, around the wreckage'. He congratulated himself on his response to the cries of the dying that 'I made the attempt, sir, as soon as any man could do so, and I am not scared of saying it. I did not hang back or anything else.'[97] Third Officer Herbert Pitman also told his men 'to get their oars and pull back toward the wreck' but was prevented from doing so by the passengers protesting against such 'a mad idea' which might have resulted in the boat being 'swamped with the crowd that was in the water. And it would add another forty to the list of drowned.' He at least felt some remorse that instead of trying to save lives, they had 'simply took our oars in and lay quiet'. They then 'just simply lay there doing nothing'.[98]

Ismay had wanted to return home as soon as possible with the surviving crew once the *Carpathia* reached New York but was prevented from doing so by a Senate Inquiry set up to investigate the disaster, chaired by a populist Republican, William Alden Smith, senator for Michigan. The four surviving officers and another twenty-seven crewmen subpoenaed to give evidence wanted to get home as quickly as possible and were reluctant to co-operate until persuaded by the British attaché, Lord Eustace Percy, and by Lightoller that they should give evidence.[99] These officers and crew took offence at some of the questions they were asked. Harold Lowe's contemptuous response to an enquiry as to whether he knew what an iceberg was made from was, 'Ice, I suppose.'[100] When the chairman of the inquiry, William Alden Smith, showed a complete ignorance of ships by assuming that watertight compartments were designed not to keep the ship afloat but to shelter passengers, he was nicknamed 'Watertight Smith' by the British press. In such ways he was considered to have 'set the whole world laughing by the appalling ignorance betrayed by questions'[101] and to have 'made himself ridiculous in the eyes of British seamen. British seamen know something about ships. Senator Smith does not.'[102] The inquiry was further criticised because 'it has no technical knowledge, and its proceedings show a want of familiarity with nautical matters and with the sea'.[103]

The British Wreck Commissioner's inquiry into the sinking of the *Titanic*, appointed by the Board of Trade and chaired by Lord Mersey, which met in the London Scottish Regiment Drill Hall, was much more professional and technical in its approach than the American Senate Inquiry but was no more trusted by the crew. Charles Lightoller, however, believed that the British inquiry was little more than a whitewashing exercise since 'a washing of dirty linen would help no one. The Board of Trade had passed that ship as in all respects fit for the sea.'[104] If the White Star Line were found negligent, any claims for damages might break up the company and cause the loss of the transatlantic passenger trade to France and Germany. The attempt by the White Star Line to detain the crew, described as 'human salvage' when they arrived in Plymouth on *Lapland* on their way home, to prevent them from speaking to the press until they had been debriefed by the company, was seen as a move to control the narrative.[105] Lightoller himself was determined not to be apportioned any blame but carefully toed the company line, for which he received no thanks, and:

> personally, I had no desire that blame should be attributed either to the Board of Trade or the White Star Line, though in all conscience it was a difficult task, when handled by some of the cleverest legal minds in England, striving tooth and nail to prove the inadequacy here, the lack there, when one had known, full well, and for many years, the ever-present possibility of just such a disaster. I think in the end the Board of Trade and the White Star Line won.[106]

The officers and crew may have been contemptuous of both the official inquiries, but there was a determination that the sacrifice and manliness of the crew should not be forgotten amidst all the adulation of their social betters:

> that aristocrat fought to get into a boat but was held back by pistols. Now the papers are filled with their heroism. We poor folk who died while stoking the fires in the engine room until the very last minute, we third-class passengers who truly showed heroism, about us they write nothing.[107]

Rather than nothing being said about the crew, they and their actions on the night of the catastrophe had come under intense scrutiny, revealing the best and the worst of these workers under stress.

Chapter Seven

Deathly Distinction and Discrimination

Death is often said to be the great leveller, but that was not the case for the victims just as there was no equality among the survivors. Much may have been made of the equality of all passengers and crew in facing their fate at a time when 'the rich died and the poor died alike',[1] and it was said that 'they sleep tonight together, peasant and millionaire' sharing 'a democratic grave',[2] but this was clearly not true. Even in death, they were to be treated differently. The disaster may have shown 'the manner in which millionaires die on an equality with the other brave men of humbler class', but the emphasis was still on the wealthy and famous.[3] After all:

> Naturally the survivors noticed particularly the action of the more notable of their fellow passengers who were known to them on that account, and it was of their conduct that they testified specifically, though it probably was only a fair sample of the conduct of many less conspicuous who died in the same noble company.[4]

Nor were the survivors to be treated equally even though they had experienced a common ordeal. Even before they were hauled up to safety on *Carpathia* from the lifeboats, they were categorised according to their status in the hierarchy of passengers. It was lucky for them that this Cunard liner was there to rescue them as Harold Cottam, the wireless operator, was about to go off duty and leave his wireless set unmanned when he heard the distress message from *Titanic* since he had been working until the early hours on the previous two days and had 'planned to get to bed early that night'. Indeed, he was taking off his boots when the signal came through but fortunately he was still wearing the earphones. Working through another night to maintain radio contact, his first sight of the survivors was of women and children 'crying and they seemed overcome by the calamity. As they were raised to the deck several of them collapsed.'[5] Where these women and the few men with them were sent for treatment depended on their perceived class. The English doctor who attended the first-class passengers on *Carpathia* was stationed in the first-class dining room, the Italian doctor in the second-class dining room and the Hungarian doctor in the third. Whilst first- and second-class passengers were to be reassured by their stewards that nothing was amiss and were encouraged to remain in their staterooms, it was the role of the inspector, steerage stewards and master of arms to 'control our own steerage passengers and keep them out of the third-class dining hall, and also keep them out of the way and off the deck to prevent confusion'. Meanwhile, the purser and chief stewards received the rescued passengers at the gangway, noted down their names and class of travel, and supervised the stewards who directed them to the various dining rooms where they could find accommodation and any necessary medical attention. Soup, coffee and tea were available throughout the ship.[6] The supplies of stimulants, restoratives and other necessities were much appreciated. Harold Bride, with his frostbitten legs, benefitted from a shot of liqueur before being taken to the ship's hospital whilst Archie Gracie welcomed a hot drink while his clothes were being dried in the bakery oven.[7] Caroline Bonnell was pleased that 'as soon as we got on deck, we were rolled in blankets and given brandy and water. And nothing have I ever tasted was quite so good as that brandy and water.'[8] The coffee was also laced with brandy, which may be why third-class steward Sidney Daniels 'didn't care what it was then, just something to warm me up' even though he 'used to hate coffee'.[9] Emily Ryerson appreciated that 'the kindness and the efficiency of all the arrangements on the *Carpathia* can never be too highly praised'.[10]

Although segregated by cabin class in the same way as they had been on *Titanic*, some of the passengers found themselves mixed with those from different social classes. Semi-conscious and possibly semi-nude, there was nothing to mark out Robert Daniel as anything but a steerage passenger and he was summarily despatched to a bunk shared with a sailor. Only when he was able to explain his circumstances was he loaned more respectable clothing by one of the ship's doctors and allowed to join his fellow first-class passengers. Without the distinction afforded by his smart clothing, all of it lost with the sinking,

Daniel could not immediately be identified as a gentleman.[11] Other first-class passengers also found themselves among unfamiliar bedfellows, especially when berthed in the hospitals for medical treatment. Imanita Shelley complained when her mother, Lutie Parrish, who had travelled in second class on *Titanic*, was given a bed in the hospital intended for third-class passengers on *Carpathia* while being treated for a leg injury. However impressed she may have been by the doctors on the ship and 'how hard they worked, unceasingly to do for us', Mrs Shelley was disgusted by how many 'foreigners' there were and by the pervasive smell of antiseptics in the steerage hospital. Mrs Shelley had earlier been concerned about the cracked and bleeding lips of other women sharing a lifeboat with her, fearful of contracting a disease, until she realised that her own lips were also bleeding from the cold, not from a lower-class infection.[12]

The officers on *Carpathia* gave up their cabins for the use of first-class women from *Titanic*. Eleanor Widener, Marian Thayer and Madeline Astor shared Captain Rostron's own cabin, whilst Bruce Ismay claimed the doctor's cabin for himself. Rostron later recalled that 'their husbands, all millionaires, had perished, and, in addition, one lady had lost a son' though another of them was reunited with her son, Jack Thayer. The passengers on *Carpathia*, despite having set out on a pleasure cruise to the Mediterranean, rose to the occasion and 'our people understood they must not remain spectators, that here was a situation unparalleled in which they must play a part'. They tried to comfort the victims of the sinking, persuaded them to drink something warming and used 'their persuasion and common sense' so successfully in 'seeking to soften the grief which wrapped them round about'.[13] More practically, they loaned them dry and warm clothing. The barbershop was raided for ties, collars, hairpins and combs, while 'one good Samaritan' distributed toothbrushes. Even so, many men and women remained in the clothes in which they had left the ship until they reached New York, however incongruous dishevelled evening dress or dressing gowns may have been.[14] All the male passengers gave up their cabins and many of the ladies doubled up to leave their berths for the use of the rescued. Even so, many of the men rescued from *Titanic*, as well as the men from *Carpathia*, had to find places to sleep wherever they could, in the smoking rooms, dining rooms, library or even on deck.[15] One man wandered around the ship searching for somewhere to sleep. Finding a mattress and some blankets, he made himself comfortable, only to wake up the next morning surrounded by rescued women who had been allocated that part of the ship.[16] The steerage passengers were given no choice about having to share. Those already on *Carpathia* were grouped together while all spare steerage berths were prepared for the survivors from third class on *Titanic*.[17]

Leaders also emerged among the survivors intent on taking control of the situation rather than being forever the victims. Rostron encouraged the first-class passengers to form a committee of seven members 'to assist in caring for the rescued'. The committee, headed by Frederick K. Seward, was made up mainly of men – H.B. Steffanson, F.O. Spedden, Karl Behr, I.G. Frauenthal and George A. Harder, with Margaret Brown as the token woman.[18] Their work was focused on the steerage passengers. Karl Behr found it 'harrowing to talk with these despairing people from whom I had to get names, home addresses and the names of lost relatives'.[19] Some of the women, observing how poorly clad were many of the steerage passengers saved from *Titanic*, organised sewing bees to make clothes for them from requisitioned blankets and sheets. Others saw to the nursing, feeding and clothing of the children in third class, relieving their mothers. For some of the upper-class survivors, being involved in such practical tasks gave them something to do and was a familiar activity for those who in their normal lives had been involved with charitable work and practical philanthropy.

A founding member of the Denver Woman's Club, promoting literacy, education, women's suffrage and human rights in Colorado, Margaret Brown was an inveterate fundraiser for the causes she believed in and had not been above working in soup kitchens for destitute miners. On *Carpathia*, she clashed with one of the ship's doctors who informed her that, as he was overseeing the distribution of clothing, there was no need for her to be involved in any social work on the ship. Seeing the doctor's view of relief as being a limited one, she was determined to help with the emotional as well as the practical difficulties of the survivors. It was not only steerage passengers, but also women from the other classes of passengers who came to seek advice and 'poured out their grief and story of distress'. As they 'unburdened their sorrows that lay like a weight on their breasts', they also sought help and assurance about more practical concerns. Without funds, many people were worried that they would not be able to make it to their final destinations. The committee persuaded Ismay to agree that the White Star Line would provide help with such transport. Many of the women in both first and second class, having lost all their money when the ship went down, were fearful of being treated like destitute immigrants subject to the Alien Law on arrival in the United States.[20] Even the wealthiest of passengers were recorded as having lost everything at sea on the passenger manifest for *Carpathia* on arrival in New York. Reassurance that they would not lose status was important.[21]

Rather than make for the nearest port of Halifax, it was decided that *Carpathia* should return to New York, original destination of *Titanic*, with its better transport links and more facilities for the accommodation and medical care of the survivors. Rostron was also determined that the ship should avoid the icebergs with all their dangers and bitter associations, 'and I knew very well what the effect of that would be on people who had had the experiences these people had had.'[22] Instead, Halifax was to accommodate the dead rather than the living once the bodies recovered from the sinking were landed there. Had the survivors also been taken there it may have eased the identification of the dead and enabled some of the survivors to know the fate of those they had lost more quickly, though it could also have worsened the condition of people who were already 'hysterical and in a bad state'.[23]

Once the ship arrived in port, class distinctions again granted privileges to the wealthier passengers. Just as they had been the last to embark in Southampton, they were now the first to disembark in New York. The Waldorf Astoria Hotel sent eight limousines to collect passengers with bookings there. Madeleine Astor was met by her stepson Vincent and a fleet of cars. Three special trains were chartered to go from Pennsylvania station to Philadelphia, the first exclusively for Eleanor Widener, who had been met by her brother-in-law, and the second for the Thayers. The third train was for other prominent Philadelphians, escorted by the Philadelphia chief of police to the taxis that took them to the station.[24] Once the first-class passengers had disembarked it was the turn of those in second class. Only then were the steerage passengers and then finally the crew allowed to go onshore.

For the more impoverished passengers, who had to wait to go ashore until their social betters had disembarked, arrangements had been made to help them by a number of aid agencies. The Red Cross and Salvation Army had officers waiting at the pier. Commissioner Evangeline Booth, Territorial Commissioner for the Salvation Army in the United States, personally oversaw the work of her officers just as she had previously taken a lead in the response in the aftermath of the 1906 San Francisco earthquake when she had spearheaded fundraising for relief work. She reported that amongst those she helped was a co-religionist:

> Mrs. Abbott, a Salvationist in uniform, was rescued after five hours drifting on a raft, during which time her two sons, aged sixteen and a half and thirteen and a half, were drowned before her eyes; they died, I am assured, like true Salvationists. Mrs. Abbott is now seriously ill in hospital, owing to long exposure on the raft; she was frozen up to the hips.[25]

The Municipal Lodging House was thrown open to provide free food and lodgings, while the White Star Line offered railroad tickets to their final destinations for all steerage passengers. Ambulances took the more badly injured to New York hospitals. Over 100 were treated at St Vincent's Hospital, mainly for exposure and shock.[26]

Esther Hart, who had lost her carpenter husband Ben, was grateful to the Women's Relief Committee in New York for their practical help in supplying shelter and clothing, where 'everything a woman needed was there in abundance, from a blouse to a safety pin, underclothing, stays, stockings, garters, suspenders, hair pins, boots of all sizes, each pair with laces or a button hook in them as was necessary'. Mrs Satterlee, who had taken Esther and her small daughter Eva under her wing, drove them herself to a hotel and invited them for lunch at her own house but appreciated that Mrs Hart was too upset to accept her offer.[27] It was not only steerage passengers like the Harts who received help; Edward and Ethel Beane, a bricklayer and dressmaker travelling in second class, were left destitute, having lost all their money and clothes. They had deposited $300 with the purser but were unable to produce a receipt. The White Star Line offered them $20 conditional on Beane signing a form waiving any further claim for compensation. Mrs Stott, who lived at their hotel and had offered to help them, declared that this was unacceptable despite the official insisting that:

> Mr. Beane seemed pretty well fixed and wanted to know who I was anyway. He said these benevolent societies had been giving the line a lot of bother, but I stuck to my point, and we are going to file a claim.

Meanwhile, she paid the couple's fare to Rochester and arranged for them to be given a box of suitable clothing from the Women's Relief Committee. As members of an ad hoc committee set up to deal with the immediate needs of the survivors, the priorities of these philanthropic women were to see that 'clothing, a railroad ticket, perhaps, and a little money is bestowed in each case along with a deal of comforting' primarily to immigrants holding a certificate of assent from the Commissioners of Immigration, who had suspended the usual immigration formalities on this one unprecedented occasion.[28]

The third-class survivors may have been spared the indignities of medical inspection at Ellis Island, but their inferior status as immigrants was not forgotten nor were contemporary American attitudes to immigration softened after the disaster.[29] In 1912, there was considerable concern and fear about 'new' immigrants from southern and eastern Europe considered less likely to assimilate into American society than the 'old' immigrants from the British Isles, Germany, Scandinavia and the Netherlands. Working-class Americans feared that they would compete for jobs and depress wages. The Dillingham Commission, appointed by Congress, recommended a literacy test to keep out undesirable immigrants. The underlying assumption was that migrants from southern and eastern Europe were less likely to be fluent in English or more likely to be illiterate. The Senate passed the resultant bill on 19 April 1912, the same day that the inquiry into the sinking began at the Waldorf Astoria, only for it to be vetoed by President Taft with support from the House of Representatives. It did not escape the notice of the more radical immigrant newspapers that 'the same people who sentimentalized over the actual death of those who lost their lives in the *Titanic* are eager to kill off all opportunity for thousands who desire to come here'.[30]

In successfully returning the rescued men, women and children to New York, the captain and crew of *Carpathia*, having already held a discreet committal service for the four men who were brought up dead from the lifeboats, had been careful to avoid the debris and floating victims of *Titanic* ostensibly so as not to upset the survivors. Rostron claimed that 'the only wreckage we saw there was very small stuff – a few deck chairs and pieces of cork from lifebelts, and a few lifebelts knocking about, and things of that description, all very small stuff indeed. There was very little indeed,' but that 'we saw only saw one body'.[31] He did not attempt to recover the body of this man, as 'the *Titanic*'s passengers then were knocking about the deck and I did not want to cause any unnecessary excitement or any more hysteria among them, so I steamed past, trying to get them not to see it.'[32] Nevertheless, the sea was thickly strewn with what was left of the victims. Passengers on *Bremen* were horrified to see 'a number of bodies so clearly that we could make out what they were wearing and whether they were men or women'; these included 'one woman in her nightdress with a baby clasped closely to her breast' and another 'with her arms tightly around the body of a shaggy dog'. Dozens of men 'encased in life preservers, clinging together as though in the last struggle for life' were seen, whilst another three bodies were still clutching a steamer chair. The ship's officers ignored the pleas of passengers to pick up the bodies of these victims since rescue vessels were on their way.[33]

Three ships were chartered by White Star to search for the bodies of the victims. When the *Mackay-Bennett* arrived at the debris field it found 'a flock of seagulls in the fog' made up of corpses still wearing their white life jackets.[34] Although partially preserved by the cold of the waters, the bodies were bleached by the sun and damaged, both from the sinking itself, as well as from knocking against each other and the wreckage of the ship. In almost a week since the sinking, the corpses had drifted across a wide expanse of ocean.

The crew of the morgue ships had little experience in the recovery of bodies. The *Mackay-Bennett* was a cable repair ship laying and repairing the transatlantic telegraph cables. Frederick Hamilton, cable engineer, was aware of how distressing this work was for the crew aboard the rescue ships:

A large amount of money and jewels has been recovered, the identification of most of the bodies has been established, and details set out for publication. It has been an arduous task for those who have had to overhaul and attend to the remains; the searching, numbering, and identifying of each body, depositing the property found on each in a bag marked with a number corresponding to that attached to the corpse, the sewing up in canvas and securing of weights, entailed prolonged and patient labour. The Embalmer is the only man to whom the work is pleasant, I might add without undue exaggeration, enjoyable, for to him it is a labour of love, and the pride of doing a job well.[35]

Each body had to be numbered in the order that they were taken on board and a record made of relevant physical characteristics, identifying marks on clothing and personal effects. The corpses were left clothed until they were embalmed, but their personal possessions were removed and placed in numbered cloth bags locked away in the sick bay by the purser.[36] The ship recovered 306 bodies, of which 116 were returned to the sea. Of the other search ships chartered, *Minia* recovered 17 bodies, its crew sleeping with the coffins stacked around them, *Montmagny* found 4, and *Algerine* retrieved one, the last of the 328 bodies to be recovered.

The *Mackay-Bennett* carried with it a clergyman who could perform the service for burial at sea for the bodies of those passengers and crew to be placed in canvas sacks weighted down with grate iron. Canon Cameron Hind justified such burials as being a peaceful and dignified end despite a 'common impression of the awfulness of a grave in the mighty deep' and as an act of compassion towards the poorer families in steerage in sparing them the cost of a funeral.[37] Frederick Lardner, captain of the *Mackay-Bennett*, was blunter in explaining that the burials at sea were either because the men were crew who might have preferred the tradition of being consigned to the deep or else because 'we couldn't care for them'.[38] It was a more honest explanation based on the state of many of the bodies and a shortage of embalming fluid but behind it was an assumption that this only applied to the less privileged of the corpses. He also admitted that 'the unidentified seemed unidentifiable, the identified were too mutilated to bring to shore'.[39]

Even in death, class distinction on the *Titanic*, often defined by what the victim wore, governed the disposal of the corpses that were recovered after the sinking of the liner on 15 April 1912. Sensationalist accounts of the sinking concentrated on how 'amidst the acres and acres of wreckage hundreds of dead bodies floated. Many of them were among the first cabin passengers, still dressed in their evening clothes which they had worn when the ship struck the iceberg.'[40] Social status mattered in death as in life and it was the better-dressed passengers who were to be noticed even as floating corpses. The dead were still judged by the clothes and the quality and style of those clothes which gave them their identity and their perceived place in the world, although when the corpses of passengers known to have still been in evening dress, such as Milton Long, were recovered and recorded, the nuances of upper-class sartorial styles were not always to be distinguished when their clothing was described by men unfamiliar with the correct forms of upper-class fashion, who simply recorded them as clothed in dark suits.[41] Eight of the bodies recovered were described as wearing evening dress or tuxedo suits. One of these, a dark-haired man estimated to be aged 25, wearing evening dress trousers, jacket, waistcoat, a black double-breasted overcoat and a silver watch and ring, was never identified; his clothes bore no identification marks, unlike those of most first-class passengers, and he was buried at sea.[42] Presumably, his body was too badly battered or decomposed to be recognisable or brought ashore.

Only one identifiable first-class passenger, 43-year-old New York businessman William Fisher Hoyt, was buried at sea during the initial recovery of the bodies of the victims. He had been picked up by lifeboat 14, bleeding heavily from his nose and mouth, but he was already too close to death and he soon died, despite his rescuers taking off his collar and loosening his shirt to help him to breathe more easily. He was buried at sea when the *Carpathia* rescued the survivors of the lifeboat. Although he was identified by his distinctive watch and membership cards from the New York Athletic and the Fidelity and Casualty Company of New York, his brother was later to have trouble establishing his fate.[43]

Another first-class passenger, Thomson Beattie, was also buried at sea a month later, on 16 May 1912, when the *Oceania* came across a lifeboat in which:

> Two sailors could be seen, their hair bleached by exposure to sun and salt, and a third figure, wearing evening dress, flat on the benches. All three were dead and the bodies had been tossing on the Atlantic swell under the open sky ever since it had seen the greatest of ocean liners sink.

The three bodies were badly decomposed, their facial features unrecognisable and their arms came off when touched. The corpses were quickly sewn into canvas bags and draped with the Union Jack before being committed to the deep. Still wearing his saltwater-stained but once spruce dinner jacket, the 36-year-old landowner and businessman Beattie was buried at sea with the less dapperly dressed crew members alongside whom he had struggled for survival and died.[44]

First-class passengers, who could be identified from their effects or simply because they were well dressed, were embalmed and placed into coffins on the poop deck ready for a dignified landing, formal identification and burial. Their corpses were given all the respect they could have expected in life. A different fate awaited the victims from other classes. Instead of being reverentially placed in coffins, second- and third-class passengers were sewn up in canvas sacks. Their position in the social hierarchy was determined by the quality or coarseness of the clothing they wore and the value of their personal effects, just as their appearance and what they wore had determined their treatment in life. What distinguished the different classes of male travellers was not the type of garments they wore but lay in their quality and detail. When the first bodies were recovered, how they were dressed was immediately noticed and judgments quickly made:

> Everybody had on a lifebelt and bodies floated very high in water in spite of the sodden clothes and things in pockets. Apparently the people had lots of time and discipline must have been splendid, for some had on their pyjamas, two and three shirts, two pairs of pants, two vests, two jackets and an overcoat. In some pockets a quantity of meat and biscuits were found, while in the pockets of most of the crew quite a lot of tobacco and matches besides keys to the various lockers and stateroom doors were found. On this day we buried 15 bodies some of them very badly smashed and bruised.[45]

For the men on the rescue ships, 'hauling the soaked remains in saturated clothing over the side of the cutter is no light task' even before the gruesome work of examining the bodies and their clothing to try to identify them and judge their precise status.[46]

It is from the inventories of the insurance and compensation claims lodged by the first-class passengers who survived or by their heirs that we get an idea of the contents of their wardrobes, what they brought with them when travelling, what was considered essential by social etiquette and what would have indicated the social status of their corpses. A man needed at least five to ten business or lounge suits for ordinary day wear in addition to at least one evening suit and often more, reflecting the fashions of the time. For some well-dressed men a cutaway evening suit and a more modish, less formal dinner jacket or tuxedo suit were both essential. Dozens of shirts and ties were needed to maintain a smart appearance, together with accessories. Lucian Smith's widow claimed for a dress suit, 7 lounge suits and 36 shirts that had belonged to her husband and also for 5 evening dresses, 2 evening gowns, 4 tailored suits and 6 hats in addition to a $1,000 wedding trousseau that included underwear, shoes and gloves which she personally lost.[47] John Snyder lost an expensive dress suit, a fashionable tuxedo suit, 5 lounge suits, 8 silk shirts, 6 fancy dress shirts, 4 plain shirts, 3 flannel shirts, 3 fancy linen shirts and 19 neckties, but only 2 pairs of shoes.[48] In contrast to such extravagance in clothing and even the less expensive claim of second-class passenger Emilio Portaluppi for his loss of 4 worn and 2 new suits in addition to a signed portrait of Garibaldi,[49] was that of Chinese sailor Yum Hee, travelling in steerage, for his one suit and set of working clothes.[50] Of course, the quality and value of this clothing varied from one gentleman to another. Indeed, some of the claims may have inflated the value of the lost clothing, including for new suits, suggesting that some men, as well as their wives and daughters, had indulged in shopping sprees among European tailors. There were distinct national tastes in clothing. Americans preferred broad shoulders, heavy seams, conspicuous flap pockets and low-cut waistcoats, whilst the British preference was for more distinctive patterned cloths and bolder colours but a more subtle and discrete cut and fit for their suits. Such style distinctions would help with the identification of some of the recovered bodies, though many fashion-conscious American men would have purchased their clothes in Europe and died indistinguishable in the same sartorial style as well-off Englishmen.[51]

Whilst a wealthy young dandy like Victor Peñasco would have owned the latest, most fashionable clothing in immaculate condition, despite him having left his valet behind in Paris, other passengers would have been more economical and travelled with older, much-worn clothing, some of it repaired.[52] For those first-class passengers without the assistance on board of their personal menservants, it was possible to call on the services of a clothes presser, 28-year-old Ernest Roskelly Olive, who earned £6 a month and as a trained tailor's cutter, son of a St Pancras tailor who was described as a 'sartorial artist', could effect any repairs needed as well as ensuring that the clothes of his passengers were sharply pressed.[53] It was the obvious quality of their clothing that would have distinguished the recovered bodies of first-class victims from others. Second-class passengers, many of them from professional, clerical, academic and business backgrounds, followed a similar dress code but spent less on maintaining respectability without the style and quality of the clothing of their social betters. Whilst Alfred Nourney spent $30 on each of his ten suits[54] and Lucien Smith $85 for his,[55] a decent made-to-measure suit could be got for 30–90 shillings or $7.30–$21.90, with suits in the range of 40–50 shillings or $9.73–$12.16 the most common in 1912. A suit made from lower-grade serge or tweed could cost about £1. Readymade clothes were also becoming more common with suits costing from 14s 9d to £1 or $3.59–$4.87, and many working men would pick up second-hand clothing for considerably less.[56] The clothing of many passengers travelling in third class was coarser than that of those travelling in higher classes and much less stylish, which made it even easier to distinguish them from their social betters. The worn clothing of many emigrants travelling in third class is represented by the humble suitcase recovered from the *Titanic* wreck in 2000 of William Henry Allen, a 35-year-old Birmingham toolmaker. Neatly packed for a new life, his case contained his best black woollen three-piece suit, stiff shirt collars, smart shoes and worn work shoes, socks and darning wool, as well as a pocket watch and sterling silver matchbox still containing matches.[57] Inequality in clothing truly denoted class differences among the passengers on *Titanic*.

The style and fabric of women's clothing was also what marked out the social status of passengers in each class. However, it was not so important as a factor in identifying what class a passenger belonged to as the majority of the recovered bodies were of third-class women passengers, most of them wearing respectable blouses, skirts and jackets under their coats. A working-class woman could expect to spend up to 44 shillings for a costume, 8s for a dress and 10s 7d for the hat without which she would never venture into company.[58] These women could not compete in extravagance with socialite Charlotte Drake Cardeza, who had boarded with 14 trunks, 4 suitcases, and 3 crates of baggage containing at least 841 individual items, for which she was claiming $177,352.75 in insurance. Her claim ran to twenty pages. It listed 32 dresses, 10 suits, 6 gowns, 6 fur coats, 90 pairs of gloves, 32 pairs of shoes, 23 veils, 11 hats, 41 pairs of stockings, 18 nightgowns, 46 hat pins, 44 handkerchiefs, 29 ostrich feathers, and 2 pairs of garters. She also claimed for a $300 white lace embroidered umbrella, a 6.5-carat diamond ring valued at $20,000, 69 other pieces of jewellery, and $5,600 in cash.[59] By comparison, Margaret Brown's claim for 6 dinner gowns, 15 dresses, 3 satin evening gowns, a sealskin jacket, 2 kimonos and 14 hats seems modest.[60] Passengers on the *Carpathia* noticed the first-class women and what they wore when saved, and that 'there were few men in the boats. The women were the gamest lot I have ever seen. Some of the men and women were in evening clothes, and others among those saved had nothing on but night clothes and raincoats.'[61] The clothing of humbler passengers, and indeed their presence, went unremarked.

It was from the inferior style and quality of his clothes that Edwin Keeping, valet to George Widener, was identified despite his body having been initially thought to be that of his master. A letter addressed to George Widener at the Paris Ritz had been found in the pocket of a badly mutilated body and was assumed to be that of Widener. However, the black suit and striped shirt worn by the man were of 'inferior quality' to anything Widener would have owned and his grey overcoat had the initials 'E.K.' sewn into it. Now identified as the manservant rather than the master, the body was buried at sea instead of being brought ashore as would have happened if it had been Widener. Even so, an element of doubt remained, especially when Widener's younger son George arrived in Halifax to claim his father's body. Only once young Widener had examined the man's personal effects, including a locket with photographs of Keeping's wife and 3-year-old daughter, a gold pocket watch and chain, a diamond and ruby tiepin and a cigarette case, was he satisfied that it was the valet and not his father who had been committed to the deep.[62]

There were similar problems in identifying the body of Richard Frazar White because of the damage to the cadaver from the wreck. Keeping's face had been rendered unrecognisable by collision with the wreckage, White's features and body had aged in the sea. He was returning from a trip to Europe with his cotton manufacturer father Percival, intended to celebrate the end of his studies at Bowdoin College and in advance of his graduation. When Richard's body was recovered wearing a brown suit and white shoes, it was so battered and bruised that he was thought to be aged 37 although he was actually a fresh-faced 21-year-old. He was identified by his bloodstone ring, fraternity tiepin and gold watch. However, his family were not satisfied that it was indeed him and his best friend and fellow Delta Kappa Epsilon fraternity member, Frank Arthur Smith, was despatched to Halifax, where he spent his thirtieth birthday identifying the body. Meanwhile, Bowdoin College sent a copy of his physical examination report, which listed his physical characteristics, not sparing such personal but conclusive details as his knock-knees and round shoulders.[63]

Without any personal identification from someone who knew the deceased, the evidence of clothing could be deceptive. Leonard Mark Hickman of Fritham, Hampshire, had emigrated to Manitoba in 1908. On a visit home, he had persuaded two of his brothers and four friends to emigrate to Canada as farm labourers with him. Although they had booked third class, the 1912 coal strike meant that they had to transfer to another ship and were upgraded to second class. Out of the seven young men travelling together, only one body was recovered and identified as that of Leonard Hickman. An active member of a friendly society in Neepawa, Manitoba, Hickman was so popular with his fellow members of the Foresters Lodge that they paid for his body to be buried in Neepawa, where he had settled. However, when the body arrived at the church it was that of a fair-haired older man rather than the dark-haired, clean-shaven, 24-year-old Leonard Hickman. Too late to cancel the funeral, the burial went ahead as planned although Hickman's employer, Harold Honeyman, realised that they were burying the wrong man. Viewing of the body was not allowed because 'it was in the water for two weeks, and more than one week enroute from the scene of death'. Nevertheless, the local newspaper reported that:

The body was remarkably well preserved and the features were readily recognized by acquaintances who were permitted to view the remains. Thus was laid to rest the remains of Leonard Hickman, an efficient

English farm labourer. Had he been a state dignitary or a millionaire, there might have been more pomp, but there could not have been more genuine sorrow and respect manifested.[64]

Only after the dead man's possessions were returned to the Hickman family in Hampshire did the wife of Leonard's elder brother Lewis, aged 32, recognise a silver watch and chain, tie clip, cigarette case and an amber cigarette holder as the property of her husband. The initial confusion had arisen because Leonard's membership card for the Foresters had been found in the pocket of the green overcoat the dead man was wearing over his dark suit and 'fancy vest'.[65]

The bodies of members of the crew were treated unceremoniously:

> The first bodies taken ashore were those of the crew. These bodies had not been embalmed or even sewn up in canvas (they had been kept in the ice-filled hold) and presented a gruesome sight that it would be impossible to picture. The bodies were carried on stretchers by members of the *Mackay-Bennett* crew and at times as many as 30–40 bodies were in a heap on the deck where they had been taken from the ice-filled hold. It is reported that to get the bodies on to the stretchers and later into the coffins many of the frozen limbs had to be broken.[66]

Yet, in the confusion of the recovery of the corpses of victims, errors of classification were made and the social order subverted: some members of the crew were brought back for burial on land in the finest of Savile Row tailoring, in the coffins reserved exclusively for first-class passengers. Some of them, seeking warmer clothing that might help them to survive in the icy waters, had presumably helped themselves to the bespoke suits and heavy overcoats of the gentlemen they had served from the abandoned staterooms, and, being in death exceedingly dapper and well turned out, had been afforded the respect accorded exclusively to first-class passengers, only for their true identities to emerge when their personal effects were properly examined before their corpses were prepared for embalming and burial.[67]

However, there were too few coffins or canvas sacks and too little embalming fluid for all the recovered bodies to be treated equally and brought ashore.

Under Canadian port regulations, a corpse could not be taken ashore from a ship unless it had been embalmed so not all the bodies recovered could be landed. The severely disfigured and unidentified corpses were selected for burial at sea, though primarily from the lower classes. Only 0.8 per cent of the people buried at sea came from first class, but these men made up 15.6 per cent of the bodies embalmed and brought to shore for burial. Second-class passengers made up 11.3 per cent of those brought ashore and 6.7 per cent were buried at sea. Third-class passengers represented 13.2 per cent of those brought to shore and 19.3 per cent of the men, women and children buried at sea. The figures certainly point to a bias based on class among the passengers, and even more so in attitudes towards the crew, whose bodies were the most numerous to be recovered, and they made up 43.6 per cent of those who were brought to shore, and 59.6 per cent of those buried at sea.[68] Without the confusion over their identities based on purloined clothing, even more of the crew may have been buried at sea. Class prejudice and deference to social elites dictated how the dead would be treated.

Priority was given to the recovery and preservation of the bodies of first-class passengers since proof of their deaths was more likely to be needed for insurance claims and the probate of their estates. Frederick Larnder, the captain of the *Mackay-Bennett*, admitted this:

> No prominent man was recommitted to the deep. It seemed best to embalm as quickly as possible in those cases where large property might be involved. It seemed best to be sure to bring back to land the dead where the death might give rise to such questions as large insurance and inheritance and all the litigation.[69]

If the body of a wealthy passenger was not recovered, there was always the possibility of legal difficulties in settling an estate. Although his wife and her maid survived the sinking, Victor Peñasco perished and his body was never recovered, which caused problems for his family. Unable to hold a funeral service and in the absence of a grave, his family had annual masses held in his memory in a number of Madrid churches. His family were said to have later paid for and registered an unidentified and unidentifiable, badly battered and decomposed body that was picked up at sea as his corpse in order to prove his death and obtain the death certificate necessary for his wife to inherit and even remarry. The death of Victor Peñasco y Castellana, 'gentleman, born 24 October 1887 in Madrid, son of Hilario Peñasco de la Puente and Purificación Castellana, drowned at sea in the shipwreck of the *Titanic*, 15 April 1912', was registered in folio 15 of the Halifax death registers and attested by the Spanish vice-consul in Canada.[70] This legal fiction was eased by the strong political connections of his family. His grandfather, Víctor Peñasco y Otero, from whom the family wealth derived, was a wealthy merchant, a member of the Madrid City Council, Commander of the Order of Isabel la Católica, and had been a close friend of the liberal Progressive politician General Juan Prim, prime minister in 1868–9. His father, Hilario Peñasco de la Puente, had been a lawyer and conservative councillor of the city of Madrid. His widowed mother, Purificación Castellana, daughter of the surgeon Laureano de la Castellana Moreno, had subsequently married Julián Suárez Inclán, the brother-in-law of the liberal politician José Canalejas, who was prime minister from 1910 until his assassination in 1912. His wife, María Josefa Pérez de Soto y Vallejo, was the daughter of the financier Manuel Pérez de Soto, President of the Madrid Provincial Council.[71] With such connections backed by great wealth there was no problem in securing the inheritance though little concern was given to the disposal of the unknown corpse appropriated as that of Victor Peñasco, which was quickly consigned back to the oblivion from which it had come. In the anonymity of death, the poised arrogance of the elegant young man met its hubris in the squalid depersonalisation of the decomposed corpse in which distinctions of wealth were reduced to the same level.

As insurance companies often required an identified body, it was not always easy to make a claim against policies. The family of Ervin G. Lewy, a Chicago jeweller, had to press their claim hard for an insurance payout of $20,000 from the Illinois Life Insurance Company in the absence of a body, and because 'there were no undertaker's or doctor's certificates of death ... the company had to strain several points in allowing the claim'.[72] By contrast, the Metropolitan Life Insurance Company of Buffalo, New York, was quick to pay out £1,000 to the brother of third-class passenger and coach trimmer Henry Sutehall and 'no papers or documentation of any kind were required by the company before making the payment'.[73]

Everything possible was done in Halifax to make it easy for the friends and relatives of first-class passengers to identify and repatriate the corpses for which they were searching. Waldo Sessions, the undertaker sent to collect shoe manufacturer Walter Porter, was impressed by the efficiency of the operation. Within an hour of arriving at the curling rink in Halifax where the bodies, some of them 'black from exposure and injuries', were laid out in rows, he had identified Porter and transferred his body to the railroad station to return him to Worcester, Massachusetts, for burial, keen to get away before 'the rush'. It helped that he had a letter of introduction to the medical examiner of Halifax, Dr Finn, from a local physician who had been Finn's roommate as a fellow medical student at Columbia College, but influence was to expedite matters for the wealthy and important:

> The White Star Line people are giving the people there every possible courtesy and the officials and all the people of Halifax are extremely courteous. The hotels are all crowded and the city is packed with people. I was surprised to find Mr. Porter's body in such a fine state of preservation. Everybody is trying to assist in the identification of bodies and in getting them to parts of the country where they belong. All the ordinary red tape accompanying the transportation of bodies through the country is being waived to railroads and state officials. Usually there are strict laws to be complied with and hermetically sealed caskets are demanded by the law in the transportation of bodies on trains. All of this is being waived by the officials and it helps greatly.[74]

Everything was 'systematic' and 'very much business-like'. At the Mayflower Curling Rink, the coffins were laid out in rows on the main floor waiting to be viewed and for identifications to be made by friends and family of the deceased. A large empty room upstairs was where 'the packets of clothing were distributed in rows upon the floor' in case they might be needed to help with the identification of the people who had once worn the garments. The canvas bags containing personal effects were in the custody of the Provincial Cashier.

When a body had been claimed, the contents of the effects bags would be released once an affidavit had been made by the duly authorised representative of the executor or next of kin. The medical examiner meanwhile issued death certificates and the registrar released burial permits. This temporary morgue also contained a desk for railway tickets and a lunch counter serving refreshments to the 'weary workers'.[75]

Even in mourning, class distinction remained strong. As families waited for news of victims and survivors, they were popularly depicted as united by a common sorrow at a time when 'wealth and society rubbed elbows in the crowd that besieged the steamship line officials, and both classes were in deep sorrow'.[76] Thronging the pavement outside the White Star Line offices in Broadway, New York, were 'multitudes of pallid men and women with swollen eyes'.[77] When the news of the disaster had reached New York, the theatres on Broadway had emptied as 'many friends and relatives of the passengers of the *Titanic* motored in evening dress from the opera and from the theatre to the offices of the White Star Company'.[78] They were joined by the relatives of third-class passengers who 'came in a swarm to fight their way into the jammed offices and wail for information', though 'they chattered and wept and wailed in vain'.[79] Amongst this melee, 'fashionably gowned women whose friends rode in the deluxe state rooms of the liner are mingling with and confiding their grief to women in shawls and shabby bonnets.'[80] Yet, the wealthy received all the attention, with only the names of first- and second-class survivors being posted. A similar array of the rich in top hats, frock coats and modish millinery and the poor in flat caps and shawls crowded outside the White Star Line offices in Cockspur Street and Leadenhall Street waiting for news.[81] In Liverpool, with which many crew members had strong local connections, 'it was an all absorbing topic which appealed equally to all classes, rich and poor, young and old'.[82] Yet, the emphasis in the press remained on the wealthy. It was observed that 'nowhere is the fate of the liner being discussed more feelingly than in the big London hotels, where the most notable of the travellers stayed while in the Metropolis'.[83] Similarly, from Paris it was reported that 'there is hardly a leading hotel without visitors having relatives and friends on board'.[84]

It was an important part of the public mourning process to hold a proper funeral and the wealthier of the passengers were returned home to be appropriately buried by their families. The funeral of John Jacob Astor on 4 May 1912 was a suitably lavish affair. Flags were at half-mast and business in New York stopped while the funeral took place. Police officers had to control the 'curious crowd' of onlookers and keep them at a 'respectful distance'. The day after Astor was buried next to his mother, a funeral service was preached at Trinity Church in Manhattan. Astor's son Vincent had insisted that only the formal service of the Episcopal Church should be used in a gesture towards dignified simplicity, but one tradition of Astor funerals was not followed:

> 'Nearer My God to Thee', which for years has been sung at the funerals of the Astors, was omitted, as it was feared the strains of the hymn, which was the last played by the bandsmen on the *Titanic*, might cause the collapse of Mrs. Madeline Force Astor, the bereaved bride.[85]

Equally impressive that same day was the funeral of department store buyer George Graham:

> One of the largest funerals ever witnessed at Harriston was held on Saturday upon the arrival of a special train from Toronto, bringing the remains of Mr George Graham. The train was made up of five coaches, including The *Eatonia*, the private car of the company president, Mr J.C. Eaton. It arrived at the Canadian Pacific Railway depot at 11 a.m. and from which the remains were conveyed to the Methodist Church, where services were conducted, after which the remains were taken to the Harriston cemetery. The floral tributes were beautiful and required special conveyances. All business in the town was suspended and the town flag was at half-mast.[86]

Despite his aristocratic connections, Tyrell Cavendish was cremated also on 4 May at North Bergen in New Jersey at a simple funeral service conducted according to the rites of the Episcopal Church, and his ashes were returned to London to be interred in the newly built East Columbarium at Golders Green Cemetery.[87] His wife also built the Tyrell William Cavendish Memorial Hall for the villagers of Thurston in Suffolk, where the couple had bought a house they had never occupied and which Julia Cavendish sold not long after she lost her husband.[88] The body of another Englishman rather than his ashes was returned to his home for a burial that was more lavish than that of first-class passenger Cavendish. Over 500 people attended the funeral on 30 May of 19-year-old Cornish miner William Carbines at St Ives. The St Ives Town Band led the lengthy funeral cortège, with 'the body, dressed in a black suit, with collar and tie, visible through a glass slide' in an oak coffin stained to resemble mahogany. The curtains and blinds were drawn in all the houses on the route of the procession as a mark of respect.[89]

If there was no corpse to be interred, the rites of mourning were still observed and sumptuous memorials erected. On the first Sunday after the disaster, a grieving Eleanor Widener attended a memorial service for her husband and son in the chapel of the Widener Home for Crippled Children in Philadelphia. Although her father-in-law was too distraught to leave his room, the service was attended by other members of the Widener and Elkins families, prominent Philadelphian families and ninety-eight disabled boys and girls.[90] George and Harry Widener were both remembered by brass cenotaphs in the family mausoleum at Laurel Hill Cemetery near Philadelphia, giving them in death the same prominence among the Wideners they had enjoyed in life. Eleanor Widener Dixon commemorated her father and brother by commissioning Louis Comfort Tiffany to design and manufacture stained glass windows for St Paul's Episcopal Church, Elkins Park, in 1913. George was commemorated in a window depicting Christ the Good Shepherd, whilst, appropriately for a book lover, the window dedicated to Harry features St John the Evangelist holding his Gospel.[91] Harry was to be further commemorated through the Harry Elkins Widener Memorial Library at his beloved Harvard and the Harry Elkins Widener Memorial Building of Arts and Crafts at Hill School.[92] On his cenotaph in the Cimetière Mont-Royal, the thrusting businessman Thornton Davidson was hailed as having 'died in the foundering of the SS *Titanic* April 15 1912 and thus this man died leaving his death as an example of a noble courage and a memorial of virtue'. Keen motorists and progressive managers Thomas Pears and Washington Roebling were both commemorated by inscriptions added to existing family tombs but Charles G. Roebling, a prominent member of the Trinity Episcopal Church in Trenton, later had the west wall of the church rebuilt as a memorial to his son.[93] The dynamic ex-mayor of Chelsea and patron of the arts Christopher Head was remembered for his interest in gardening and town planning by a simple memorial sundial in the Cadogan Place gardens, of which he had been honorary secretary. Even the personable yet hard-drinking and heavy gambling Walter Clark was to be commemorated in the Walter Clark Memorial Community Church at Lakewood, California, built by his family in 1937 in a town they had developed.

The 150 corpses who remained unidentifiable or whose families had not requested and paid for them to be returned home were buried in Halifax. Any unclaimed effects were burned along with the packets of clothing recovered from the corpses. Intended to prevent these relics falling into the wrong hands and becoming morbid mementos of the sinking, the result of this policy was to destroy what remained of the identity of the victims and reduce them to a common level of anonymity. Ten passengers thought to be Jewish were buried at Baron de Hirsch and nineteen Roman Catholics at Mount Olivet cemeteries in individual graves, but the majority of the burials were at Fairview Cemetery in three long trenches. With 121 bodies to be committed, shortcuts were necessary and the funerals were timely considering that 'the weather is becoming so warm that the undertakers are finding it difficult in preserving the bodies, especially some of those which were hurriedly embalmed at sea'.[94] The White Star Line had informed the bereaved that 'it has been arranged for the bodies, it has been possible to bring to shore by the steamer to Halifax, to be buried in single graves with head stone bearing the name of deceased, at the Company's own expense'.[95] Such a gesture may have been appreciated by the bereaved, but less tactful was the letter received from the company by the brother of Sixth Officer James Paul Moody, informing him that:

> Should you after further consideration desire the remains of your brother to be returned will you kindly telegraph us in the morning at the same time sending us a deposit of £20 for any expenses and land charges on the other Side and we will at once cable New York asking them to arrange this if practicable. We also think it right to point out that the arrangements and expenses for taking charge of the remains after arrival of the steamer at Liverpool or Southampton would be on your account.

They suggested that Moody's remains should be buried in Halifax and that they would send his family 'a photograph of the tombstone'. What makes the letter seem especially callous is that the body of James Moody was never recovered.[96]

For the ordinary members of the *Titanic* crew, public memorials, raised by subscription, recognised their loss. At Southampton, where many of the crew had lived, a memorial to the ship's musicians was unveiled in April 1913, featuring a weeping woman next to an iceberg and the opening bars of the hymn 'Nearer My God to Thee'. Then, in April 1914, the *Titanic* Engineers' Memorial, featuring a statue of Nike, the Greek Winged Goddess of Victory, and carved panels showing the engineer officers of the ship who died in the disaster, was dedicated in front of 100,000 people. There was also a plaque commemorating the postal staff lost on *Titanic* erected in the Southampton Docks Post Office, which has since been relocated to the Guildhall. It was not until 27 July 1915 that all the crew were commemorated, rather than particular occupations, by a fountain of Portland stone unveiled on Southampton Common, and, after vandalism, moved to its current site in the ruins of the bombed-out Holyrood Church.[97] A Memorial to the Engine Room Heroes of the *Titanic* was erected in Liverpool, close to the White Star Line offices, but by the time it was completed in 1915 it was no longer just a monument to the lost of the *Titanic* but had also become a war memorial as the Merchant Navy suffered heavy losses during the First World War. Consisting of a granite obelisk with representations of the elements on four corners, naturalistic life-sized statues of stokers and engineers stand on its east and west sides in a celebration of working-class heroism on *Titanic* and in the war at sea.[98] The Great War also delayed until 26 June 1920 the construction and dedication of a *Titanic* Memorial in Belfast to both crew and members of the guarantee group, who were technically passengers, from the city. It features a statue of Death, or Fate, holding a laurel wreath over the head of a drowned sailor who is raised above the waves by a pair of mermaids.[99] In New York, the *Titanic* Lighthouse Memorial was erected on the roof of the headquarters of the Seamen's Institute Church in 1913.[100] In many ways, this plethora of dedicated structures anticipated the style and intent of the memorials that within a few years were to be erected in honour of the casualties of the Great War with their commemoration of the war dead of all ranks.

It was the humble yet heroic figures of the crew that were publicly memorialised. For passengers, the monuments tended to be personal to individuals rather than to all those lost. The memorial fountain to Butt and Millet in Washington, DC may have been on federal land and dedicated to the two close friends on the grounds that they were both federal government officials, Butt as presidential aide and Millet as vice-chairman of the United States Commission of Fine Arts, yet was still a tribute to two individuals, indicated by bas relief figures representing military valour and the arts.[101] A memorial to those male passengers deemed to have sacrificed their lives was planned within weeks of the disaster as 'the tribute of woman to heroic manhood'.[102] The Women's *Titanic* Memorial Fund was endorsed by the wives of prominent politicians with First Lady Helen Taft symbolically donating the first dollar to the appeal 'in gratitude to the chivalry of American manhood'.[103] The statue, designed by Gertrude Vanderbilt Whitney, and unveiled by Mrs Taft on 26 May 1931, is of a 13-foot-tall partly clad male figure holding out his arms as if to welcome death.[104] Despite criticisms at the launch of the appeal asking, 'Why not instead of having the memorial solely for the heroes of the wreck, have it also for the heroines?' the monument remained 'a worthy remembrance of that splendid group, from the bellboy and the stoker to the army officer and capitalist, who faced death with intrepidity which upholds our ideals and gives fresh impetus for the life of our nation'.[105] In its paean to masculine chivalry it reflects the attitudes of its time and reinforces the myth of upper-class male nobility harnessed to save the defenceless and weak woman, however different the reality. Even the monuments perpetuate the class and gender divisions revealed by the sinking of the *Titanic*.

What happened in the early hours of 15 April 1912 derives its significance in revealing a snapshot of the realities behind the myths of a society and its attitudes at a moment of crisis. It did not change the world, other than reforms of benefit to maritime safety, but it brings into focus the tensions and fixed positions of a patriarchal and class-ridden world that was already facing challenges to its certainties and its illusions about itself. Walter Lord, in his haunting recreation of the sinking in *A Night to Remember*, wrote that:

> Before the *Titanic*, all was quiet. Afterward all was tumult. That is why, to anybody who lived at the time, the *Titanic* more than any other single event marks the end of the old days, and the beginning of a new, uneasy era.[106]

Despite the symbolism Lord attached to the disaster, it was not the totemic end of an era, nor did the world suddenly change; and it is an overstatement to say that it 'marked the end of a general feeling of confidence'. It was rather a moment captured in time of a society as it saw itself whatever the underlying reality. The emphasis on chivalry and manliness may have been reaction to the demands from suffragettes, the unions and political reformers for social change, but was also a reflection of the society that produced it. In their relationships with other passengers, their social attitudes and their preconceptions of how to behave in a disaster, the victims and survivors on *Titanic* were actors in a drama playing roles that were conditioned by the expectations of the world to which they belonged. That world came crashing down for them with the breaking up of the stage set, the ship, against which their complex relationships and dramas had been played out, leaving only the stark reality of life and death where any perceived protection from modern technology and opulence was nothing more than illusory. That is what makes the story of the *Titanic* as a vignette of the wider world so fascinating and the hubris its sinking evoked so compelling, to this day.

Notes

Chapter One: Sunken Palace of the Sea

1. *The Sphere*, 4 May 1912.
2. Ibid., 10 May 1912.
3. *Sunday Times*, 21 April 1912.
4. *Roscommon Messenger*, 1 January 1910.
5. R. Davenport-Hines, *Titanic Lives* (2012), p. 174.
6. A. Gracie, *The Truth about the Titanic* (1913), p. 253.
7. F. Young, *Titanic* (1912), p. 24.
8. *Belfast Evening Telegraph*, 15 April 1912.
9. N. Barratt, *Lost Voices from the Titanic* (2009), p. 99.
10. L. Duff-Gordon, *Discretions and Indiscretions* (1932), p. 149.
11. Ibid., p. 154.
12. *Northern Daily Mail*, 11 April 1912.
13. R. Davenport-Hines, *Titanic Lives* (2012), p. 73.
14. *Seattle Daily Times*, 22 April 1912.
15. *Belfast Evening Telegraph*, 15 April 1912.
16. A. Gracie, *The Truth about the Titanic* (1913), p. 11.
17. *Seattle Daily Times*, 22 April 1912.
18. *Western Daily Press*, 4 April 1912.
19. L. Duff-Gordon, *Discretions and Indiscretions* (1932), p. 150.
20. Hearing Before a Subcommittee of the Committee on Commerce, United States Senate: Sixty-second Congress, Second Session, Pursuant to S Res 283, Directing the Committee on Commerce to Investigate the Causes Leading to the Wreck of the White Star Liner *Titanic*, 1912, pp. 486–7. Hereafter cited as American Inquiry.
21. *El Paso Herald*, 20 May 1912.
22. *Debrett's Peerage, Baronetage, Knightage and Companionage* (1911); *Windham Club Rules and Regulations with a List of Members* (1911).
23. A. Gracie, *The Truth about the Titanic* (1913), p. 12.
24. L. Beesley, *The Loss of the SS Titanic* (1912), p. 12.

25. A. Gracie, *The Truth about the Titanic* (1913), pp. 5–6.
26. K. Brown, *Poxed and Scurvied* (2011), pp. 148–9.
27. Ibid., p. 149.
28. *Acton Gazette*, 11 July 1958.
29. *New York Tribune*, 30 April 1912.
30. *Trenton Evening Times*, 17 April 1912.
31. *Ilford Graphic*, 12 May 1912.
32. *Belfast Evening Telegraph*, 15 April 1912.
33. N. Barratt, *Lost Voices from the Titanic* (2009), p. 100.
34. *Semi-Monthly Magazine*, May 1912.
35. L. Beesley, *The Loss of the SS Titanic* (1912), p. 41.
36. N. Barratt, *Lost Voices from the Titanic* (2009), p. 101.
37. *Belfast Evening Telegraph*, 15 April 1912.
38. *Newark Star*, 20 April 1912.
39. *New York Times*, 16 January 1913.
40. *Economist*, 20 April 1912.
41. W.H. Martin and S. Mason, *Edward FitzGerald's Rubáiyát of Omar Khayyám: a Famous Poem and its Influence* (2011), pp. 124–5.
42. L. Beesley, *The Loss of the SS Titanic* (1912), p. 14.
43. *Philadelphia Inquirer*, 21 April 1912.
44. *English Review*, May 1912.
45. *Southern Daily Echo*, 23 April 1912.
46. *Illustrated London News*, 11 May 1912.
47. A.E. Larabee, 'The American Hero and His Mechanical Bride: Gender Myths of the Titanic Disaster', *American Studies* 31/1 (1990), 6.
48. T. McCluskie, *Anatomy of the Titanic* (1998), p. 22.
49. A. Gill, *Titanic* (2010), p. 148.
50. *Daily Mirror*, 16 April 1912.
51. L. Beesley, *The Loss of the SS Titanic* (1912), p. 6.
52. A. Gill, *Titanic* (2010), p. 165.
53. S. 6412, An Act to Regulate Radio Communication, 20 May 1912.
54. *Chicago Daily Journal*, 16 April 1912.
55. A. Gracie, *The Truth about the Titanic* (1913), p. 11.
56. *Dundee Evening Telegraph*, 29 June 1935.
57. British Inquiry final report, pp. 45–6. Report of a Formal Investigation into the Circumstances Attending the Foundering on 15th April, 1912, of the British Steamship *Titanic*, Cd 3352, pp. 45–6. Hereafter cited as British Inquiry.
58. *English Review*, May 1912.
59. British Inquiry, Q 21267.

60. Ibid., Q 21321.
61. K. Brown, *Passage to the World* (2013), p. 233.
62. *The Times*, 26 February 1903.
63. *Economist*, 26 April 1902.
64. *Fairplay*, 25 May 1905.
65. *Economist*, 1 June 1907.
66. *Evening Telegraph*, 23 April 1912.
67. *Chicago Record-Herald*, 19 April 1912.
68. *Liverpool Daily Post*, 1 December 1899.
69. *Daily Sketch*, 5 June 1912.
70. *The Standard*, 7 January 1907.
71. *Review of Reviews*, March 1912.
72. *Daily Mirror*, 17 April 1912.
73. *Irish Independent*, 23 April 1908.
74. D. Finamore and G. Wood, *Ocean Liners* (2017), pp. 32, 34.
75. *Irish Independent*, 18 September 1909.
76. A. Gracie, *The Truth about the Titanic* (1913), pp. 4–5.
77. *Northern Daily Mail*, 8 April 1912.
78. *Sunday Independent*, 18 February 1912.
79. *Freeman's Journal*, 3 March 1909.
80. *The Times*, 1 November 1909.
81. *Freeman's Journal*, 13 July 1909.
82. S.F. Bullock, *Thomas Andrews Shipbuilder* (1912), p. 21.
83. Ibid., p. 61.
84. *English Review*, May 1912.
85. Thomas Hardy, *Selected Shorter Poems* (1968), pp. 45–6.
86. *Binghamton Press*, 29 April 1912.
87. N. Barratt, *Lost Voices from the Titanic* (2009), p. 107.
88. American Inquiry, p. 530.
89. D. Hyslop, A. Forsyth and S. Jemima, *Titanic Voices* (1994), p. 27.
90. *Acton Gazette*, 11 July 1958.
91. Ibid., 25 July 1958.
92. American Inquiry, p. 530.
93. *Binghamton Press*, 29 April 1912.
94. D. Hyslop, A. Forsyth and S. Jemima, *Titanic Voices* (1994), p. 126.
95. Ibid., p. 89.
96. *Scarborough News*, 12 April 2019; for other correspondence of James Moody see I. Sheil, *Titanic Valour: The Life of Fifth Officer Harold Lowe* (2011).
97. V. Jessop, *Titanic Survivor* (1998), p. 117.

98. *Belfast Evening Telegraph*, 15 April 1912.
99. British Inquiry, Q 18825.
100. L. Beesley, *The Loss of the SS Titanic* (1912), p. 36.

Chapter Two: Manly Heroes in Evening Suits

1. L. Marshall, *The Sinking of the Titanic* (1912), p. 46.
2. *North American*, 20 April 1912.
3. M. Everett, *Wreck and Sinking of the Titanic* (1912), p. 188.
4. *Washington Post*, 19 April 1912.
5. *Daily Mirror*, 13 May 1912.
6. *Leicester Daily Post*, 17 April 1012.
7. *Washington Post*, 18 April 1912.
8. *Denver Post*, 27 May 1912.
9. *Philadelphia North American*, 4 May 1912.
10. L. Marshall, *The Sinking of the Titanic* (1912), p. 54.
11. W.T. Stead, *The Blue Island: Experiences of a New Arrival Beyond the Veil* (1922), pp. 37–8.
12. F. Young, *Titanic* (1912), p. 82.
13. *New York Times*, 10 September 1911.
14. A. Gracie, *The Truth about the Titanic* (1913), p. 30.
15. *Chicago Herald Record*, 22 April 1912; *New York Times*, 22 April 1912.
16. *Brooklyn Daily Eagle*, 19 April 1912.
17. *Washington Times*, 19 April 1912.
18. *Worcester Evening Gazette*, 19 April 1912.
19. *Worcester Telegram*, 20 April 1912.
20. *New York Times*, 21 April 1912.
21. Ibid., 8 May 1912.
22. Ibid., 20 April 1912.
23. *Washington Times*, 20 April 1912.
24. *Toronto World*, 17 April 1912; *The Times*, 19 April 1912.
25. J.H. Marsh, *The Canadian Encyclopaedia* (1999), p. 1052.
26. *Montreal Daily Herald*, 19 April 1912.
27. *Montreal Herald*, 8 May 1912.
28. J.H. Marsh, *The Canadian Encyclopaedia* (1999), p. 1001.
29. *New York Times*, 24 April 1912.
30. *Dr Alfred Pain – In Memoriam*, Hamilton, published privately, 1912.
31. M. Kerby and M. Baguley, 'When death gave way to glory: Philip Gibbs, RMS Titanic and the Western Front', *International Journal of Maritime History* 34/1 (2022), 46–62.

32. M. Girouard, *The Return to Camelot* (1981), pp. 4–6.
33. *Secretary's First Report of Harvard Class of 1907* (1908), pp. 6, 121, 145, 147–8, 151, 161, 176, 217.
34. *Bowdoin Orient* 42 (23 April 1912), 20.
35. *Toronto World*, 17 April 1912.
36. *The Times*, 4 March 1912.
37. W.H. Atherton, *Montreal 1535–1914: Biographical*, vol. 3 (1914), pp. 80–3.
38. *Montreal Standard*, 17 April 1912.
39. *Dr Alfred Pain – In Memoriam*, Hamilton, published privately, 1912.
40. *Washington Herald*, 18 April 1912.
41. *New York Times*, 16 April 1912.
42. *Leicester Daily Mercury*, 6 November 1911.
43. *Daily Mail*, 16 April 1912.
44. *Walsall Advertiser*, 11 May 1912.
45. *The Times*, 18 April 1912.
46. F. Young, *Titanic*, pp. 83–4.
47. *Trenton Evening Times*, 19 April 1912.
48. 'Nearer My God to Thee', *Clifton Magazine* (2012), 20–21.
49. *The Bridgwater Mercury*, 20 April 1912; *Chicago Daily Journal*, 16 April 1912.
50. TNA, FO 369/522, consular despatch from C.W. Bennett to Foreign Office, 19 April 1912.
51. *Daily Mirror*, 15 May 1912; *Daily Sketch*, 17 April 1912; *New York Times*, 21 April 1912.
52. *Toronto Star*, 19 April 1912.
53. A. Gracie, *The Truth about the Titanic* (1913), p. 3.
54. American Inquiry, p. 395.
55. Ibid., p. 3.
56. *San Francisco Call*, 16 April 1912.
57. Russell, Edith, 'I Was Aboard the Titanic', *Ladies' Home Companion* (May 1964), 88–97; Russell, Edith, 'J'ai Survécu au Naufrage du Titanic', *Moustique*, 12 October 1958, pp. 5–9; 19 October 1958, pp. 5–9; 26 October 1958, pp. 12–15, 14.
58. *USA Today*, 10 April 2017.
59. *Anaconda Standard*, 26 April 1912.
60. Ibid., 26 April, 1912.
61. *Daily Northwestern*, 17 April 1912.
62. L. Beesley, *The Loss of the SS Titanic* (1912), pp. 61–2.
63. *American Medicine* 18 (1912), 271.
64. *New York Times*, 21 September 1911.
65. *Daily Republican*, 19 April 1912.
66. R. Rondeau, *Titanic Lives: On Board, Destination Canada* (2012), p. 74.

67. *Surrey Comet*, 3 September 2004.
68. L. Beesley, *The Loss of the SS Titanic* (1912), p. 21.
69. Ibid., p. 21.
70. *Calgary Herald*, 20 April 1912.
71. *The Times*, 18 April 1912; *Western Daily Mercury*, 18 April 1912.
72. *The Times*, 26 April 1912.
73. L. Beesley, *The Loss of the SS Titanic* (1912), p. 67.
74. J.H. Mowbray, *Sinking of the Titanic* (1912), p. 185.
75. *Anaconda Standard*, 26 April 1912.
76. *Western Times*, 16 April 1912.
77. J.H. Mowbray, *Sinking of the Titanic* (1912), p. 97.
78. L. Marshall, *The Sinking of the Titanic* (1912), p. 100.
79. S. Martínez Cotos, 'Shots under Titanic's Shadow: The Tragedy of a Spanish Multimillionaire Family and its Unknown Connection with an Assassination', *Titanic Commutator* 205 (2014), 4–12.
80. J. Geller, *Women and Children First* (1998), p. 61.
81. *El Heraldo de Madrid*, 13 April 1917.
82. *La Correspondencia militar*, 22 April 1912.
83. *El Heraldo de Madrid*, 23 April 1912.
84. *Washington Times*, 16 April 1912; *New York Times*, 16 April 1912; ibid., 17 April 1912.
85. J.H. Mowbray, *Sinking of the Titanic* (1912), p. 179.
86. *Denver Post*, 27 May 1912.
87. *New York Post*, 19 April 1912.
88. *Uttoxeter Advertiser and Ashbourne Times*, 8 May 1912.
89. A. Gracie, *The Truth about the Titanic* (1913), p. 27.
90. A.E. Newton, 'A Word in Memory, a Remembrance of Harry Elkins Widener', *The Atlantic* (1918), 355.
91. Ibid., 356.
92. *Telegraph*, 5 June 1912.
93. *Harvard Library Bulletin* 6 (1951), 248–9.
94. Emma Smith, *Portable Magic: A History of Books and their Readers* (2022), pp. 106–107.
95. P.A.B. Widener II, *Without Drums* (1940), p. 88.
96. A.E. Newton, 'A Word in Memory, a Remembrance of Harry Elkins Widener', *The Atlantic* (1918), 354.
97. *London Review of Books*, 5 June 1997.
98. A.E. Newton, 'A Word in Memory, a Remembrance of Harry Elkins Widener', *The Atlantic* (1918), 354.
99. *American Courier*, 8 January 1913.

100. *New York Times*, 10 July 1914.
101. A.E. Newton, 'A Word in Memory, a Remembrance of Harry Elkins Widener', *The Atlantic* (1918), 351.
102. Ibid., 355.
103. *Register of Wills*, Montgomery County, PA, Book 40, p. 85, 18 May 1912.
104. A.E. Newton, 'A Word in Memory, a Remembrance of Harry Elkins Widener', *The Atlantic* (1918), 355.
105. *The New York Times*, 22 September, 1912.
106. *Boston Sunday Herald*, 10 October 1915; 'Commencement—Dedication of the Library', *The Harvard Graduates' Magazine* 24 (1915), 81–82.
107. *Detroit Saturday Night*, 30 October 1915.
108. *New York Times*, 2 June 1912.
109. *The Nation*, 99 (1914), 101.
110. S. Biel, *Down with the Old Canoe* (1996), p. 95.
111. H. Cabot Lodge, 'The Meaning of a Great Library', *Harvard Graduates' Magazine* (1915), 38.
112. *Hudson Observer*, 20 April 1912.

Chapter Three: The Shame of Survival

1. F. Young, *Titanic* (1912), p. 197.
2. Ibid., p. 188.
3. *Worcester Telegram*, 20 April 1912.
4. J.H. Mowbray, *Sinking of the Titanic* (1912), p. 33.
5. L. Delap, 'Thus Does Man Prove His Fitness to Be the Master of Things: Shipwrecks, Chivalry and Masculinities in Nineteenth- and Twentieth-Century Britain', *Cultural and Social History* 3/1 (2006), 61.
6. S.L. Takis, 'Titanic: A Statistical Exploration', *Mathematics Teacher* 92 (1999), 660–64; TNA, BT 27/780B, Outward Passenger List, Southampton, *Titanic*, 10 April 1912; TNA BT 27/776, Outward Passenger List, Queenstown, *Titanic*, 11 April 1912; TNA, BT 100/259 Agreements and Crew List, *Titanic*, April 1912; TNA, BT 334/52 Register of Deceased Passengers, *Titanic*, 1912.
7. *Philadelphia Evening Bulletin*, 29 April 1912.
8. *Daily Mail*, 30 April 1912.
9. L. Beesley, *The Loss of the SS Titanic* (1912), pp. 81–2.
10. *Daily Mirror*, 17 April 1912.
11. L. Beesley, *The Loss of the SS Titanic* (1912), p. 82
12. Ibid., p. 78.
13. American Inquiry, p. 79.
14. L. Beesley, *The Loss of the Titanic* (1912), p. 72.

15. B.S. Frey, D.A. Savage and B. Torgler, 'Behavior under Extreme Conditions: The Titanic Disaster', *Journal of Economic Perspectives* 25/1 (2011), 217, 220.
16. *Express*, 21 January 2009.
17. *The Daily News*, 14 May 1912.
18. Ibid., 20 May 1912.
19. L. Duff-Gordon, *Discretions and Indiscretions* (1932), p. 167.
20. *The Irish Independent*, 19 April 1912.
21. *Western Daily Mercury*, 29 April 1912.
22. *New York Times*, 22 April 1912.
23. G. Jacub, 'The Shootings on the Titanic: The Only First Class Passenger to be Shot', https://www.williammurdoch.net/articles_31_shootings_on_the_Titanic_02.html
24. *Philadelphia Inquirer*, 20 April 1912.
25. J. Geller, *Women and Children First* (1998), p. 60.
26. *Daily Mail*, 20 April 1912.
27. American Inquiry, p. 209.
28. Ibid., p. 211.
29. Ibid., p. 404.
30. British Inquiry, Q 13872.
31. Ibid., Q 14004.
32. Ibid., Q 14007.
33. *San Francisco Chronicle*, 12 May 1912.
34. *The Bulletin*, 20 April 1912.
35. *Chester Times*, 20 April 1912.
36. *Dowagiac Daily News*, 20 April 1912.
37. Ibid., 26 April 1912.
38. Ibid., 20 April 1912.
39. *New York Herald*, 20 April 1912.
40. *Calgary Herald*, 30 April 1912.
41. *Brooklyn Daily Eagle*, 19 April 1912.
42. *Newark Evening News*, 18 April 1912.
43. *The Bulletin*, 19 April 1912.
44. Ibid., 20 April 1912.
45. *Hartford Courant*, 16 April 1912.
46. N. Barrett, *Lost Voices* (2009), pp. 182–5.
47. *The San Francisco Examiner*, 1 December 1912.
48. *Brooklyn Daily Eagle*, 19 April 1912.
49. L. Marshall, *The Sinking of the Titanic* (1912), p. 165.
50. Ibid., p. 79.

51. *Washington Times*, 22 April 1912.
52. *The Daily News*, 14 May 1912.
53. *The Toronto World*, 20 April 1912.
54. *The Times*, 20 April 1912; American Inquiry, p. 220.
55. *Daily Sketch*, 20 April 1912.
56. *The Witney Gazette*, 11 May 1912.
57. *New York Times*, 18 April 1912.
58. *Chicago Inter Ocean*, 21 April 1912.
59. *New York Herald*, 19 April 1912.
60. W.T. Sloper, 'Ship to Shore: William Sloper's Account of the Titanic Disaster', *Oceanographic Navigation Research Society* (1984), 301–413.
61. *Chicago Examiner*, 19 April 1912.
62. W.T. Sloper, 'Ship to Shore: William Sloper's Account of the Titanic Disaster', *Oceanographic Navigation Research Society* (1984), 301–413.
63. *Cork Examiner*, 6 May 1912.
64. American Inquiry, p. 220.
65. *Burlington Free Press and Times*, 10 July 1913.
66. American Inquiry, p. 220.
67. *Semi-Monthly Magazine*, May 1912.
68. *Dowagiac Daily News*, 20 April 1912.
69. *The Times*, 20 April 1912.
70. *Brooklyn Daily Eagle*, 23 April 1912.
71. *The Salt Lake Tribune*, 28 February 1912.
72. *Chicago American*, 25 April 1912.
73. *New York Sun*, 27 April 1912.
74. *Evening Bulletin*, 16 April 1912.
75. *Washington Herald*, 19 April 1912.
76. L. Beesley, *The Loss of the SS Titanic* (1912), p. 85.
77. A. Gracie, *The Truth about the Titanic* (1913), p. 244.
78. American Inquiry, p. 373.
79. *Calgary Herald*, 21 April 1912.
80. American Inquiry, p. 370.
81. A. Gracie, *The Truth about Titanic* (1913), pp. 67–8.
82. *Evening Banner*, 26 April 1912.
83. A. Gracie and J.B. Thayer, *Titanic: A Survivor's Story and The Sinking of the SS Titanic* (1998), p. 345.
84. *The Times*, 20 April 1912.
85. *New York Sun*, 19 April 1912.
86. *Washington Post*, 19 April 1912.

87. Ibid., 22 April 1912.
88. *New York Press*, 19 April 1912.
89. *The Times*, 20 April 1912.
90. *The Richmond Times-Dispatch*, 22 April 1912.
91. A. Gracie and J.B. Thayer, *Titanic: A Survivor's Story and The Sinking of the SS Titanic* (1998), pp. 340–341.
92. *Washington Post*, 19 April 1912.
93. *New York Press*, 19 April 1912.
94. *New York Tribune*, 19 April 1912.
95. *Baltimore Sun*, 19 April 1912.
96. *Richmond Times-Dispatch*, 22 April 1912.
97. *New York Times*, 19 April 1912.
98. *San Francisco Examiner*, 19 April 1912; *Indianapolis Star*, 19 April 1912.
99. *Philadelphia Inquirer*, 23 April 1912.
100. *New York World*, 19 April 1912.
101. *New York Sun*, 19 April 1912.
102. *Richmond Times-Dispatch*, 22 April 1912.
103. *New York Herald*, 27 October 1914.
104. *New York Times*, 20 April 1912.
105. *The Times*, 21 May 1912.
106. *New York Herald*, 19 April 1912.
107. *New York American*, 19 April 1912.
108. British Inquiry, Q 12923.
109. *Evening World*, 22 April 1912.
110. L. Duff-Gordon, *Discretions and Indiscretions* (1932), p. 177.
111. Final report, British Inquiry, p. 53.
112. L. Duff-Gordon, *Discretions and Indiscretions* (1932), p. 158.
113. *Newark Star*, 24 April 1912.
114. L. Duff-Gordon, *Discretions and Indiscretions* (1932), p. 165.
115. H.G. Wells, *The Labour Unrest* (1912), p. 5.
116. *London Illustrated News*, 18 May 1912.
117. *Washington Times*, 19 April 1912.
118. *Providence Journal*, 20 April 1912.
119. *Camden Post-Telegram*, 15 May 1912.
120. *Evening Bulletin*, 20 April 1912.
121. A. Gracie and J.B. Thayer, *Titanic: A Survivor's Story and The Sinking of the SS Titanic* (1998), p. 341.
122. British Inquiry, Q 10520.
123. American Inquiry, p. 212.

124. *Evening Bulletin*, 20 April 1912.
125. N. Barrett, *Lost Voices* (2009), p. 224.
126. *Rahway Daily Record*, 19 April 1912.
127. *New York Times*, 19 April 1912.
128. N. Barrett, *Lost Voices* (2009), pp. 265–6.; Records of District Courts of the United States, Admiralty Case Files, In the Matter of the Petition of the Oceanic Steam Navigation Company, Limited, for Limitation of its liability as owner of the steamship *Titanic*, minutes, 1912–13, https://catalog.archives.gov/id/6254783 accessed 3 August 2023.
129. *Chicago Daily Journal*, 19 April 1912.
130. American Inquiry, p. 229.
131. A. Gracie and J.B. Thayer, *Titanic: A Survivor's Story and The Sinking of the SS Titanic* (1998), p. 356.
132. *Worcester Evening Gazette*, 20 April 1912.
133. American Inquiry, p. 396.
134. *The Times*, 18 October 1937.
135. *Baltimore Sun*, 19 April 1912.
136. *The New York Times*, 22 April 1912.
137. *Washington Times*, 19 April 1912.
138. *Baltimore Sun*, 18 April 1912.
139. N. Barrett, *Lost Voices* (2009), p. 280.
140. *New York Times*, 23 April 1912.
141. *Baltimore Sun*, 21 January 1915.
142. *Woman's Journal*, 27 April 1912.
143. R. Davenport-Hines, *Titanic Lives* (2012), p. 330.
144. *Denver Post*, 16 April 1912.
145. *Morning Post*, 22 December 1863.
146. L. Delap, '"Thus Does Man Prove His Fitness to Be the Master of Things": Shipwrecks, Chivalry and Masculinities in Nineteenth- and Twentieth-Century Britain', *Cultural and Social History* 3/1 (2006), pp. 49–50.
147. British Inquiry, final report, p. 53.

Chapter Four: Dutiful and Undaunted en Deshabille

1. *The Times*, 20 April 1912.
2. R. Davenport-Hines, *Titanic Lives* (2012), p. 339.
3. American Inquiry, p. 396.
4. Ibid., p. 529.
5. Ibid., p. 492.

6. Public Archives of Nova Scotia, Medical Examiner for City of Halifax, Record of Bodies and Effects: Passengers and Crew, S.S. *Titanic*, RG 41, Series C, vol. 76 no. 172, 1912, https://archives.novascotia.ca/titanic/fatalities/archives/?ID=172 accessed 2 August 2023.
7. *Walsall Advertiser*, 11 May 1912.
8. D. Byatt, *Promises to Pay: The First Three Hundred Years of Bank of England Notes* (1994), p. 114.
9. *Daily Mirror*, 17 April 1912.
10. *Daily Mail*, 16 April 1912.
11. T. Roosevelt, *The Works of Theodore Roosevelt, Strenuous Life* (1901), p. 5.
12. *The Times*, 20 April 1912.
13. A. Gracie, *The Truth about the Titanic* (1913), p. 124.
14. S. Molony, *The Irish Aboard Titanic* (2000), p. 46.
15. American Inquiry, p. 396.
16. A. Gracie, *The Truth about the Titanic* (1913), p. 46.
17. *The Auburn Citizen*, 23 April 1912.
18. American Inquiry, p. 529.
19. *The Bulletin*, 30 April 1912.
20. A. Gracie, *The Truth about the Titanic* (1913), p. 256.
21. C.H. Lightoller, *Titanic and Other Ships* (1935), p. 281.
22. *Leeds Mercury*, 19 April 1912.
23. *Connaught Telegraph*, 25 May 1912.
24. *West Briton and Cornwall Advertiser*, 18 April 1912.
25. P. Gibbs, *The Deathless Story of the Titanic* (1912), p. 2.
26. *San Francisco Chronicle*, 17 April 1912.
27. *New Orleans Times Picayune*, 26 April 1912.
28. *New York Times*, 21 April 1912.
29. *Denver Post*, 18 April 1912.
30. L. Duff-Gordon, *Discretions and Indiscretions* (1932), p. 154.
31. *Dundee Evening Telegraph*, 29 June 1935.
32. *Cornell Alumni News*, 14 (1912), 339.
33. *New York Times*, 23 April 1912.
34. L. Duff-Gordon, *Discretions and Indiscretions* (1932), p. 167.
35. American Inquiry, p. 492.
36. *Worcester Evening Gazette*, 19 April 1912.
37. A. Reynolds, 'True Manhood and Manly Boys: Boys' Adventure Stories, Imperialism, and the Titanic', *Articulāte* 12 (2007), 247.
38. *Boston Post*, 20 April 1912.

39. *Daily Home News*, 23 April 1912.
40. *Montreal Daily Star*, 20 April 1912.
41. N. Barratt, *Lost Voices from the Titanic* (2009), p. 196.
42. *Milwaukee Journal*, 19 April 1912; *New York Herald*, April 1912.
43. V. Jessop, *Titanic Survivor* (1998), p. 132.
44. *New York Times*, 19 April 1912.
45. Ibid.
46. Ibid., 20 April 1912.
47. *Bristol Times and Mirror*, 27 April 1912.
48. *The Times*, 20 April 1912.
49. *Baltimore Sun*, 20 April 1912.
50. J.G. Wilson and J. Fiske, *Appleton's Cyclopædia of American Biography* (1918), vol. 8, p. 343.
51. *Primitive Methodist Leader*, April 1912.
52. *New York Herald*, 19 April 1912.
53. *Sacramento Union*, 29 May 1912.
54. *Los Angeles Evening Herald*, 9 October 1912.
55. *Salt Lake Tribune*, 24 April 1912.
56. *The Daily Courier*, 18 November 1912.
57. *Los Angeles Evening Herald*, 23 November 1912.
58. *Chicago Tribune*, 21 April 1912.
59. *The West Briton*, 13 May 1913.
60. L. Beesley, *The Loss of the SS Titanic* (1912), p. 41.
61. *Evening World*, 22 April 1912.
62. *Washington Times*, 10 April 1913.
63. *Worcester Evening Gazette*, 19 April 1912.
64. *New York Herald*, 21 April 1912.
65. *New York Times*, 20 April 1912.
66. Ibid., 20 April 1912.
67. *Daily Sketch*, 30 April 1912.
68. *New York Herald*, 21 April 1912.
69. M. Everett, *Wreck and Sinking of the Titanic* (1912), p. 170.
70. *Henley and South Oxfordshire Standard*, 7 June 1912.
71. *Daily Sketch*, 30 April 1912.
72. *New York Herald*, 21 April 1912.
73. *Philadelphia Inquirer*, 20 April 1912.
74. *Denver Post*, 7 September 1922.
75. Ibid., 28 October 1932.
76. *New York Times*, 20 April 1912.

77. *Shields Daily News*, 27 April 1912.
78. *New York Times*, 20 April 1912.
79. Ibid.
80. American Inquiry, pp. 237–9.
81. *New York Times*, 20 April 1912.
82. Ibid.
83. Ibid.
84. K. Iverson, *Molly Brown, Unravelling the Myth* (1999), p. 171.
85. *Votes for Women*, 26 April 1912.
86. *La Correspondencia militar*, 18 April 1912.
87. J. Geller, *Women and Children First* (1998), p. 59.
88. S. Martínez Cotos, 'Shots under Titanic's Shadow: The Tragedy of a Spanish Multimillionaire Family and its Unknown Connection with an Assassination', *Titanic Commutator* 205 (2014), 9.
89. *New York Herald*, 21 April 1912.
90. *Western Daily Mercury*, 30 April 1912.
91. *The Bulletin*, 30 April 1912.
92. *Washington Post*, 28 April 1912.
93. *Denver Post*, 18 April 1912.
94. *New York Sun*, 21 April 1912.
95. *Daily Mail*, 18 April 1912.
96. Ibid., 20 April 1912.
97. A. Gracie, *The Truth about the Titanic* (1913), p. 146.
98. *Daily Mail*, 23 April 1912.
99. *Daily Herald*, 26 April 1912.
100. *Daily Mail*, 25 April 1912.
101. *The Freewoman*, 2 May 1912.
102. *Woman's Journal*, 4 May 1912.
103. *Daily Mail*, 25 April 1912.
104. *Cleveland Plain Dealer*, 17 April 1912.
105. *New York Herald*, 26 April 1912.
106. *Chicago Tribune*, 22 April 1912.
107. M. Soames (ed.), *Speaking for Themselves: The Personal Letters of Winston and Clementine Churchill* (1999), p. 64.
108. *St Louis Dispatch Post*, 26 April 1912.
109. A.E. Wright, *The Unexpurgated Case against Women's Suffrage* (1913), pp. 106–107.
110. *Daily Mail*, 17 April 1912.
111. *Votes for Women*, 26 April 1912.

112. *Woman's Journal*, 27 April 1912.
113. *Progressive Woman*, May 1912.
114. *New York Times*, 20 April 1912.

Chapter Five: Class, Prejudice and Conflict

1. *New York Times*, 7 November 1915.
2. A.E. Newton, *The Amenities of Book-collecting and Kindred Affections*, Atlantic Monthly Press, New York (1918), p. 345.
3. P.A.B. Widener II, *Without Drums*, New York, Putnam (1940), p. 9; L.A. Morris, 'Harry Elkins Widener and A.S.W. Rosenbach: Of Books and Friendship', *Harvard Library Bulletin* NS 6/4 (1995), 27.
4. *Washington Herald*, 21 April 1912.
5. R. Rondeau, *Titanic Lives On Board, Destination Canada* (2012), p. 9.
6. *The Toronto World*, 20 April 1912.
7. *The Times*, 19 April 1912.
8. *Toys and Novelties*, 9 (1913), 22.
9. L. Beesley, *The Loss of the SS Titanic* (1912), p. 39.
10. Ibid., pp. 2–3.
11. R. Davenport-Hines, *Titanic Lives* (2012), pp. 195–6.
12. K. Brown, *Passage to the World* (2013), pp. 130–1.
13. *New York Tribune*, 30 April 1912.
14. Ibid., p. 194.
15. *Western Morning News*, 18 April 1912.
16. *Liverpool Daily Post*, 4 May 1912.
17. *Liverpool Echo*, 17 April 1912; A. Scarth, *Titanic and Liverpool* (2009), p. 106.
18. L. Beesley, *The Loss of the SS Titanic* (1912), pp. 37–8.
19. R. Davenport-Hines, *Titanic Lives* (2012), p. 200.
20. *West Briton and Cornwall Advertiser*, 18 April 1912.
21. *Western Morning News*, 17 April 1912.
22. N. Barratt, *Lost Voices from the Titanic* (2020), p. 179.
23. T. Fitch, J.K. Layton and B. Wormstedt, *On a Sea of Glass* (2012), p. 217.
24. R. Davenport-Hines, *Titanic Lives* (2012), pp. 225, 227.
25. *Belfast Telegraph*, 16 April 2012.
26. L. Beesley, *The Loss of the SS Titanic* (1912), pp. 36–7.
27. *Boxing*, 13 April 1912.
28. Ibid., 11 May 1912.
29. *New York Times*, 21 April 1912.
30. *Rochester Democrat and Chronicle*, 15 April 1931.
31. D. Hyslop, A. Forsyth and S. Jemima, *Titanic Voices* (2006), p. 85.

32. J. Geller, *Women and Children First* (1998), p. 61.
33. British Inquiry, final report, pp. 40, 70.
34. L. Duff-Gordon, *Discretions and Indiscretions* (1932), pp. 162–3.
35. British Inquiry, Q 6176.
36. Ibid., Q 6195.
37. Ibid., Q 9771.
38. Ibid., Q 9926.
39. American Inquiry, p. 460.
40. *Ottawa Citizen*, 24 April 1912.
41. *New York Herald*, 19 April 1912.
42. British Inquiry, Q 9887.
43. Ibid., Q 9925.
44. Ibid., Q 10076.
45. Ibid., final report, p. 70.
46. Ibid., Q 9776.
47. Ibid., p. 73.
48. *Newark Star*, 20 April 1912.
49. N. Barratt, *Lost Voices from the Titanic* (2020), pp. 179–80.
50. *Irish Independent*, 9 May 1912.
51. American Inquiry, p. 441.
52. Ibid., p. 459.
53. British Inquiry, p. 73.
54. *New York Times*, 20 April 1912.
55. *Semi-Monthly Magazine*, May 1912.
56. American Inquiry, p. 443.
57. *Washington Post*, 21 April 1912.
58. Letter from H. Bride to W.R. Cross, traffic manager, Marconi, 27 April 1912, American Inquiry, p. 77.
59. British Inquiry, Q 16784.
60. *New York Times*, 19 April 1912.
61. *Baltimore Sun*, 19 April 1912.
62. L. Marshall, *The Sinking of the Titanic* (1912), pp. 55–6.
63. *Washington Times*, 19 April 1912.
64. *Le Matin*, 3 May 1912.
65. *Western Daily Mercury*, 29 April 1912.
66. American Inquiry, p. 372.
67. Ibid., p. 198.
68. Ibid., p. 226.
69. Ibid., p. 485.

70. *New York Times*, 19 March 1891.
71. *American Marine Engineer*, 1/9 (September 1906), 13.
72. *New York Times*, 8 August 1906.
73. A. Gracie, *The Truth about the Titanic* (1913), p. 166.
74. *The Times*, 20 April 1912.
75. A. Gracie, *The Truth about the Titanic* (1913), pp. 91–2.
76. S. Biel, *Down with the Old Canoe* (1996), p. 77.
77. A. Gracie, *The Truth about the Titanic* (1913), pp. 75–6.
78. *New York Times*, 22 April 1912.
79. *Worcester Evening Gazette*, 20 April 1912.
80. *The Review of Reviews*, April 1912; J.W. Foster, *The Age of Titanic* (2002), pp. 153–6.
81. *The War Cry*, 27 April 1912.
82. *Atlanta Constitution*, 22 April 1912.
83. *New York Times*, 29 April 1912.
84. *Lutheran Herald*, 25 April 1912.
85. *Binghampton Press*, 29 April 1912.
86. *Charlotte News*, 7 February 1907.
87. *Town and Country*, 26 December 1906.
88. *Walsall Advertiser*, 11 May 1912.
89. A. Gracie, *The Truth about the Titanic* (1913), p. 34.
90. *Uttoxeter Advertiser and Ashbourne Times*, 8 May 1912.
91. *New York Times*, 20 April 1912.
92. *Washington Herald*, 19 April 1912.
93. *New York Sun*, 19 April 1912.
94. *Independent*, 25 April 1912.
95. *Baltimore Sun*, 21 April 1912.
96. *The Daily Herald*, 30 April 1912.
97. *Worcester Evening Gazette*, 20 April 1912.
98. *Worcester Daily Times*, 20 April 1912.
99. *Atlanta Constitution*, 19 April 1912.
100. *The Bulletin*, 20 April 1912.
101. Ibid., 19 April 1912.
102. *New York Times*, 27 April 1912.
103. American Inquiry, p. 140.
104. R. Davenport-Hines, *Titanic Lives* (2012), p. 283.
105. T. Fitch, J.K. Layton and B. Wormstedt, *On a Sea of Glass* (2012), p. 217.
106. *Chicago Daily News*, 24 April 1912.
107. *The Masses*, June 1912.

108. *Literary Digest*, May 1912.
109. *Christian Socialist*, 25 April 1912.
110. *Baltimore Sun*, 22 April 1912.
111. *Religious Telescope*, 24 April 1912.
112. *Literary Digest*, 4 May 1912.
113. *American Review of Reviews*, June 1912.
114. M. Everett, *Wreck and Sinking of the Titanic* (1912), p. 24.
115. *Evening Telegraph and Post*, 16 April 1912. These were John Jacob Astor, Isidor Straus, George Widener, Benjamin Guggenheim and John Borland Thayer. Washington Roebling was confused with his uncle. Alfred Vanderbilt was not aboard but had intended to travel.
116. *Yorkshire Post*, 17 April 1912.
117. *Toronto Daily Star*, 19 April 1912.
118. *Literary Digest*, 4 May 1912.
119. *Denver Post*, 16 April 1912.
120. *Crisis*, June 1912.
121. United States Congress, Senate Committee on Education and Labor, *Conditions in the Paint Creek District, West Virginia*, p. 2266.
122. *Miners' Magazine*, 2 May 1912.
123. *Coming Nation*, 27 April 1912.
124. *Ladies' Garment Worker*, May 1912.
125. *Daily Herald*, 22 April 1912.
126. *Cambridge Daily News*, 20 April 1912.
127. H.G. Wells, *The Labour Unrest* (1912), p. 5.

Chapter Six: Heroes or Incompetents

1. British Inquiry, final report, p. 50.
2. *The Evening World*, 17 April 1912.
3. American Inquiry, p. 75.
4. *Shipping Gazette and Lloyd's List*, 7 August 1912.
5. *Daily Herald*, 26 April 1912.
6. TNA, BT 100/259, crew list, April 1912; TNA, BT 334/53, Register of Deceased Crew, Titanic, 1912.
7. TNA, BT 27/780B, list of passengers boarding *Titanic* at Southampton, 10 April 1912.
8. *Larne Times*, 27 April 1912.
9. W. Blair, *Titanic, Behind the Legend* (2011), p. 38.
10. *Lincoln Daily News*, 29 April 1912.
11. S.F. Bullock, *Thomas Andrews Shipbuilder* (1912), pp. 59–60.

12. *The Times*, 22 April 1912.
13. *Belfast Newsletter*, 3 October 1912.
14. S.F. Bullock, *Thomas Andrews Shipbuilder* (1912), p. 73.
15. Ibid., p. 70.
16. Ibid., p. 71.
17. Ibid., p. 73.
18. Ibid., pp. 3–4, 29–30.
19. *Colne and Nelson Times*, 24 May 1912.
20. J.H. Mowbray, *Sinking of the Titanic* (1912), p. 225.
21. *The Musicians' Report and Journal*, July 1912.
22. *Worcester Evening Gazette*, 20 April 1912.
23. *New York Times*, 21 April 1912.
24. *Le Matin*, 20 April 1912.
25. *Daily News*, 14 May 1912.
26. *Toronto Daily Star*, 24 April 1912.
27. *New York Times*, 21 April 1912.
28. *English Review*, May 1912.
29. C.H. Lightoller, *Titanic and Other Ships* (1935), p. 223.
30. American Inquiry, p. 735.
31. *New York Times*, 19 April 1912.
32. N. Barratt, *Lost Voices from the Titanic* (2020), p. 142.
33. *New York Times*, 19 April 1912.
34. *Asbury Park Evening Press*, 22 April 1912.
35. British Inquiry, Q 20128, Q 20167, Q 20170.
36. A. Gracie, *The Truth about the Titanic* (1913), p.19.
37. American Inquiry, pp. 352–4.
38. *New York Times*, 20 April 1912.
39. D. Hyslop, A. Forsyth and S. Jemima, *Titanic Voices* (1994), p. 112.
40. Ibid., p. 115.
41. H. Holman, *Titanic Voices* (2011), p. 41.
42. L. Duff-Gordon, *Discretions and Indiscretions* (1932), p. 152.
43. American Inquiry, p. 346.
44. H. Holman, *Titanic Voices* (2011), pp. 294, 299.
45. *Philadelphia Enquirer*, 20 April 1912.
46. A. Gracie, *The Truth about the Titanic* (1913), p. 7.
47. Ibid., p. 6.
48. L. Beesley, *The Loss of the SS Titanic* (1912), p. 37.
49. *Cornishman*, 2 May 1912.
50. V. Jessop, *Titanic Survivor* (1998), p. 127.

51. American Inquiry, p. 358.
52. *Hastings & St. Leonards Observer*, 4 May 1912.
53. N. Barratt, *Lost Voices from the Titanic* (2020), p. 162.
54. *Lloyd's Weekly News*, 21 April 1912.
55. *Semi-Monthly Magazine*, May 1912.
56. N. Barratt, *Lost Voices from the Titanic* (2020), p. 157.
57. Ibid., pp. 154–5.
58. *The Examiner*, 26 April 1912.
59. United States Archives, New York, RG 21, Records of District Courts of the United States, Admiralty Case Files, In the Matter of the Petition of the Oceanic Steam Navigation Company, Limited, for Limitation of its Liability as owner of the steamship *Titanic*, minutes, 1912–13, https://catalog.archives.gov/id/6254783 accessed 3 August 2023.
60. *Cambria Daily Leader*, 24 June 1913.
61. British Inquiry, p. 40.
62. American Inquiry, p. 202.
63. C.H. Lightoller, *Titanic and Other Ships* (1935), p. 225.
64. *New York Herald*, 19 April 1912.
65. British Inquiry, Q 10586.
66. *Chicago Examiner*, 19 April 1912.
67. *Daily News*, 14 May 1912.
68. C.H. Lightoller, *Titanic and Other Ships* (1935), p. 214.
69. British Inquiry, Q 4421.
70. Ibid., Q 2960.
71. American Inquiry, p. 1148.
72. Ibid., p. 28.
73. British Inquiry, Q 22961.
74. L. Marshall, *The Sinking of the Titanic* (1912), p. 212.
75. *Aberdeen Daily Journal*, 6 May 1912.
76. *Reynolds' Weekly*, 5 May 1912.
77. *United Mine Workers Journal*, 2 May 1912.
78. S.H. Allen, *International Relations* (1920), p. 201.
79. American Inquiry, p. 425.
80. Ibid., p. 429.
81. Ibid., pp. 202, 238.
82. A. Gracie, *The Truth about the Titanic* (1913), p. 134.
83. *New York Times*, 20 April 1912.
84. American Inquiry, p. 396.
85. Ibid., p. 236.

86. *New York Herald*, 24 April 912.
87. American Inquiry, p. 345.
88. S. Gregson, 'Women and Children First: The Administration of Titanic Relief in Southampton 1912–1959', *English Historical Review* 127 (2012), 90.
89. *Daily Mail*, 19 April 1912.
90. D. Hyslop, A. Forsyth and S. Jemima, *Titanic Voices* (1994), p. 70.
91. British Inquiry, Q 21353.
92. Ibid., Q 10787.
93. C.H. Lightoller, *Titanic and Other Ships* (1935), p. 215.
94. American Inquiry, p. 492.
95. TNA, BT100/259, agreement of crew, April 1912.
96. *Western Independent*, 21 April 1912.
97. American Inquiry, p. 223.
98. Ibid., pp. 171–3.
99. TNA, FO 369/522, despatch from Alfred Mitchell-Innes to Foreign Office, 1 May 1912.
100. *New York Times*, 29 May 1912.
101. *Daily Graphic*, 4 May 1912.
102. *Daily Mirror*, 15 May 912.
103. *Daily Mail*, 26 April 1912.
104. C.H. Lightoller, *Titanic and Other Ships* (1935), p. 257.
105. *Daily Herald*, 28 May 1912.
106. C.H. Lightoller, *Titanic and Other Ships* (1935), p. 217.
107. *Jewish Daily Vorwärts*, 28 April 1912.

Chapter Seven: Deathly Distinction and Discrimination

1. *Baltimore Sun*, 22 April 1912.
2. *Chicago Tribune*, 22 April 1912.
3. *San Francisco Examiner*, 21 April 1912.
4. *Chicago Tribune*, 22 April 1912.
5. *The Times*, 19 April 1912.
6. A.H. Rostron, *Home from the Sea* (1931), p. 60.
7. A. Gracie, *The Truth about the Titanic* (1913), p. 112.
8. *Washington Times*, 19 April 1912.
9. D. Hyslop, A. Forsyth and S. Jemima, *Voices from the Titanic* (1994), p. 155.
10. American Inquiry, p. 494.
11. *New York Times*, 19 April 1912.
12. *New York Herald*, 20 April 1912.

13. A.H. Rostron, *Home from the Sea* (1931), p. 13.
14. L. Beesley, *The Loss of the SS Titanic* (1912), p. 212.
15. A.H. Rostron, *Home from the Sea* (1931), p. 69.
16. Ibid., p. 76.
17. Ibid., p. 60.
18. *New York Times*, 30 May 1912.
19. N. Barratt, *Lost Voices from the Titanic* (2009), p. 186.
20. *Newport Herald*, 30 May 1912.
21. National Archives, Washington, DC, RG 85, Passenger and crew lists for vessels arriving at New York, New York: Immigration and Naturalization Service Volume 4183, Manifest of Carpathia, April 1912. https://catalog.archies.gov/id/300348 accessed 3 August 2023.
22. American Inquiry, p. 29.
23. A.H. Rostron, *Home from the Sea* (1931), p. 75.
24. *Cleveland Plain Dealer*, 19 April 1912.
25. *The War Cry*, 27 April 1912.
26. *New York Herald*, 19 April 1912; ibid., 20 April 1912.
27. *Ilford Graphic*, 12 May 1912.
28. *New York Times*, 21 April 1912.
29. J.P. Eaton and C.A. Haas, *Titanic: Triumph and Tragedy* (1994), pp. 179–80.
30. *Jewish Advocate*, 10 May 1912.
31. British Inquiry, Q 25496, Q 25497.
32. American Inquiry, p. 29.
33. M. Logan, *The Sinking of the Titanic* (1912), pp. 246–7.
34. J.H. Mowbray, *Sinking of the Titanic* (1912), p. 259.
35. N. Barratt, *Lost Voices from the Titanic* (2009), p. 234.
36. Public Archives of Nova Scotia, sworn testimony of Frank Higginson, purser of CS *Mackay-Bennett* signed by Dr William D. Finn, City of Halifax and Town of Dartmouth, RG 41, vol. 81, no. 1233 https://archives.novascotia.ca/titanic/archives/?ID=20 accessed 3 August 2023.
37. *Chronicle Herald*, 30 April 1912.
38. *Washington Times*, 30 April 1912.
39. J.H. Mowbray, *Sinking of the Titanic* (1912), p. 261.
40. Ibid., p. 80.
41. Public Archives of Nova Scotia, Medical Examiner for City of Halifax, Record of Bodies and Effects: Passengers and Crew, SS *Titanic*, RG 41, Series C., vol. 76, no. 126 https://archives.novascotia.ca/titanic/fatalities/archives/?ID=126 accessed 3 August 2023.

42. Public Archives of Nova Scotia, Medical Examiner for City of Halifax, Record of Bodies and Effects: Passengers and Crew, SS *Titanic*, RG 41, Series C, vol. 75, no. 39, 1912 https://archives.novascotia.ca/titanic/fatalities/archives/?ID=39 accessed 3 August 2023.
43. *New York Times*, 27 April 1912.
44. *The Times*, 30 May 1912.
45. *Halifax Evening Mail*, 30 April 1912.
46. N. Barratt, *Lost Voices from the Titanic* (2009), p. 234.
47. National Archives, New York City, Record Group 21: Records of District Courts of the United States, Admiralty Case Files, In the Matter of the Petition of the Oceanic Steam Navigation Company, Limited, for Limitation of its Liability as owner of the steamship *Titanic*, claim of James Hughes for Eloise Smith, 1913 https://www.titanicinquiry.org/lol/claims/smith-c30-2.php accessed 2 August 2023.
48. Ibid., claim of John P. Snyder, 1913. https://catalog.archives.gov/id/6210884?objectPage=4 accessed 2 August 2023.
49. Ibid., claim of Emilio Portaluppi, 1913. https://catalog.archives.gov/id/6210891?objectPage=4 accessed 2 August 2023.
50. Ibid., claim of Yum Hee, 1913. https://catalog.archives.gov/id/6210878?objectPage=4 accessed 2 August 2023.
51. United States, Bureau of Foreign and Domestic Commerce, *Daily Consular and Trade Reports* (1912), p. 230.
52. *New York Times*, 11 April 1912.
53. TNA, BT 100/259/409, *Titanic* crew list, April 1912.
54. *Brooklyn Daily Eagle*, 23 April 1912.
55. National Archives, New York City, Record Group 21: Records of District Courts of the United States, Admiralty Case Files, In the Matter of the Petition of the Oceanic Steam Navigation Company, Limited, for Limitation of its Liability as owner of the steamship *Titanic*, claim of James Hughes for Eloise Smith, 1913 https://www.titanicinquiry.org/lol/claims/smith-c30-2.php accessed 2 August 2023.
56. United States, Bureau of Foreign and Domestic Commerce, *Daily Consular and Trade Reports* (1912), pp. 929, 931.
57. K. Brown, *Passage to the World* (2013), p. 131.
58. TNA, T 172/886, 'Lord Sumner's Committee on the Cost of Living Report', 1918.
59. National Archives, New York City, Record Group 21: Records of District Courts of the United States, Admiralty Case Files, In the Matter of the Petition of the Oceanic Steam Navigation Company, Limited, for Limitation of its Liability as owner of the steamship *Titanic*, claim of Charlotte Drake Cardeza, 1913. https://catalog.archives.gov/id/6210868?objectPage=4 accessed 2 August 2023.

60. Ibid., claim of Margaret Brown, 1913. https://catalog.archives.gov/id/6210870?objectPage=5 accessed 2 August 2023.
61. J.H. Mowbray, *Sinking of the Titanic* (1912), p. 86.
62. Ibid., p. 266.
63. Public Archives of Nova Scotia, Medical Examiner for City of Halifax, Record of Bodies and Effects: Passengers and Crew, SS *Titanic*, RG 41, Series C, vol. 76, no. 169, 1912. https://archives.novascotia.ca/titanic/fatalities/archives/?ID=169 accessed 2 August 2023.
64. *The Neepawa Press*, 13 May 1912.
65. Public Archives of Nova Scotia, Medical Examiner for City of Halifax, Record of Bodies and Effects: Passengers and Crew, SS *Titanic*, RG 41, Series C, vol. 76, no. 256, 1912. https://archives.novascotia.ca/titanic/fatalities/archives/?ID=256 accessed 2 August 2023.
66. *Nova Scotian Evening Mail*, 21 April 1912.
67. D.A. Butler, *Unsinkable* (1998), p. 201.
68. J. Bier, 'Bodily Circulation and the Measure of a Life: Forensic Identification and Valuation after the Titanic disaster', *Social Studies of Science* 48/5 (2018), 635–662.
69. J.H. Mowbray, *Sinking of the Titanic: Thrilling Stories Told by Survivors* (1912), pp. 261–2.
70. J. Geller, *Women and Children First* (1998), p. 62.
71. S. Martínez Cotos, 'Shots under Titanic's Shadow: The Tragedy of a Spanish Multimillionaire Family and its Unknown Connection with an Assassination', *Titanic Commutator* 205 (2014), 9.
72. *Chicago Tribune*, 11 May 1912.
73. *Washington Herald*, 20 April 1912.
74. *Worcester Telegram*, 2 May 1912.
75. J.H. Mowbray, *Sinking of the Titanic* (1912), pp. 206–207.
76. *San Francisco Examiner*, 19 April 1912.
77. *Cleveland Plain Dealer*, 17 April 1912.
78. *Shields Daily News*, 16 April 1912.
79. *Philadelphia Enquirer*, 19 April 1912.
80. *Cleveland Plain Dealer*, 17 April 1912.
81. *Daily Telegraph*, 17 April 1912.
82. *Liverpool Daily Post*, 16 April 1912.
83. *The Globe*, 16 April 1912.
84. *Daily Telegraph*, 18 April 1912.
85. *Standard Union*, 4 May 1912.
86. *St. Mary's Journal*, 7 May 1912.

87. *New York Times*, 4 May 1912.
88. *The Times*, 20 May 2023.
89. *St. Ives Times & Express*, 31 May 1912.
90. *Philadelphia Inquirer*, 22 April 1912.
91. *New York Times*, 28 April 1912; ibid., 21 May 1912; ibid., 17 June 1913.
92. Ibid., 27 June 1933.
93. *Daily State Gazette*, 15 August 1912.
94. *New York Times*, 3 May 1912.
95. *St. Ives Times & Express*, 10 May 1912.
96. *Northern Echo*, 15 April 2015.
97. D. Hyslop, A. Forsyth and S. Jemima, *Titanic Voices* (2006), pp. 300–309.
98. R. Pollard and N. Pevsner, *Lancashire: Liverpool and the South-West* (2006), p. 100.
99. S. Barczewski, *Titanic: A Night Remembered* (2011), pp. 222–3.
100. *New York Times*, 28 April 2020.
101. *Washington Post*, 26 October 1913.
102. Ibid., 29 April 1912.
103. *New York Times*, 4 May 1912.
104. Ibid., 27 May 1931.
105. *Baltimore Sun*, 9 May 1912.
106. W. Lord, *A Night to Remember* (1955), p. 99.

Bibliography

Archive Sources

The National Archives, Kew
TNA, BT, Board of Trade
TNA, FO, Foreign Office
TNA, MT, Transport
TNA, T, Treasury

National Archives (USA), Washington, DC
RG 85, Passenger and crew lists for vessels arriving at New York, New York: Immigration and Naturalization Service Volume 4183, 1912, https://catalog.archives.gov/id/300348 (available online, accessed 3 August 2023)

National Archives (USA), New York City
RG 21, Records of District Courts of the United States, Admiralty Case Files, In the Matter of the Petition of the Oceanic Steam Navigation Company, Limited, for Limitation of its Liability as owner of the steamship *Titanic*, 1913, https://catalog.archives.gov/id/278328 (available online, accessed 3 August 2023)

Public Archives of Nova Scotia
RG 41, Series C, Medical Examiner for City of Halifax, Record of Bodies and Effects: Passengers and Crew, SS *Titanic*, 1912, https://archives.novascotia.ca/titanic/fatalities (available online, accessed 3 August 2023)

Titanic Inquiries

Report of a Formal Investigation into the Circumstances Attending the Foundering on 15th April, 1912, of the British Steamship *Titanic* of Liverpool, after striking ice in or near latitude 41° 46'N., longitude 50° 14'W., Cd 3352, 1912 (British Inquiry)

Hearing Before a Subcommittee of the Committee on Commerce, United States Senate: Sixty-second Congress, Second Session, Pursuant to S Res 283, Directing the Committee on Commerce to Investigate the Causes Leading to the Wreck of the White Star Liner *Titanic*, 1912 (American Inquiry)

Primary Printed Sources

Allen, Stephen Haley, *International Relations*, Princeton, Princeton University Press, 1920
Atherton, William Henry, *Montreal 1535–1914: Biographical*, Chicago, S.J. Clarke, 1914
Beesley, Lawrence, *The Loss of the SS Titanic: its Story and its Lessons*, Boston, Houghton Mifflin, 1912
Bullock, Shane F., *Thomas Andrews Shipbuilder*, Dublin and London, MacNeil, 1912
Cabot Lodge, Henry, 'The Meaning of a Great Library', *Harvard Graduates Magazine* (1915), 31–38
Duff-Gordon, Lucy, *Discretions and Indiscretions*, London, Jarrolds, 1932
Everett, Marshall, *Wreck and Sinking of the Titanic, the Ocean's Greatest Disaster*, New York, L.H. Walter, 1912
Gibbs, Philip, *The Deathless Story of the Titanic*, London, *Lloyd's Weekly News*, 1912
Gracie, Archibald, *The Truth about the Titanic*, New York, M. Kennerley, 1913
Gracie, Archibald and Thayer, John Borland, *Titanic: A Survivor's Story and The Sinking of the SS Titanic*, Chicago, Academy Chicago Publishers, 1998
Harvard, University of, *Secretary's First Report of Harvard Class of 1907*, Cambridge, Massachusetts, Crimson Publishing, 1908
Jessop, Violet, *Titanic Survivor: the Memoirs of Violet Jessop Stewardess*, Thrupp. Sutton Publishing, 1998
Lightoller, C.H., *Titanic and Other Ships*, London, Ivor Nicholson & Watson, 1935
Marshall, Logan, *The Sinking of the Titanic and Great Sea Disasters*, Philadelphia, J.C. Winston, 1912
Mowbray, Jay Henry, *Sinking of the Titanic, Most Appalling Ocean Horror*, Harrisburg, Minter, 1912
Newton, Alfred Edward, 'A Word in Memory, a Remembrance of Harry Elkins Widener', *The Atlantic* (1918), 351–6
_____, _____, _____, *The Amenities of Book-collecting and Kindred Affections*, New York, Atlantic Monthly Press, New York, 1918
Paine, Alfred, *Dr Alfred Pain – In Memoriam*, Hamilton, published privately, 1912
Rostron, Arthur H., *Home from the Sea*, London, Cassell, 1931
Sloper, William T., 'Ship to Shore: William Sloper's Account of the Titanic Disaster', *Oceanographic Navigation Research Society* (1984), 301–413
Soames, Mary (ed.), *Speaking for Themselves: The Personal Letters of Winston and Clementine Churchill*, London, Black Swan, 1999
Stead, W.T., *The Blue Island: Experiences of a New Arrival Beyond the Veil*, London, Hutchinson & Co., 1922
United States, Bureau of Foreign and Domestic Commerce, Daily Consular and Trade Reports, US Government Printing Office, Washington, DC, 1912
Wells, H.G., *The Labour Unrest*, London, Associated Newspapers, 1912

Widener, Peter A.B., II, *Without Drums*, New York, Putnam, 1940
Wilson, James Grant and Fiske, John, *Appleton's Cyclopædia of American Biography*, New York, D. Appleton, 1918
Wright, A.E., *The Unexpurgated Case against Women's Suffrage*, New York, Paul E. Hoeber, 1913
Young, Filson, *Titanic*, London, Grant Richards, 1912

Secondary Printed Works

Barczewski, Stephanie, *Titanic: A Night Remembered*, London, Continuum International Publishing Group, 2011
Barratt, Nick, *Lost Voices From the Titanic: The Definitive Oral History*, London, Random House, 2009
Biel, Stephen, *Down with the Old Canoe: A Cultural History of the Titanic Disaster*, New York, Norton, 1996
Bier, J., 'Bodily Circulation and the Measure of a Life: Forensic Identification and Valuation after the *Titanic* Disaster', *Social Studies of Science* 48/5 (2018), 635–662
Blair, William, *Titanic: Behind the Legend*, Belfast, National Museums of Northern Ireland, 2011
Brown, Kevin, *Poxed and Scurvied: Health and Sickness at Sea*, Barnsley, Seaforth, 2011
_____, _____, *Passage to the World: The Emigrant Experience, 1807–1940*, Barnsley, Seaforth, 2013
Butler, Daniel Alan, *Unsinkable: the Full Story of RMS Titanic*, Barnsley, Frontline Books, 1998
Byatt, Derrick, *Promises to Pay: The First Three Hundred Years of Bank of England Notes*, London, Spink, 1994
Davenport-Hines, Richard, *Titanic Lives: Migrants and Millionaires, Conmen and Crew*, London, Harper Press, 2012
Delap, Lucy, 'Thus Does Man Prove His Fitness to Be the Master of Things: Shipwrecks, Chivalry and Masculinities in Nineteenth- and Twentieth-Century Britain', *Cultural and Social History*, 3/1 (2006), 45–74
Eaton, John P. and Haas, Charles A., *Titanic: Triumph and Tragedy*, New York, Norton, 1994
Finamore, Daniel and Wood, Ghislaine, *Ocean Liners*, London, V&A Publishing, 2017
Fitch, Tad, Layton, J. Kent and Wormstedt, Bill, *On a Sea of Glass: the Life and Loss of the RMS Titanic*, Stroud, Amberley, 2012
Foster, John Wilson, *The Age of Titanic: Cross-Currents in Anglo-American Culture*, Dublin, Merlin, 2002
Frey, Bruno S., Savage David A. and Torgler, Benno, 'Behavior under Extreme Conditions: The Titanic Disaster', *Journal of Economic Perspectives* 25/1 (2011), 209–22
Geller, Judith B., *Women and Children First*, Sparkford, Patrick Stephens, 1998

Gill, Anton, *Titanic: the Real Story of the Construction of the World's Most Famous Ship*, London, Channel 4 Books, 2010

Girouard, Mark, *The Return to Camelot, Chivalry and the English Gentleman*, New Haven, Yale University Press, 1981

Gregson, Sarah, 'Women and Children First: The Administration of Titanic Relief in Southampton 1912–1959', *English Historical Review*, 127 (2012), 83–109

Hardy, Thomas, *Selected Shorter Poems*, London, MacMillan, 1968

Homan, Hannah, *Titanic Voices*, Stroud, Amberley, 2011

Hyslop, Donald, Forsyth, Alastair and Jemima, Sheila, *Titanic Voices*, Southampton, Southampton City Council, 1994

Iverson, Kristen, *Molly Brown: Unravelling the Myth*, Boulder, Johnson Books, 1999

Kerby, M. and Baguley, M., 'When death gave way to glory: Philip Gibbs, RMS Titanic and the Western Front', *International Journal of Maritime History*, 34/1 (2022), 46–62

Larabee, A.E., 'The American Hero and His Mechanical Bride: Gender Myths of the Titanic Disaster', *American Studies* 31/1 (1990), 5–23

Lord, Walter, *A Night to Remember*, London, Longmans, Green & Co., 1955

McCluskie, Tom, *Anatomy of the Titanic*, London, PRC Publishing, 1998

Marsh, James H., *The Canadian Encyclopaedia*, McClelland & Stewart, 1999

Martin, W.H. and Mason, Sandra, *Edward FitzGerald's Rubáiyát of Omar Khayyám: a Famous Poem and its Influence*, Anthem Press, London, 2011

Martínez Cotos, Sergio, 'Shots under *Titanic*'s Shadow: The Tragedy of a Spanish Multimillionaire Family and its Unknown Connection with an Assassination', *Titanic Commutator* 205 (2014), 4–12

Molony, Senan, *The Irish Aboard Titanic*, Dublin, Wolfhound Press, 2000

Morris, L.A., 'Harry Elkins Widener and A.S.W. Rosenbach: Of Books and Friendship', *Harvard Library Bulletin* NS 6/4 (1995), 7–28

Pollard, Richard and Pevsner, Nikolaus, *Lancashire: Liverpool and the South-West, The Buildings of England*, London, Yale University Press, 2006

Reynolds, Alison, 'True Manhood and Manly Boys: Boys' Adventure Stories, Imperialism, and the Titanic', *Articulate* 12 (2007), 242–50

Rondeau, Rob, *Titanic Lives: On Board, Destination Canada*, Halifax, Nova Scotia, Formac, 2012

Roosevelt, Theodore, *The Works of Theodore Roosevelt, The Strenuous Life*, New York, P.F. Collier, 1901

Scarth, Alan, *Titanic and Liverpool*, Liverpool, Liverpool University Press, 2009

Sheil, Inger, *Titanic Valour: The Life of Fifth Officer Harold Lowe*, Stroud, History Press, 2011

Smith, Emma, *Portable Magic: A History of Books and their Readers*, Harmondsworth, Penguin, 2022

Takis, Sandra L., 'Titanic: A Statistical Exploration', *Mathematics Teacher* 92 (1999), 660–64

Index

Abbott, Rhoda Mary, 185
Abelseth, Olaus, 145
Aberconway, Laura, 117–18
Accidents at sea, previous involvement of *Titanic* passengers and crew, 44–6
Adams, Cornelia, 135
Algerine, 188
Allen, William Henry, 192
Allison, Bess, 103–104
Allison, Hudson, 103–104, 124–5
Allison, Lorraine, 103–104
Allison, Trevor, 103–104
Altruism, 92, 116–19, 138
American Inquiry *see* Senate Inquiry
Andrews, Thomas, 158
   conduct during sinking, 154–6
   naval architect, 22–5, 154–6
   routine on *Titanic*, 154, 162
Anti-suffragism, 117–20
Appleton, Charlotte, 98
Art collecting, 11, 39, 123
Asplund, Carl, 103
Asplund, Clarence, 103
Asplund, Filip, 103
Asquith, Herbert, 116, 144
Asquith, Violet, 94
Assaf, Marian, 132
Astor, John Jacob, 9, 98, 111
   business practices, 31–3
   death, 28–9, 32–3, 44, 103, 145
   dilettante, 31
   funeral, 200
   man of action, 31–3
   marriage scandal, 31–2
   reputation, 28–9, 31–3, 44, 55, 64
Astor, Madeline, 31–2, 63, 76, 111, 182, 184, 200
Astor, Vincent, 131, 184, 200
Aubart, Léontine Pauline, 28, 33

Bacon, Francis, *Essaies*, 53–5
Bailey, Percy, 128
Barber, Nellie, 9, 24
Barkworth, Algernon, 79–80
Baron de Hirsch Cemetery, Halifax, 202
Baxter, Hélène, 37–8, 141, 174
Baxter, Quigg, 26, 37–8, 141

Beane, Edward, 129–30, 185–6
Beane, Ethel, 185–6
Beattie, Thomson, 124, 189–90
Beauchamp, Earl *see* Lygon, William
Beckwith, Richard, 42, 69–70
Beckwith, Sallie, 70
Beedem, George, 24
Beesley, Lawrence, 10, 46, 125–6, 129, 164–5
Behr, Karl, 26, 42, 69–71, 88, 183
Bidois, Rosalie, 32
Billiard, James van, 103
Birkenhead, 92
Bishop, Dickinson, 67
Bishop, Helen, 67, 114
Björnström-Steffansson, Mauritz Håkan, 11, 43, 78–9, 98
Blackwell, Stephen, 40
Blair, David, 170
Blank, Henry, 43, 69
Blondel, Merry-Joseph, 11
Board of Trade, 8, 16–17, 149–50, 170–1, 178–9
Bonnell, Caroline, 49, 181
Book collecting, 11–12, 50, 53–7, 123
Booth, Bramwell, 140
Booth, Evangeline, 185
Botsford, Hull, 126
Bourke, John, 100
Bourke, Kate, 100
Bourke, Mary, 100
Bowen, Dai, 130
Bowerman, Edith, 113
Bowerman, Elsie, 113
Boxhall, Joseph, 160
Brailey, William, 156
Bremen, 187
Brereton, George, 43, 74
Brewe, Arthur, 29, 97
Bricoux, Roger, 156
Bride, Harold, 15, 101–102, 135, 158–60, 181
Britannic, 17
'British first' *see* Xenophobia
British Seafarers' Union, 176
British Wreck Commissioner's Inquiry, 25, 83–4, 133–5, 152, 167–8, 178–9
Brown, Caroline, 98
Brown, Edward, 87

Brown, Margaret, 11, 97–8, 110–13, 174, 183–4
Buckley, Daniel, 75–6, 134
Bucknell, Emma, 64, 66–7, 97, 110, 164
Burial at sea, 186–7, 189–90, 196
Buss, Kate, 99
Butt, Archibald, 81, 145, 167
   death, 52–3, 59, 64, 72
   lifestyle, 28–9, 43, 51–2
   man of action, 52, 64
   memorial, 204
   presidential aide, 52, 123, 204
Byles, Thomas, 51

Calderhead, Edward P., 111, 125
Californian, 159
Candee, Helen Churchill, 78, 97–8, 112, 143
Capitalism, 27–8, 31, 54–5, 63–4, 120–1, 145–9, 152–3, 204
Carbines, William, 201
Cardeza, Charlotte Drake, 9, 77, 193
Cardeza, Thomas, 77
Carlisle, Alexander, 16–17, 19
Carpathia, 156, 169, 178
   accommodation for *Titanic* survivors, 77, 82, 89
   aid to *Titanic* survivors, 80, 104, 107, 109–10, 180–4
   burials, 186–7, 189
   captain *see* Rostron, Arthur
   J. Bruce Ismay on board, 88–9, 91
   Marconi operator, 160, 180–1
   passengers' committee of *Titanic* survivors, 71, 112, 183
   reached by *Titanic* lifeboats, 115, 174, 180–1
   rescue of *Titanic* passengers, 85, 180–4
   searching for missing friends aboard, 124, 127, 163
   segregation of survivors, 82, 89, 181–3, 193
   steerage, 11, 131, 180–4
Carraú, Francisco Mauro Severiano, 114
Carraú-Esteves, José Pedro, 114
Carter, Ernest, 97, 125–6
Carter, Lillian, 97, 105
Carter, Lucille, 89–90, 91, 103, 123
Carter, William Ernest, 6, 11, 38, 43, 47–8, 75, 89–90, 123
Carter, William Thornton, 103
Case, Howard Brown, 43–4, 49–50, 81
Cassebeer, Eleanor, 23, 141, 154
Caton, Annie, 165
Cavendish, Julia, 9, 24, 49, 95, 96, 112, 141–2, 174, 200–201
Cavendish, Tyrell William:
   aristocratic background, 142–3
   clubman, 6–7
   education, 36
   funeral, 200
   gentlemanly behaviour, 49, 52, 59, 95
   marriage, 141–2

   political ambitions, 39
   recovery of corpse, 95
   Tyrell William Cavendish Memorial Hall, 200–201
   will, 96
Chalmers, Alfred, 171
Chambers, Norman, 163
Cherry, Gladys, 108–10
Chesterton, G.K., 13, 86
Chinese Merchants Association of America, 118
Chisholm, Roderick, 154
Chivalry, 1–2, 33, 50, 92, 101, 117–18, 120–1, 138, 145–6, 204–205
Churchill, Winston, 119
Cinematography, 41, 46
Circassienne au Bain, 11
Clark, James Ross, 106
Clark, Virginia, 43–4, 48, 82, 95, 106, 163
Clark, Walter Miller, 36, 43–4, 48, 81, 95, 106, 163, 204
Clarke, Fred, 156
Class consciousness:
   antagonism, 63–6, 120–1, 148–51
   discrimination after death, 190, 196–8
   discrimination among survivors, 180–4
   distinction by clothing, 2–3, 130, 188–90, 192–3, 195–6
   elitism, 35–6, 49, 60–1, 63–6, 123, 144–5, 180, 196
   entitlement, 86, 90, 149
   segregation, 11, 128–9, 133–4
   snobbery, 90, 107, 123, 130–1, 136, 182
   social hierarchy, 2–4, 128–31, 140, 174, 199
Cleaver, Alice, 103–104
Collander, Erik, 126
Collett, Stuart, 98–9
Colley, Edward, 98
Collyer, Charlotte, 10, 76, 134–5, 138, 165–6
Collyer, Harvey, 10
Collyer, Marjorie, 10, 76
Compensation claims, 191–2
Complacency, 12–13, 44–6, 49, 92, 154, 163
Compton, Alexander G., 43
Conan Doyle, Arthur, 63
Conrad, Joseph, 12–13, 16, 22, 158
Conspicuous consumption:
   art and books, 11–13, 54–5
   clothing, 5, 9, 50–1, 55, 113–14, 191–3
   dining, 5–6, 40–1, 113, 123, 128–9
   display of wealth, 6, 25–6, 51–2, 113–14
   elite travel, 13, 17, 19, 40–1, 47, 50–1, 113–14
   luxury goods, 11–12, 54–5
   opulence, 3–6, 12–13, 22–3, 25, 146–7
Cornell, Malvina, 98
Corpses:
   burial, 196, 199–203
   discrimination by class, gender and clothing, 188–90, 193, 195–7
   identification, 54, 184, 187–90, 193–9

recovery, 186–91, 193–8
unidentified, 188, 189, 196–7, 202
Cottam, Harold, 160, 180–1
Cotterill, Harry, 128
Cowardice, 59–61, 63–6, 71–92, 134–5, 137–9
Craig, Norman Carlyle, 39, 96
Crawford, Alfred, 110, 173
Crew:
  accommodation, 24–5
  captain *see* Smith, Edward
  doctors, 8–9
  engineers, stokers and trimmers, 165–6
  hierarchy, 153–4
  incompetence in manning lifeboats, 108–10, 111–12, 173–5
  interpreter, 132
  lift attendants, 164–5
  Marconi operators, 14–15, 135–6, 158–6
  officers, 3, 5, 25, 46, 65–6, 87–8, 94, 143, 152–3, 156–9, 166–70, 173, 176–9
  orchestra, 5, 156–8
  physical training instructors, 7–8, 164
  post office, 160–1
  recruitment, 175–6
  reluctance to pick up survivors, 109–10, 112, 171, 177–8
  restaurant staff, 161–3
  stewardesses, 155–6, 165
  stewards, 133, 153–4, 162–5, 173–5
  unfamiliar with *Titanic* layout, 132–4, 176–7
Cribb, Laura Mae, 11, 133
Crowe, George, 137
Cullen, Charles, 162
Cumings, Florence, 163
Cumings, John Bradley, 163
Cunard, 15, 17–18, 20, 24, 42, 180
Cunningham, Andrew, 163, 175

Daly, Eugene, 26
Daniel, Robert, 81–3, 168–9, 181–2
Davidson, Charles Peers, 186
Davidson, Oriana, 95, 99
Davidson, Shirley, 185–6
Davidson, Thornton, 99
  anti-Catholicism, 140–1
  athlete, 8, 79, 162, 164
  clubman, 7, 26, 36–7, 38, 125
  memorial, 201
  stockbroker, 36–7, 124–5
Dick, Albert, 68
Dick, Vera, 68
Dillingham Commission, 186
Divorce, 31–2, 90–1, 101
Dixon, Eleanor Widener, 201
Dock, Wharf, Riverside and General Workers' Union, 149–50
Dodge, Ruth, 99, 115–16, 144–5

Dodge, Washington, 66, 69, 144
Dogs, 3, 33, 63, 67, 81, 188
Dorkings, Edward, 139
Douglas, Mahala, 6, 88
Dowdell, Elizabeth, 57–8
Drachstedt, Baron Alfred von *see* Nourney, Alfred
Duff-Gordon, Cosmo, 6, 83–6
Duff-Gordon, Lucy, 4, 6, 63, 83–6, 101, 103, 131, 163
Dulles, William Crothers, 12, 29, 55
Durnford, William, 8

Emigration, 17–18, 129–30, 186
Endres, Caroline Louise, 32
Entrepreneurs, 28–31, 33–5, 36–7, 40, 102, 122–3
Etches, Henry, 33, 162
Eugenics, 118, 144, 147–8
Eustis, Elizabeth, 163
Evans, Cyril, 159
Evans, Edith, 98, 105
Everett, Marshall, 28, 147

Fairview Cemetery, Halifax, 202
Fatherhood, 60–1, 107–108
Finn, Dr, 198
Fitzpatrick, Cecil, 64, 137
Flynn, John Irwin, 125
Foreman, Benjamin, 141
Fortune, Alice, 124, 138
Fortune, Charles, 124
Fortune, Ethel, 124, 138
Fortune, Mabel, 124, 138
Fortune, Mark, 124
Fortune, Mary, 124, 138
Francatelli, Laura, 84–5
Frankfurt, 160
Franklin, Philip, 48–9
Frauenthal, Henry William, 9, 44–5, 78
Frauenthal, Isaac G., 78, 183
Frey, Bruno, 62–3
Frölicher-Stehli, Maximilian, 43
Funerals, 199–201
Futrelle, Jacques, 5, 32, 61
Futrelle, May, 60, 61
Fynney, Joseph, 127

Gamblers, 42–4, 73–4
Gaskell, William, 127
Gatti, Gaspare (Luigi), 6, 154, 161
Geddes, Richard, 162–3
Gender:
  discrimination, 61, 117–21, 174, 204
  see also Manliness; Women
Gentlemen's clubs, 6–7, 36, 124–5
Gibson, Dorothy, 74–5
Giglio, Victor, 33, 162
Giles, Ralph, 47

Givard, Hans, 128
Gracie, Archibald:
  athleticism, 8, 79, 162, 164
  escort for unaccompanied women, 97–8
  observes speed of *Titanic*, 42
  personal courage, 32, 79, 139
  prejudices, 138–9, 142–3
  social activities on *Titanic*, 5, 7, 52–3, 81, 100–101
  survival, 79, 139, 164
Graham, Edith, 49–50
Graham, George, 125, 200
Greenfield, William, 43
Guggenheim, Benjamin, 10, 26, 28–9, 33, 51, 162

Hamilton, Frederick, 187–8
Harbeck, William, 46
Harder, Dorothy, 168–9
Harder, George Achilles, 32, 68–9
Hardy, John, 135
Hardy, Thomas, 23
Harland & Wolff, 13, 16–21, 24, 154, 155, 170
Harland & Wolff Guarantee Group, 24, 154
Harris, Mary, 148–9
Hart, Ben, 10, 185
Hart, Esther, 10, 185
Hartley, Wallace, 156–7, 158
Hawke, 45, 156, 177
Hays, Charles Melville, 37, 99
  lack of confidence in big ships, 20, 42, 95
  railroad mogul, 26, 28–9, 33–5, 81, 124
Hays, Clara, 95, 99
Hays, Margaret, 77, 107
Head, Christopher:
  art connoisseur, 12, 39
  character, 39–40, 202
  education, 36
  insurance, 39, 47, 147
  Mayor of Chelsea, 39–40, 202
Hearst, William Randolph, 89
Hee, Yum, 191
Hendrickson, Charles, 84
Heroism:
  cerebral, 53–7
  challenges to narrative of, 63–5, 148–9
  Christian, 142–3
  lower class, 107, 145
  martial, 49, 51–3, 142–3
  practical, 154–6
  romantic, 1–2, 51, 64–5, 70–1, 113–15
  stoical, 1–2, 27–8, 49–53, 59–60, 62, 64–7, 116
  womanly, 99–100, 108–13, 121
Hichens, Robert, 112, 174
Hickman, Leonard Mark, 194–5
Hickman, Lewis, 194–5
Hind, Cameron, 188
Hingston, Aileen, 185–6
Hippach, Ida, 32

Hippach, Jean, 32
Hocking, George, 106, 128
Hoffman, Louis *see* Navratil, Michel
Homer, Harry, 43, 74
Honeyman, Harold, 194
Honeymooners, 25–6, 41, 50–1, 67–8, 99–100, 113–14
Hoyt, Frederick, 43
Hoyt, Jane, 65
Hoyt, William Fisher, 178, 189
Hume, John, 156

Immigration *see* Emigration
Imperial Merchant Service Guild, 153
Inebriation, 37, 43–4, 81–2, 167, 174
Insurance claims, 39, 147, 191–2, 196–8
International Convention for the Safety of Life at Sea, 173
International Mercantile Maritime Company, 18–21, 48–9
International Navigation Company, 18
Irish Home Rule, 39, 109, 129
Ismay, Joseph Bruce, 34, 154
  chairman of White Star Line, 18–20
  conduct during sinking, 6, 25, 70–1, 82, 86–90, 91, 165, 178, 182, 184
  conduct on *Carpathia*, 88–9, 91
  criticism of, 16–17, 25, 42, 83, 86–90, 92
Ismay, Thomas, 19

Jarvis, Denzil, 126
Jessop, Violet, 24, 104
Jewan, Mary, 104
Johnstone, James, 143
Jones, Thomas, 108–10, 173–4
Joughlin, Charles, 132

Keeping, Edwin, 193
Kelly, Fanny Maria, 106
Kelly, Margaret, 133–4
Kemish, George, 166
Kent, Edward, 43, 97–8
Kimball, Edwin N., 42
Kincaid, Anna, 128, 133
Krins, Georges, 15

Labour movement, 29, 34, 122, 148–51
Lapland, 179
Lardner, Frederick, 188, 196
Laroche, Joseph Philippe Lemercier, 136
Laroche, Juliette, 136
Laroche, Simone, 136
Lattarulo, Vincent, 138
Leader, Alice, 108
Lengyel, Árpád, 82
Leslie, Noël *see* Rothes, Noël, Countess of
Lesueur, Gustave, 77

Levett, George, 177
Lewy, Ervin G., 197
Lifeboats:
  alleged rushing onto, 52, 63–6, 137–8
  legislation, 16, 170–3
  on *Titanic*, 12, 16–17, 170–5
Lightoller, Charles Herbert:
  accounts of sinking, 27, 47–8, 62, 89
  controlling crowds with gun, 65–6
  difficulty in finding way around *Titanic*, 133, 176, 179
  evidence to Inquiries, 178–9
  ideas about why *Titanic* sank, 159, 179
  opinion about Captain Smith, 168
  policy in filling lifeboats, 66, 72–3, 170
  promoted to second officer, 169–70
  survivor, 152
Lines, Elizabeth, 42, 88
Long, Milton, 45, 80, 189
Lord, Walter, 204–205
Loring, Joseph, 80
Lowe, Harold, 65, 73, 76, 87, 137–8, 177–8
Lundahl, Johan, 145
Lundström, Edwin, 145
Lusitania, 15, 17, 37, 47, 130, 156, 158
Lygon, William, 144

Mackay-Bennett, 187–8, 195–6
Manliness:
  athleticism, 7–8, 36, 38–40, 51, 79, 117, 130–1, 162, 164
  business success, 36–7
  civic duty, 38–40
  clothing and appearance, 1–2, 33, 51, 65, 75, 82
  clubman, 6–7, 36–7
  courtesy, 1–2, 50, 117–21, 142–3
  definition of, 35–6
  education, 35
  escorting women, 78, 97–9, 111
  gallantry, 27–8, 35, 66, 72, 84, 87, 92, 93, 94, 116–21
  leadership, 152–3, 183
  lower class, 107, 114
  risk-taking, 40–4
  selflessness, 117–20
  smoking, 28, 32, 49–50, 60
  sportsmanship, 38
  stiff upper lip, 1–2, 27–8, 52–3, 59–60, 62, 64–7, 116
  upper-class trait, 28, 57, 62, 143
Marconi International Marine Communication Company, 158, 160
Marconigrams, 14–15, 48
Marriage, 31–2, 91, 101, 141–2
Marriott, John, 177
Marshall, Logan, 29, 50
Marvin, Daniel, 26, 41, 93–4
Marvin, Mary, 26, 41, 93–4, 104

Matania, Fortunino, 1–2, 26, 27, 93
Maugé, Paul Achille Maurice Germain, 161–2
Mayflower Curling Rink, Halifax, 197–9
Mayné, Berthe, 37
McCaffry, Thomas, 124
McCawley, Thomas, 7, 164
McGough, James, 111, 125
McNamee, Eileen, 99–100
McNamee, Neal, 99–100
Mellors, William, 80
Memorials, 39, 50–1, 56–7, 200–204
Men and Religion Forward Movement, 139–40
Merritt, Abraham, 83–4
Mersey Inquiry *see* British Wreck Commissioner's Inquiry
Mersey, Lord, 84, 133, 134, 152, 167–8, 178
Mesaba, 159
Meyer, Edgar, 102–103
Meyer, Leila, 102, 174
Millet, Francis, 4, 5, 28, 43, 52, 123, 204
Minia, 188
Mock, Philip, 32
Modernity, 13–14, 22–5
Molson, Harry, 45, 72, 124–5
Montmagny, 188
Moody, James Paul, 25, 104, 152, 202–203
Moore, Clarence, 7, 28, 38, 43, 52, 72, 81
Morgan, John Pierrepoint, 18–19, 149
Morrow, Thomas Rowan, 129
Mount Olivet Cemetery, Halifax, 202
Moy Foi, Henry, 118
Müller, Ludwig, 132
Murdoch, William, 66, 152, 167, 169–70
Muscular Christianity, 139–40

National Sailors' and Firemen's Union, 172, 176
Navratil, Edmond (Momo), 107–108
Navratil, Michel (Lolo), 107–108
Navratil, Michel (alias Hoffman, Louis), 107
News reporting, 28–9, 48–9, 51, 59–61, 64, 81–4, 94, 96, 136, 145
Newsom, Helen, 26, 69–70
New York, 45–6
Noblesse oblige, 28, 57, 146, 183
Nomadic, 22
Nourney, Alfred, 26, 43, 76–7, 192

O'Loughlin, William Francis Norman, 8
Oliva, Fermina, 114, 131
Olive, Ernest Roskelly, 192
Olympic:
  collision with *Hawke*, 45, 177
  design, 15, 154
  previous sailing of *Titanic* passengers on, 9, 45, 47, 69, 127
  previous service of *Titanic* crew on, 8, 24, 156, 169–70, 177

strike by crew over safety, 172
Titanic trying to beat arrival time to New York, 42, 88
Olympic-class ships, 15, 17, 19–22
Owen, 'Doc', 73

Pain, Alfred, 35, 38
Paintin, James, 24
Panic, 52, 63–6, 133–5, 144, 157
Parish, Lutie, 23–4, 182
Parkhurst, Charles, 146–7
Parr, William, 154
Partner, Austin, 45–6, 47
Pascoe, Charles, 173–4
Passengers:
  ethnic diversity, 129
  first-class, 4–6, 122–5, 127
  seasoned travellers, 46–8
  second-class, 10, 125–8
  third-class, 10–11, 127, 128–35
Paternalism, 93–9, 107, 117
Payne, Vivian, 34
Pears, Edith, 41, 95–6
Pears, Thomas, 15, 36, 40–1, 95–6, 201
Peñasco, Pepita *see* Pérez de Soto, María Josefa (Pepita)
Peñasco, Victor:
  alleged cowardice, 64–5
  body bought as proof of his death, 196–7
  dandy, 50–2, 55, 191–2
  family wealth and connections, 50, 196–7
  fluency in English language, 131
  gentlemanly behaviour, 50–1, 64–5, 114–15
  honeymoon, 26, 113–14
  piety, 51, 139, 196
Penrose, John, 163–4
Percy, Eustace, 178
Pérez de Soto, María Josefa (Pepita), 26, 51, 64–5, 113–15, 131, 196–7
Pernot, René, 10
Peuchen, Arthur, 72–3, 103, 124–5, 137, 168, 174
Phillips, Jack, 135–6, 158–60
Pickard, Ben, 132, 134
Pirrie, James William, 16, 19, 20, 155
Pitman, Herbert, 178
Plunkett, Horace, 154–5
Poingdestre, John, 170
Ponesell, Martin, 128
Portaluppi, Emilio, 191
Porter, Walter, 198
Post, Louis, 148
Progressivism, 36, 40, 147–8
Pulbaum, Franz, 126

Racial prejudice:
  anti-black, 135–6
  anti-Chinese, 138–9
  anti-Italian, 65–6, 134–5, 136–7
  anti-Japanese, 138
Radio Act (1912), 14–15
Recovery ships, 187–8
Red Cross, 185
Redemption:
  moral, 31–5, 91–2, 114
  professional, 158–60
  religious, 51, 140
Reed, John, 145–6
Relief agencies, 184–6
Religious prejudice:
  anti-Catholicism, 139–41
  anti-Semitism, 141–2
  Protestantism, 36, 139–41, 146–7, 201–202
Reuchlin, Johan George, 18
Rheims, George, 80–1
Robber barons, 29–31, 33–7, 43, 54, 123
Robbins, Victor, 32
Roebling, Washington, 10, 36, 40, 49–50, 201–202
Rogers, Harry, 127
Rogers, J.M. *see* Yates, Jay
Romaine, Charles H., 43, 74
Roosevelt, Theodore, 52, 97
Rosenbach, A.S.W., 53, 105
Ross, John Hugo, 124–5
Rostron, Arthur, 169, 171, 182–4, 187
Rothes, Noël, Countess of, 98, 108–10, 114–15, 131, 173–4
Roussillon, Pierre, 161–2
Rubáiyát of Omar Khayyám, 11–12
Rule, Samuel, 165
Ryan, Edward, 75
Ryerson, Arthur, 29, 103
Ryerson, Emily, 88, 94–5, 99, 181
Ryerson, John, 103

Salomon, Abraham, 84
Salvation Army, 140, 185
Sangorski, Francis, 11–12
Satterlee, Mrs, 185
Scawn Blunt, Wilfrid, 91–2
Scott, Kathleen, 39
Senate Inquiry, 137, 152–3, 178–9, 186
Sessions, Waldo, 198
Seward, Frederick, 74, 183
Shaw, George Bernard, 63, 72, 98, 157, 169
Shelley, Imanita, 23–4, 170–1, 182
Shipbuilding, State subsidies, 17–18
Shipping, growth of big business, 18–19
Shootings, alleged, 64–5, 76, 144–5
Shutes, Elizabeth, 3, 143
Silverthorne, Spencer, 44, 125
Sim, William Sowden, 171–2
Simonius-Blumer, Alfons, 43
Simpson, John Edward, 8–9
Sjöstedt, Ernst, 126

Sloan, Mary, 155, 165
Sloper, William T., 74–5
Smith, Edward:
 culpability for disaster, 42, 66, 88, 143–4, 152, 159, 167–9, 176–7
 heroic image, 168–9
 monument, 39
 personal steward, 24
 popularity with passengers, 32, 43, 88, 94, 108, 123, 166–7
Smith, Eloise, 26, 82, 86, 94–5, 174, 191
Smith, Frank Arthur, 194
Smith, James Clinch, 35, 43, 97–8
Smith, Lucian Philip, 26, 86, 94–5, 191
Smith, William Alden, 153, 178
Snape, Lucy, 165
Snyder, John, 67–8, 191
Snyder, Nelle, 67–8
Socialism, 128–9, 145–6, 149–51
Spedden, Frederic Oakley, 183
Speed, cult of, 19–20, 40–2
Spencer, William Augustus, 12, 55
Spiritualism, 30–1
Staehelin-Maeglin, Max, 43
Stagg, Jack, 163
Stanley, Frank, 10
Stead, Alfred, 86–7
Stead, Estelle, 30
Stead, William Thomas, 19, 28–9, 30, 32, 86–7, 98, 140, 163
Stengel, Annie, 78
Stengel, Charles Henry, 84, 85
Stephenson, Martha, 163
Stokes, Philip, 127
Stott, Mrs, 185–6
Straus, Ida, 4, 15, 81, 100–101
Straus, Isidor, 15, 81, 100–101, 145
Suffrage movement, 109, 111, 113, 117–21
Survival:
 by chance, 66
 by class, 61–3, 133–4, 175
 by gender, 61
 by nationality, 62–3
 by obeying orders, 68–71
 by port or starboard side of boat, 66
 crew, 175
 jumping ship and swimming to lifeboat, 71–2, 77–81
 shame, 59–61, 174–5
 treatment of survivors on *Carpathia*, 180–4
Sutcliffe, John, 11–12
Sutehall, Henry, 197–8
Sutton, Frederick, 29
Swane, George, 127

Taft, Helen, 204
Taft, William, 14, 52, 186

Talbot, Edward, bishop of Winchester, 13
Tanner, John, 106
Taussig, Tillie, 64
Taylor, Percy, 156
Technology, faith in, 22–5, 40–2
Thayer, Jack, 80, 81, 87, 89, 182
Thayer, John Borland, 26, 28–9, 47, 81, 89, 95, 123
Thayer, Marian, 29, 81, 123, 167, 182
Tillett, Ben, 149–50
Titanic:
 à la carte restaurant, 5, 43, 123, 154, 162
 as stage set, 3, 25–6, 111, 205
 cabins, 3–5, 9, 10, 22, 23–4
 Café Parisien, 6
 cargo, 11–12
 collision with *New York*, 45–6
 construction, 13–22
 Dining Room, 5–6, 128–9
 emigrant ship, 10–11, 17–18, 129–30
 floating hotel, 4–6, 12–13, 25–6
 Gymnasium, 7–8, 32, 94, 130, 162, 164
 Ismay screens, 21, 176–7
 language barriers on board, 131–2
 Library, 10
 medical facilities, 8–9
 microcosm of society, 3–4, 25–6, 122
 physical barriers between classes, 133–4
 Promenade Deck, 176–7
 radio communication, 14–15
 Royal Mail ship, 25, 160–1
 sinking, 15–16, 26
 Smoking Room, 5–7, 10–11, 26, 42–4, 49, 52–3, 69, 89, 145, 156
 speed, 20, 42, 88, 146, 167–9, 172
 Squash Court, 8, 70, 155, 164
 Swimming Pool, 8
 technological progress, 13–14, 22–5
 Turkish bath, 8, 12, 81, 165
 unfinished state, 23–4
 unsinkable, 15–17, 27, 44–5, 48–9, 66
 Veranda Café, 6
 wayfinding difficulties, 132–4, 176–7
 see also Crew; Passengers
Trades unions, 34, 122, 148–51, 172, 175–6
Traffic, 22

United Mineworkers' Union, 172
Utopia, 138

Vanderbilt, Edith, 9–10
Vanderbilt, George, 9–10, 127

Wallis, Catherine, 8, 165
Ward, Annie, 77
Weikman, Charles, 27, 87
Weis, Gabriel, 12
Wells, H.G., 86, 150

Wennerström, August, 129, 145
West, Edwy Arthur, 107
Wheeler, Edwin, 9–10, 127
Whillems, Charles, 127
White, Alfred, 166
White, Ella, 117, 173
White, Percival, 81, 194
White, Richard Frazar, 36, 193–4
White, William Allen, 147
White Star Line:
  commercial position, 17–21, 175
  culpability, 12, 17, 25, 42, 70, 86–8, 149, 170, 179, 184–6
  employer, 153–4, 156–7, 164–6, 172–3, 176–7, 179, 202–203
  failure to provide lifeboats, 12, 17, 139, 170
  Harland & Wolff partnership, 19–21
  International Mercantile Marine Company membership, 18–19, 122
  luxury travel, 17–20, 42
  origins, 17
  recovery efforts, 187
  reputation for innovation, 13
  support for victims, 184–6, 198–9, 203
Whitney, Gertrude Vanderbilt, 204
Widener, Eleanor:
  devotion to son, 56–7, 105–106
  dinner party, 43, 122–3, 167
  family background, 122–3
  parting from husband and son, 47
  regular traveller, 46–7
  survival, 182, 184, 201
Widener, George Dunton:
  business career, 18, 26, 122–3
  death, 27–9, 47–8
  dinner party, 167
  memorial, 201
  misidentification of corpse, 193
  parting from wife, 29, 47, 105
  regular traveller, 46–7
  reputation, 64, 27–9
Widener, George Dunton Jr., 54, 193
Widener, Harry Elkins:
  bibliophile, 12, 44, 53–7, 105, 123
  card player, 43
  closeness to mother, 56–7, 105
  death, 27–9, 46–8, 54
  education, 36
  family background, 122–3
  Harry Elkins Widener Library, Harvard, 54, 55–7, 201
  insouciance about danger of sinking, 44–5, 47–8, 90
  involved in collision of *Olympic* with *Hawke*, 45
  memorials, 55–7, 140, 201
  parting from mother and father, 47
  regular transatlantic traveller, 18, 46–8
  reinvention as cerebral hero, 55–7
  target of snobbery, 123
Widener, Peter Arrell Browne, 18–19, 122–3
Wilde, Henry, 65, 152, 169
Wilhelmsburg, 92
Willard, Constance, 107
Williams, Charles Eugene, 73, 130
Williams, Duane, 29, 81
Williams, Leslie, 130–1
Williams, Richard Norris, 81, 163–4
Windeløv, Einar, 128
Women:
  bravery, 108–13, 121
  equality, 94, 99–101, 117–21
  hysteria, 113–16
  motherhood, 102–107
  need for male escorts, 97–9, 111
  perceived lack of altruism, 116, 118–20
  reluctance to leave husbands, 99–102
  reluctance to pick up survivors, 109–10, 112, 174
  sheltered from financial responsibility, 95–6
  society, role in, 93, 97
  suffrage, 109, 111, 113, 117–21
  wifely obedience, 93–4
Women and Children First, code of conduct, 35, 66, 72, 84, 87, 92, 93, 94, 116–21
Women and Children First, Fortunino Matania, 1–2, 26, 27, 93
Women's Relief Committee, 104, 185–6
Women's Social and Political Union, 113
Women's Titanic Memorial Fund, 204
Woodward, Wesley, 156–7
Woolner, Hugh, 43, 78–9, 98, 137
Wright, Almroth, 119–20
Wright, Frederick, 164
Wright, Marion, 98–9

Xenophobia, 39–40, 63–5, 142–3

Yates, Jay (alias Rogers, J.M.), 74
Yellow Peril *see* Racial prejudice, anti-Chinese
Young, Filson, 31, 39–40, 59
Yvois, Henriette, 46